Turn That Thing Off!

As personal technology becomes ever-present in the classroom and rehearsal studio, its use and ubiquity is affecting the collaborative behaviors that should underpin actor training. How is the collaborative impulse being distracted and what kind of solutions can re-establish its connections?

The daily work of a theatre practitioner thrives on an ability to connect, empathize, and participate with other artists. This is true at every level, from performing arts students to established professionals. As smartphones, social media, and other forms of digital connectedness become more and more embedded in daily life, they can inhibit these collaborative, creative skills. *Turn That Thing Off! Collaboration and Technology in 21st-Century Actor Training* explores ways to foster these essential abilities, paving the way for emerging performers to be more present, available, and generous in their work.

Rose Burnett Bonczek is Director of the BFA Acting Program and Professor of Theater at Brooklyn College, CUNY, USA.

Roger Manix is an adjunct lecturer in the BFA Acting Program at Brooklyn College, CUNY, USA, and at Parsons School of Design at The New School, New York, USA. He is the owner of Brooklyn Training Ground, an acting studio in New York.

David Storck is Professor of Performing Arts at the Savannah College of Art and Design in Savannah, Georgia, USA.

Turn That Thing Off!

Collaboration and Technology in 21st-Century Actor Training

Rose Burnett Bonczek, Roger Manix, and David Storck

Valerie Clayman Pye and
Michael Flanagan, Associate Editors

LONDON AND NEW YORK

First published 2018
by Routledge
2 Park Square, Milton Park, Abingdon, Oxon, OX14 4RN

and by Routledge
711 Third Avenue, New York, NY 10017

Routledge is an imprint of the Taylor & Francis Group, an informa business

British Library Cataloguing-in-Publication Data
A catalogue record for this book is available from the British Library

Library of Congress Cataloging-in-Publication Data
Names: Bonczek, Rose Burnett, 1958- author. | Manix, Roger,
author. | Storck, David, 1962- author.
Title: Turn that thing off!: collaboration and technology in
21st century actor training/Rose Burnett Bonczek, Roger Manix,
and David Storck.
Description: Milton Park, Abingdon, Oxon; New York:
Routledge, 2017. | Includes bibliographical references and index.
Identifiers: LCCN 2017033818 | ISBN 9781138677128 (hardback) |
ISBN 9781138677135 (pbk.) | ISBN 9781315559759 (ebook)
Subjects: LCSH: Acting—Study and teaching. | Actors—Training of. |
Artistic collaboration. | Technology—Social aspects.
Classification: LCC PN2075.B58 2017 | DDC 792.02/8071—dc23
LC record available at https://lccn.loc.gov/2017033818

ISBN: 978-1-138-67712-8 (hbk)
ISBN: 978-1-138-67713-5 (pbk)
ISBN: 978-1-315-55975-9 (ebk)

Typeset in Sabon
by Sunrise Setting Ltd, Brixham, UK

From Rose: *This book is dedicated to my incredible students; the brave, tenacious, and fiercely talented BFA actors of Brooklyn College, especially the classes of 2014 to 2018. And to Mike Cleary for his endless love and support, and for doing his job so beautifully.*

From David: *To Mom, Dad, and Susan, for their love and for showing me what teaching is all about. And to Averie and Maddie for their patience and support during the many hours I spent on this; and for making me happier than I ever thought I could be.*

From Roger: *To my students, whose dare and talent inspire me. To my teachers, who over the years encouraged me to dream big. To my family, who let this quirky little boy express himself on stage. To my community, who carry me. To the theatre, who saved me.*

Contents

Acknowledgements

The authors would like to gratefully acknowledge the following:

To the dynamic duo, Valerie Clayman Pye and Michael Flanagan; your boundless generosity and extraordinary writing and editorial skills elevated this book beyond our original vision. You are here on every single page.

To our ensemble of early readers who made invaluable contributions to the content, to our confidence, and to our spirits: Ally Callaghan, Patrick Delaney, Elaine Fadden, Eugene Solfanelli.

To those who contributed resources, research, stories and observations, and inspired portions of the book or inspired us: Lisa Anderson, Sara Brown, Sabrina Cataudella, Joshua Chase Gold, Sofiya Cheyenne, Gary Cowling, Michael Colby Jones, Cliona Dukes, Mack Exilus, Ramona Floyd, Samantha Fontana, Katherine Harte-DeCoux, Mikela Horn-Bjork, Helen Huff, Adama Jackson, Len Jenkin, Andreas Kern, Arthur Kriklivy, Belinda Mello, Terril Miller, Schann Mobley, Jay Nickerson, Lynn Olson, Mickey Ryan, Anya Saffir, Todd Thaler, Dr. Sherry Turkle, Alexandra Slater, Ian Wen.

Thanks to the colleges, universities, and organizations that supported us:

The Department of Theatre at Brooklyn College; Dr. Tobie Stein for her unwavering support, friendship and mentorship always; Eugene Solfanelli for his fierce dedication to finding solutions through compassion and wisdom (when Buddha's attack indeed!); Michael Colby Jones for his passionate commitment to our students, their growth, and their futures; Francine Zerfas for her generosity and care of our students, and for teaching them positive applications of technology; Laura Tesman and Jolie Tong for their collaborative spirits; Jackie Smerling for always having her "The Doctor is In" sign on her desk; Jeff Steifel, Michael Hairston, and Deborah Hertzberg for the many early discussions that helped shape our curricular changes, and to Tom Bullard, Pei-Wen Huang-Shea, Amy Hughes, Teresa Snider-Stein, Judylee Vivier, and our Department Chair, Kip Marsh, for their encouragement and support throughout this project.

The Savannah College of Art and Design, particularly the faculty and students of the Performing Arts Department for their encouragement and sharing; Craig Anton, Vivian Majkowski, Jennefer Morris-Lough, Martin Noyes, and Kim Steiner who listened patiently; Laurence Ballard for his expertise in both acting and technology; Michael Wainstein for effectively playing devil's advocate and keeping me (David) balanced with his comments; the MFA acting cohort, Class of 2018, for gamely trying my ideas; Colleen Mond for her logistical support; and the many colleagues who said, in essence, "Yes, write it – we need that book!"

The New School for Social Research, and their belief in the power of play to transform lives.

Geycel Best, Rita Breidenbach, Lisa Grocott, Lisa Norton, Lara Penin, Jane Pirone, Mathan Ratinam.

The Graduate School of Business and The d.school at Stanford University.

Maureen Carroll, JD Schramm.

Monash University and Riverdale Country Day School.

The World Bank, for understanding the relationship between somatic learning and solving global issues.

Our deepest thanks to Ben Piggott for encouraging and nurturing us, and for believing in us and in this book. Our great thanks to Kate Edwards for her support and guidance, and for shepherding this book through the maze.

And of course, to all our teachers, directors, collaborators, and students.

Student acknowledgements

This list represents the dedicated students from the BFA in Acting Program at Brooklyn College who generously shared their discoveries in their Digital Disconnects. Without their fearless investigation, we would not have this book. Our deepest gratitude and love to them all.

Ahsan Ali
Sarvin Alidaee
Fito Alvarado
Ashley Arnett
Ryan Bannon
Sarah Beitch
Sara Brown
Ally Callaghan
Francisco Carrillo
Lorenzo Cromwell
Patrick Delaney
Jonathan Nathaniel Dingle-El
Johnathan Dougan
Rachel Fink
Andrew Galteland
Stefanie Gil
Daniela Gonzalez y Perez
Chakeefe Gordon
Rhiannon Guilfoyle
Joanna Kozak
Amy Lopatin
Tanyamaria McFarlane
Harrison Marx
Ashley Mayers
Annabelle Mayock
Monica Mendez
Javon Q. Minter

JoMack Miranda
Rae Mizrachi
Valeri "Matt" Mozaidze
Henry Nwaru
Kaila Saunders
Connor James Sheridan
Alexandra Slater

Introduction

Let's begin with a quick experiment. Is your phone nearby, waiting to bring you the very latest text, email, or posting? If it is, would you mind turning it off for an hour or two? Can you set aside time to read without the interruption of chirps and buzzes, or glances to see who has sent you a message? Are you able to be fully in the moment with this book? It's not as easy as it used to be, is it? Times have changed; we live in the digital age. As a brilliant philosopher once said, "Life moves pretty fast. If you don't stop and look around once in a while, you could miss it." Okay, it was actually Ferris Bueller who said that (*Ferris Bueller's Day Off*). But his pre-digital age message is more pertinent than ever. The digital age comes with a high volume of stimuli poking at us, and the torrent is relentless.

> Technology makes us forget what we know about life (Day II Plenary 6).
> (Dr. Sherry Turkle, Professor at the
> Massachusetts Institute of Technology)

A great deal of debate is taking place about technology and the effects it's having on us. Technology is a lifesaver, technology is the enemy of humanity, technology allowed my autistic child to communicate for the first time, technology has made my child abandon her family and isolate herself from us . . . For every point, there is a counter point, as it should be when something new is introduced to society. No one could have completely predicted the ultimate impact of the Industrial Revolution when we were smack in the middle of it; and although a lot of research is underway right now to determine the effects of rapidly growing communication technologies, the full impact may not be known for a few more years.

However – even though data about respiratory disease among factory workers in the 1800s wasn't immediately known, you didn't have to listen very long to people in the community coughing their brains out to know that there was a problem. Similarly, when we encounter someone who can't seem to look up from their smartphone, who isn't present with you, or able to listen, who avoids eye contact and avoids direct human interaction in general, we don't need to wait for all of the data to come in to know that there's a problem. It's not the technological advancements themselves; it's how humans are responding to them. As Dr. Turkle states:

> Technology isn't the problem; how we use it is the problem. (Connected, but alone?)

As teachers ourselves, we embrace and appreciate the countless benefits that technology offers to us and to our students. Self-taping an audition in New York for a casting director in Los Angeles? Brilliant. Online casting services for actors so that more potential employers can view them? Wonderful. Online access to worldwide library archives for research? Outstanding. We get it; we use it ourselves; we support it. And we ourselves have felt that the more we use it, the more we *want* to use it. It makes so many things in life simpler and more efficient.

However . . .

The work, life, and profession of an actor is specifically and profoundly vulnerable to the negative side effects of excessive technology use. Someone who is training to create truthful human behavior *must* be acutely connected to the human experience. There is no other side to that coin. Actors are the social anthropologists of the arts. Painters study the human form so they can express it artistically; actors study human behavior so they can create truth within imaginary circumstances. If a painter never looked at their own body or that of another's, they wouldn't be able to draw the human form as it truly exists. They might be able to create an *idea* of what they believe it to be – but without direct, personal experience of it, their work can't be fully realized. Likewise, actors removed from face-to-face interactions and direct communal experiences won't be able to truly reflect human behavior. Those whose primary exposure to human behavior is filtered through a screen might *believe* that they're accurately studying people, but they would be missing a key ingredient that an actor needs to create another human being: empathy. That ability to understand and feel another person's pain or joy is diminished when it's filtered several generations down from the original behavior via screens. Distance dilutes empathy, and screens create human distance – ironically, while connecting millions of people online.

The distance we're talking about is Empathetic Distance – that is, being too far removed from the experiences of another person to be able to truly empathize with them. If the balance of our primary communication shifts from direct, in-person contact to a dominant amount of online or smartphone screen time, we're creating an empathy gap that directly impedes an actor's ability to do their job. And while the skills needed to be efficient with the current technology may become more proficient, the empathy gap leads to a succession of weakened human skills such as awareness, listening, focus, and most important of all, the ability to be present with another human being.

There may be people and professions out there for whom this isn't a problem at all; but acting isn't one of them.

If you want to stay up until 3:00 a.m. playing Minecraft, more power to you. If you spend hours on Facebook, daily, sharing news stories and opinions with your thousand "friends," kudos. If you won the last speed-texting contest at your school or company, congratulations. But. If you are studying to be an actor, or you are an actor or acting teacher, hit the brakes. What is it that this craft and this profession demands of you in order to excel in your artistry? Knowledge of human behavior and a deep understanding of the human experience. What is excessive use of technology displacing in your life, or in the lives of your acting students?

Exactly.

Technology makes us forget what we know about life.

This book is the story of how we begin to remember. It's not anti-technology. *We're* not anti-technology. We just discovered a problem and we're trying to get to the bottom of it. We've been down a lot of rabbit holes. Come with us on this journey. We've figured out how to navigate this labyrinth and we'd like to share it with you.

Before we proceed, we'd like to offer a little background on ourselves, how we came to this point, and a few things that will be helpful to understanding this book. We (Rose, Roger, and David) were colleagues in the Brooklyn College Theater Department for a time. It's where we met and formed the basis for our collaboration. Rose and David previously wrote a book together, *Ensemble Theatre Making: A Practical Guide*, and the three of us continue to bond over our mutual love for collaborative ensembles and pursuing a deeper understanding of how and why they work. Rose and Roger are still working together at Brooklyn College, while David has moved south.

Rose

When I graduated from SUNY New Paltz in 1980 with my theatre degree and moved to New York, I was desperate to not have to keep waitressing to pay the bills. Directing gigs had rarely paid well in theatre, and in 1981 being a female director who was 23, but who looked 14, didn't help very much. A friend told me about "temping," which sounded downright magical. I could type fairly well, control my own schedule, and I would be able to throw away those hateful waitress shoes. I signed up with an agency and waited for assignments that I was certain would come pouring in. I was a college graduate with excellent organizational and writing skills. What could go wrong?

At my first interview, I was bombarded with questions like, "Do you know Wang? WordStar? MultiMate?" I'm sure that to the office manager I looked like a cow that had been struck between the eyes with an electric prod. "OK, what about Lotus 1-2-3?" Blank. Exasperated, she said, "Well, what *can* you do?" I smiled proudly, "I can type and I'm creative and organized." She didn't smile back; she just said, "OK, but that won't pay as much as if you knew computers."

It was a brave new world, and I knew that if I wanted to burn those shoes, I'd better figure out this technology that paid more than typing on an IBM Selectric typewriter. Ironically, I was placed at a computer systems analysts firm because I was good at proofreading; they were like a temp agency for computer analysts and all of their clients had to have great – and accurate – resumes. So I was temping at a temp agency; but the bonus was, in all my downtime (and there was a lot of that) I did every tutorial for every computer program that they had. I learned the difference between DOS and VSAM. I taught myself several word processing programs, learned about spreadsheets, how to use their lumbering FAX machine (five minutes to send a single page), and the rest was history. Sort of. In my years of temping, I discovered that any software program had a finite shelf life. Huzzah, I'm great at WordStar; too bad, they don't use that anymore, now they want MultiMate. Woo hoo! I've mastered MultiMate; too bad, the hot software is now WordPerfect. For a brief period of time, companies also designed their own dedicated word processing machines – like, that's all the computer did *was* word processing. Even Exxon had created its own machine. I'm probably one of the few in my generation who can tell those boring tales about obsolete technology that no one wants to hear (but everyone wants to hear the cool story about when I held Exxon's check for $1.2 billion dollars in my hand before they paid a fine to the federal government . . .).

My point is: the technology changed fast even in the 1980s, and we all struggled to keep up with it even in those dark ages before the Internet. I had worked on the very first personal computers – the Radio Shack TRS 80 (which we fondly called the "Trash 80") whose screen, guts, and keyboard were all one big, molded hunk and it had 64K memory. I worked on the very first "portable computer," the Compaq – trust me, you wouldn't have wanted it to be your laptop. It weighed as much as several bowling balls and you carried it in a suitcase; but it was cutting edge then. Later, in 1990, when I worked at the *International Bibliography of Theatre*, I was one of the first people I knew that used email. It was revelatory, and I could see the potential for its applications in the arts. You could use it for communication and collaboration while you were in different parts of the country, for marketing and advertising for your theatre company, that little "edu" address opened up a world of possibilities. Having a trail of emails actually helped me win a legal case and I was awarded my directing fees after a particularly unpleasant experience with an unscrupulous producer. Email became the Internet became online video . . . In 2005, I began a little project with my friend and colleague, Steve Ansell, Gi60 (Gone in 60 Seconds) The International One Minute Theatre Festival. Gi60 is a one-minute theatre festival that performs

50 plays live (a different set of 50 on three continents), live streams, films them, then edits them to single play format to be uploaded to the Gi60 Channel on YouTube. We've produced over 1600 plays in the past 13 years, and the multiple technology platforms have allowed us to create artistic collaborations around the world. Steve's original tag for Gi60 was "The first online theatre festival."

I offer all of this to pre-empt any person who may think, "ah, she's anti-technology, that's why she's writing about this." Technology has saved my ass; it allowed me to grow a life in the city that I love, to research and get jobs, to have the artistic and financial flexibility to travel to those jobs, and technology let me plonk those waitress shoes in the garbage can of history. I've used technology to develop and maintain international creative collaborations since the early 1990s, and today, it helps me produce theatre, to see my godchildren as they grow a foot in height each year (what's in the water in Yorkshire anyway?), and yes, to write this book with my dear friends Roger and David, even though David lives in Savannah and Roger and I live in New York.

Where I draw the line is when people's *use* of technology impacts their ability to look me in the eye, have a meaningful conversation with me, or makes them run a stop sign and total my Toyota (fortunately *not* totaling me and my husband) because they're too busy texting. I draw the line when I see students silently sit in groups scrolling through devices instead of speaking with one another. I especially draw the line when young, brilliant actors who should have great careers ahead of them are so consumed with their devices that their acting skills are compromised and they won't *have* acting careers unless they change their behaviors. My heart has been broken too many times watching talented young artists allow their skills to slip down the drain as they get lost in online activity. I've gone from heartbreak, to getting really mad at how our students' relationship to their devices (and our colleagues for that matter) has become more important to them than their relationships to one another. As a mentor once said to me, "I don't worry about you. You turn your anger into action." So I had a choice; accept that collaboration, empathy, and ensemble was forever changed and compromised by excessive reliance on devices, or learn everything I could about the devices and behavioral research, and use that to change my teaching to help bring our students back into the present moment with one another. I made my choice, and I truly hope this book can be a supportive tool to help you make yours. I am eternally grateful to Roger and David; their boundless generosity, creativity, support, and humor will forever be the gold standard for collaboration.

Roger

I'm not only a theatre geek, I'm a math geek. I love playing make-believe, and I also love numbers. My love of numbers bore out of my need to find structure, to solve a problem that in fact had a definitive solution. 2 + 2 = 4, always (well, until one gets to higher Algebra, but I won't blow your mind with that). My love of theatre came out of finding the misfits in my elementary school who were in Drama Club. I fit in there, and I got to play Dracula, too? Sign me up!

My first semester at Manhattan College in The Bronx was spent as a mechanical engineer major. I liked the course work, but I didn't like living at home and commuting to an 8:00 a.m. physics class. The next semester I transferred to SUNY Albany and switched to studying mathematics. I LOVED IT! In a former life, I was a topologist. But something was nagging away inside me. I missed my band of misfits from the theatre, and whenever I went to see the college's productions, I longed to be on stage. A few years later, I happily graduated with a major in Theatre and a minor in Mathematics.

The question I still get to this day is, "Theatre and Math? They are so different. How does that work?" They're actually not that different. For both, I need to let my mind and imagination vastly expand. And scripts, just like equations, require detective work to crack them open. I was a math tutor and a waiter for years and years, all while acting in the mid-1990s downtown East Village theatre scene. I had a theatre company with my newfound band of misfits, and studied at The William Esper Studio (Esper). All without cell phones and computers. I had a black leather date book that carried my life: rehearsals, jobs, appointments, phone numbers, addresses. Most actors during this era had separate professional voicemails set up, and I did get a beeper that was connected to that voicemail. My agent had that number, but mostly my friends used it to page me, or my boyfriend at the time who would text me "1, 1, 1, 1, 1," which meant he loved me. Around 1999, I got a cell phone, and I'm proud to say I have the same number to this day. I take pride in my (718) area code. At the restaurant, the phone was in my apron, and as I was one of the first people at this restaurant with a cell phone, the rest of the wait staff would borrow it to sneak off to the bathroom to make calls. The early 2000s brought a computer in to my world, and thank god! I moved to LA for a stint, and because of email and AOL Instant Messaging, I was able to stay close to my family and east-coast pals. Not only that, my New York agent got me an audition for *Buffy the Vampire Slayer,* and I booked the job (which I eventually lost because they wanted a paler vampire. Damn Croatian/Italian olive skin!). LA was short lived, and I quickly found myself back home in NYC. After studying Meisner's work at Esper, I knew I was meant to teach. That meant graduate school, so from 2006 to 2008, I earned my MFA in Acting at Brooklyn College. Also in 2008, I received an iPhone for a birthday present, and loved it! Texting friends with ease, quick directions around the city, and portable Internet access made life really easy. For the first time in my adult life, I was connected all my waking my hours.

Think back to 2008, and what's the first thing that comes to mind? Yep, the economic crash. There I was, fresh out of grad school with an acting degree during one of the worst economic crises in decades. Lucky me. I saw a lot fear all around me during those days. I also saw a lot of people with their heads down focused on their smartphones, keeping up with the latest state of our current times. Nobody seemed to be taking a break from the bombardment of information, and it felt like putting kerosene on a fire. But what I really noticed were groups of people together, yet all on their phones. People weren't leaning in to each other as much for emotional support, but were turning to their devices for information instead. It got me asking, "Why are people spending so much time on their devices instead of supporting one another face-to-face, arm-in-arm, during this bleak time?"

I had an idea. A colleague taught at The Graduate School of Business at Stanford University. I asked if I could come out west and teach a series of workshops rooted in play to develop social and emotional intelligence with his MBA candidates. His reply: "Sure. If it works, great! If it doesn't, don't tell anyone and don't come back."

It worked. For about six years, I taught at the business school, using all the exercises I learned in my graduate improv class and hanging them on the development of the soft skills companies wanted their employees to have intact once they arrived. The workshops were consistently the highest rated by the students across the business school. They were hungry to collaborate, and saw the importance of these life skills, particularly in the face of our new economy. I recall with such clarity one student sharing, "I'm starting to feel more human by playing."

Eventually, I worked with students at the d.school at Stanford, and I saw it wasn't only business school students who needed this work, it was everyone. That realization led me to my current consulting career. Since that time, I have worked internationally, bringing play and storytelling to Fortune 500 companies, which hold traits like empathy, resilience, and innovation in high regard, and understand the technique of somatic learning to develop those traits.

It wasn't long until The New School of Social Research caught wind of the work I was doing, and invited me to play with the students at Parsons School of Design. During a meeting with one of the chairs within Parsons, I was asked if I could develop a course to teach empathy. A COURSE TO TEACH EMPATHY!? I quickly responded that I didn't think meeting once a week for two and a half hours for 15 weeks would satisfy the course objective of "you are now empathetic." What I did say was I could create an environment using techniques from the theatre that would allow the students a safe place to question their own beliefs on how they relate to themselves and to those around them. An investigation into their humanity. The class was a hit, and I've taught play at both the graduate and undergraduate level.

But pull the brakes here. We now have to have a course to teach empathy! Why is that? And academics are turning to this theatre geek to get the job done? What is it about these times that is creating a need to develop basic human skills? How are we growing further apart from each other when technology is ostensibly keeping us closer together?

I had been teaching acting and movement in the BFA program for a few years alongside Rose, who's my boss and also a dear friend, and we were seeing a steady increase in, well, a lack of humanness in our classrooms. Rose and David worked on *Ensemble Theatre Making* together, and that collaboration prompted the two of them to start the conversation of what effects technology might be having on our students. The questions I was asking along with the work I was doing in the corporate world made me a lucky fit for an invitation from Rose and David to join them on their latest adventure.

It was never a bashing of technology. Hell, my corporate consulting work depended upon technology. Last year, I was in Italy, Australia, and Hawaii working away, and I was able to video chat with my friends and family, and most importantly my dog, Maggie. I threw my back out in Hawaii. I went online and found an acupuncturist who did trigger point release. Such good comes from having our devices. What the three of us quickly realized was that it wasn't the thing that was a problem, but the *use* of the thing that might be problematic. The three of us started sending all kinds of research back and forth, shared stories about what we were seeing in the classroom, and became more and more excited that early research was supporting some of our suppositions. The years we spent together swimming in research were a delight (most of the time), and the stories shared among us three have bonded us together in the most unique ways. The book you're holding in your hands was a pure labor of love, dedication, humor, and some down and dirty hard work!

David

I can remember talking with my friends in Mrs. McCullom's fourth grade class, dreaming about a miracle device that would deliver us from the horror that we considered math homework to be. "Wouldn't it be great if there was a machine where we could type in 57,216 ÷ 12 and it would magically produce the answer for us?" No more long division! Two years later, my Dad bought our first calculator. I can still picture that calculator in my mind and remember the rush I felt as I waited several seconds for it to calculate long division and produce the answer for me. I was enthralled. My Dad, who loved new technology, eventually tried to pull me away from the calculator and introduce me to the wonder of the slide rule. It was the equivalent of trying to get me to eat a plate of cauliflower while I was in the midst of enjoying dessert. It's funny how the memory of my first encounter with new technology stays with me so clearly. It's a tribute to the power of new technology and its ability to captivate us.

The story of what led me to this book has close parallels to both Rose's story and Roger's story. Like Roger, I started college not as a theatre major, but an engineering major. My eventual undergraduate degree was in International Relations; my pursuit of theatre didn't begin in earnest until after college. Like Rose, when I first arrived in New York, I spent several years working as an office temp, using many of the same software programs that she named. During that time, I was also pursuing a career in theatre: taking classes, auditioning, and performing. I was introduced to improv in 1992 and it has been the core of my focus ever since. Still, acting has remained a part of my work. I added writing, thanks to improv, which, in a sense, is writing on your feet. In 1998, I added directing and by 1999, I was teaching improv and acting on a regular basis. That same year, I bought my first home computer: a Grape iMac. I can still vividly remember that device as well. Another big impact.

I met Rose when I took her graduate improv class at Brooklyn College. Our mutual interest in improv, collaboration, and ensemble eventually blossomed into the partnership that led us to write *Ensemble Theatre Making*. I met Roger about two years later, ironically, while substitute teaching Rose's improv class. We have been friends and colleagues ever since.

In 2011, I got my first smartphone. It gave me the same initial sensation as that first calculator and the Grape iMac. But the first time I realized that its impact on me might be much greater was with my first phantom ring. I felt a buzzing on my thigh – I must have a call. Nope, no call. I thought the phone had malfunctioned. As this phenomenon revisited me and I learned what was happening, it gave me pause. My body was creating imaginary phone calls! I love to improvise, but this was a little scary.

After the publication of *Ensemble Theatre Making*, Rose and I continued our discussions on collaboration and ensemble. Those talks, based largely on changes we were noticing in collaborative behaviors in our classrooms, led us to asking each other about the impact of smartphones and social media on our students. It turns out that Rose was having similar conversations with Roger. Soon, the three of us were down the rabbit hole together.

I'm pretty sure that I would not be able to write a book by myself. And if somehow I did, I would not enjoy it very much. The joy I find in this comes from the collaboration. Not just with Rose and Roger, but with our extended ensemble of contributors as well. However, there is a special feeling of satisfaction and love that I get from working with Rose and Roger. I am lucky to have them as friends and partners.

What I didn't realize all those years ago in Mrs. McCullom's class was that the real thrill didn't lie in fantasizing about a calculator. It came from my relationship to the friends who allowed me to indulge in that dream. Here's to the friends and colleagues who venture down rabbit holes with us.

About this book

We see each section of every course we teach as an ensemble. For learning to be maximized, we believe that every class needs to function together as an ensemble. We teach and instill the principles of ensemble and collaboration to our acting students, right alongside the acting techniques that they've come for. An ensemble, in many ways, is only as good as its ability to communicate effectively and collaborate together. Our students' capacity to relate to each other and their environment is affected by their use of smartphones, social media, and other technological advances. Technology is entering our class-rooms, even without the devices themselves – but in the habits and behavior they create in our students. We find ourselves asking three key questions:

- How are the communication habits of these natives of the digital age changing the ability of the student actor to live in the moment, both on stage and off?
- How are these same habits changing their ability to form strong ensem-bles in the 21st century acting classroom?
- And what, if anything, do we do about it?

The search for those answers led us to write this book.

You will notice a recurring feature that we fondly refer to as our grey boxes. These are for us to insert stories from our personal experiences. We used this in *Ensemble Theatre Making* and it proved to be a reader favorite, so we're continuing the practice here.

You will see that we insert quotes from students throughout the book. These quotes appear in italics with quotation marks, and are from an assign-ment requiring the students to detach themselves from the connected sphere of the digital world (the Internet, social media, etc.) and reflect on their experiences. This is what we call a Digital Disconnect. The students are then asked to write about their experiences. It's from their papers where the quotes are taken. The quotes do not come with attribution. The papers were writ-ten to us in confidence, not for the purpose of publication. Later, we realized the powerful potential they had for this book. With the permission of our brave and generous students, we are able to share these personal quotes with you, but choose to do so anonymously, to honor their privacy. Yet, at the same time, we want to acknowledge them and thank them for their contributions. To accomplish this, we have listed them in our Acknowledgements section. We are very proud, and grateful, to have their words within these pages. All other quotes (research, interviews, etc.) come with attribution. You will read more about the Digital Disconnect process in Chapter 4, but for now, it's enough to know simply what prompted these quotes.

A word of explanation on our use of the words "you, I, we, our," and "us." When we say "we," "our," and "us," we mean not only Rose, Roger, and David, but also you the readers, unless specifically indicated otherwise. In some instances, we (Rose, Roger, and David) will be referencing our personal experiences and will distinguish parenthetically whom we mean, just as we've done in this sentence. We will only use "I" in instances where the identity of the narrator has been clarified.

The deadline for the manuscript of this book was summer 2017. All of the research, observations, data, and conclusions in this book are based on the knowledge we had at that time. We fully expect that in the years to come this subject will continue to emerge, our collective understanding will evolve, and technology will adapt. It's possible that you may come across information in this book that since the time of our writing has been superseded by newer information. We welcome that and look forward to learning more ourselves, not only from our own discoveries but from the many dedicated individuals invested in bringing awareness to this vital subject. The good news is that the steps we've already taken in our classrooms, and outlined within this book, are working. We are confident that what we've written here will be built upon rather than replaced.

In the coming pages, we identify the basic human behaviors that we look for in acting students, describe what is shifting in those behaviors, explain the impact of technology on these shifts, examine why our students are choosing technology over direct human contact, specify how we can rekindle the desired behaviors, and take a peek beyond the acting classroom to the global implications. Woven throughout you'll find the results of our research, experiments, interviews, and long hours of discussion and debate.

So please, set aside some time for yourself, put away those devices, and read on. Life *does* move pretty fast, now more than ever. If you don't stop and look around once in a while, instead of looking down, you're definitely going to miss it.

Bibliography

Ferris Bueller's Day Off. Dir. John Hughes, Paramount Pictures, 1986. Film.

Turkle, Sherry. "Connected, but Alone?" Ted Conference. Long Beach Performing Arts Center, Long Beach. Feb 2012. Lecture.

Turkle, Sherry. "Day II Plenary 6: Humans First – Technology Second." Global Peter Drucker Forum. Hall of Sciences, Vienna. 6 Nov 2015. Lecture.

Chapter 1

The Collaborative Gene

Doing the Digital Disconnects has made me see the world differently and has made my senses sharper and more childlike ... I find myself more connected to the world and the life forces around me. The birds that I hear outside, the wind through the trees, the conversations that I hear on the bus and train are worth (it). I've learned how to walk and own my space without feeling afraid. I've also learned about being present and the truth in the moment and the energy that you can get and transfer to other people by being really present with the people you're with, and why have it any other way?

"Collaboration" has always been one of our favorite words. When we wrote *Ensemble Theatre Making*, our primary definition of an ensemble was "They collaborate." We are actors, directors, and teachers, and our philosophical approach to all of these professions is grounded in the practice of collaboration and ensemble. Collaboration is in our bones; we can't live without it. Let's face it; there are many paths to choose from in this life, but if you love to work closely with others, you'd be hard pressed to find a more rewarding field than theatre. This is likely the source of the thousands of (true!) clichés about "theatre people" being gregarious, open, empathic, and enthusiastic players. As teachers, we recognize the natural impulse in our acting students to *want* to collaborate. We see in them the seed of knowing *how* to collaborate. They come through the door with the ability to collaborate already within them, in their blood and bones; the rest is nurturing and strengthening that wonderful ability in the process of creating.

In *Ensemble Theatre Making*, we touched on the science and anthropology of collaboration, but after publication, questions about these areas stayed with us and we decided to explore further. We were delighted when the research showed there is a scientific basis to collaboration. It turns out that our genes collaborate with each other all the time. They collaborate to create what is called a phenotype; that is, our characteristics and personality traits that make us uniquely who we are. We are literally hard-wired to collaborate at our most basic cellular level; and so we nicknamed this concept "The Collaborative

Gene." It made complete sense to us that the work we do as theatre artists and educators stimulates and strengthens that gene, which, in turn, propels us to work together. Fittingly, it was during this research, as we pondered writing another book, that we knew we had to recruit Roger to join us.

As we continued our discussions, we began to talk about the Collaborative Gene as a little flame, burning within each of us, yearning to connect, to belong. We soon discovered that science had already coined the term "belongingness"; it is where "the self seeks connectedness and harmony with others" (McConnell). That's what the Collaborative Gene does: it gives us the *desire to belong* – and how true that statement is in theatre. Presumably, most of you reading this book discovered your tribe in theatre. Theatre gives us a place where we belong and fellow tribe members to whom we are connected on a meaningful level. There are countless stories of students in their early schooling, all the way through college, who speak of finding the people they feel most connected to through their participation in theatre. Finding the theatre is a beautiful thing. Yet, without the people who make up the tribe, theatre wouldn't exist. We find our people.

We enter this world connected to our mothers via the umbilical cord. Talk about being hard-wired! We are literally plugged in to another human being, developing and being nurtured through that connection. Upon birth, we spend the rest of our days searching for similar deep, profound connections. But without the actual physical cord (a biological connection), we are forced to seek fulfillment through collaboration (a social connection). From those early days of school searching for a buddy who understands us, trying out for sports teams, band, drama club, and so on, our need to bond is primal. What we find in partners are similarities: when we discover things we have in common with others, our sense of belongingness increases. As a result, we grow trust with others in the group, which, in turn, allows us to act bravely and with vulnerability.

Think about our lives as teachers. Where do we find belongingness within our departments? We search out the like-minded folks within our sections and begin to develop a sisterhood or brotherhood. At faculty meetings, we tend to side with those individuals we're bonded with, and can sense the intangible connections among certain faculty. Our biology literally changes when we come into contact with a member of our team we haven't seen in a while. We feel our insides light up, we may get flushed, and a smile erupts on our face as we are propelled toward embracing them. This is because we found others similar to us who are fighting for the same higher purpose. In our personal lives, think about the rich connections we have to those around us, even if we are not in pursuit of the same thing (i.e., theatre).

From our loved ones to the members of our local neighborhood, proximity and shared resources also bond us. Roger has lived in the same neighborhood in Brooklyn for almost 20 years. When he walks his dog, he runs into Juliya at the market, Barish at the produce cart, and Alex at the fish store. He is an integral part of his community. He belongs to it.

Roger

Early in my acting career, I got pretty jealous of all my non-theatre friends who were making decent money, and not struggling to make ends meet like I was. They were all off nights and weekends, while I worked nights and weekends in a restaurant until at least midnight. I missed out on all their hijinks. I also missed out on their medical insurance, paid vacation time, and annual bonuses. Doubt is an essential ingredient in every creative endeavor. But this seed of doubt, "Am I doing the right thing?" worked its way pretty deeply in to my consciousness. So much so that I left acting for almost a year and landed a job doing production accounting on *Late Night with Conan O'Brien* and production assisting on *Saturday Night Live* I thought to myself, "This can't be too bad. It's not like I'm leaving the business completely, I'll still be around creative energy similar to the theatre." The jobs were fun. The best part? I got to see incredible musical artists like Alanis Morissette, Smashing Pumpkins, and Sting perform. Plus, seeing the talents of Molly Shannon, Will Ferrell, and Cheri Oteri on a weekly basis was thrilling. But ... I witnessed all these other people express their art, while I remained a bystander. After a few months, the ache in my soul and loneliness I felt from being without my theatre tribe outweighed the perks of television. I was out of place there, because I wasn't doing what was in my heart to do – act. I didn't last long, and some of my friends were shocked that I left such a cool job with great opportunity for advancement. My theatre pals got it. They got me. Barely weeks after quitting, I was in acting, voice, and movement classes at HB Studios. I was surrounded by strangers, and it was the first time in a while that I was happy. Their vulnerability, generosity, and risk taking were nourishing. These were my people. I belonged there. I haven't strayed from the theatre since.

We have all witnessed a brave student take their first big risk in our classrooms. It changes the molecular structure of the cohort. They start to have the courage to share openly and personally about what they are experiencing, a tool that is vital for the growth of any artist. They are metaphorically linking arms, and their brains are creating new neural pathways to strengthen this feeling of belonging where the habit of trust is built.

This is the environment we want for our incoming student actors; an environment where they can feel like they belong. Once they feel safe and secure, belonging to the group, then the collaboration can begin. More specifically, what is collaboration for the ensemble actor? It is working with others in an open, cooperative, and supportive way toward a common goal. For actors to achieve this, they must be open, receptive, present, fully engaged with the environment and everyone in it, *right now* to fulfill their mission to live truthfully under imaginary circumstances. This is what we know as being *in the moment*. Scientifically, this is accomplished through the engagement of the Collaborative Gene.

When students first arrive in our classrooms, we assess their ability to communicate. After all, acting is communicating. Even before we begin their training, we are eager to know who they are, what type of student they'll be, what type of personality they have, and how effective a collaborator they will be. There is a hodgepodge of factors that contribute to the identities of these young people, and these factors affect their ability to communicate and collaborate. Some students may have previous training, most have previous performing experience, and of course, we're familiar with students who come with bad habits. There is also a range of personality types, from introverts to extroverts; from those who struggle with personal issues, to those who are fortunate enough to be well adjusted. Nevertheless, thanks to the Collaborative Gene and our many years of experiencing the range of traits that they bring to the classroom, we have come to anticipate that our students bring with them a basic set of social skills.

David

A large part of my teaching and directing is in improvisation. I typically teach more than one section of an introductory improv course each term. Performing arts majors are required to take improv, while students from outside the major are free to take it if they like. These classes are always a mix of the eager, the reluctant, and the brave. Some students have no performing experience and are interested in the course as a way to open up their creative self. I have budding game designers, architects, animators, advertisers, writers, graphic designers, photographers, and more, routinely register for improv. As you might imagine, many of them often show up on the first day feeling nervous and fearful. As I begin the first class, I reassure everyone that if they possess the ability to carry on a positive, enjoyable conversation, then they have all the skills necessary to improvise. After all, nearly all conversation is improvised. However, I point out, there is a difference between sitting on your couch talking to your best friend and being in a job interview.

Both require the same set of skills, but one tends to be much harder than the other. I go on to explain that this course will begin in a way that feels like talking to your best friend and gradually show them how to translate this ability and improve their communication skill set to the point where they can improvise a scene or participate in a job interview with nearly the same ease. (Contrary to a popularly held belief, improv skills are not strictly comedy skills, they are communication and collaboration skills. They happen to lend themselves quite well to comedy, but may also be applied to any endeavor that relies on strong collaboration or clear and effective communication.)

When students enter our classrooms for the first time, they aren't consciously exhibiting skill sets, but they sure are exhibiting behaviors. And, it turns out, those behaviors actually *are* the skill sets essential to acting. A large bunch of these behaviors may be directly related to the Collaborative Gene and our innate urge to connect. That is, the students walk through the door with them already. In a broad sense, we tend to call these behaviors "social skills." For us, these behaviors include:

Awareness:

- The ability to make and keep comfortable eye contact.
- The ability to listen and observe.
- An awareness of what is around you, of what is going on, of the moment.
- The ability to focus on a partner.
- The ability to acknowledge.
- The ability to show empathy.
- An awareness that contextual behavioral boundaries exist.

Expression:

- The ability to share their own thoughts.
- The ability to initiate a conversation, even if awkwardly.
- The ability to be responsible for one's actions.
- The ability to make and receive simple physical contact (handshakes, hugs, pats on the back, etc.).
- The ability to apologize, even if reluctantly.
- The ability to share and compromise with others.
- The ability to express negative feelings in a healthy way, with awareness of how they are received.
- The ability to be courteous and respectful.

Risk:

- The ability to be vulnerable with others.
- The ability to be spontaneous or impulsive when needed (e.g., playing a game).
- Having the courage to face the unknown or confront a fear.
- The ability to handle constructive criticism.

Levels of these behaviors vary based on maturity, and of course some are easier than others (it may be easier to listen than to apologize, for instance), but we expect to see a good number of these behaviors in abundance.

But beware: there are limitations to the Collaborative Gene. We are only hard-wired for the *potential* to exhibit these behaviors. They cannot manifest fully without being nurtured. Our families, friends, teachers, environment, even strangers – anyone or anything we interact with – can have an impact on the development of our collaborative skills. As we covered in *Ensemble Theatre Making*, a large part of the social fabric of our world is grounded in social groups or tribes to which we belong and that help us grow: schools, churches, clubs, teams, communities (it takes a village) (Bonczek and Storck). All of these groups allow us direct interaction with other people on a regular basis. We collaborate with each other, learning, practicing, failing, healing, and growing, all as part of the nurturing process needed for the full development of the Collaborative Gene.

Many of our students are leaving their familiar communities, all their ties that give them a sense of belonging, and entering into a phase of their life where they pretty much know no one. It makes perfect sense for them to stay connected to their communities in order to satisfy their innate need of belonging. They are satisfying this innate need to belong through the most accessible way they know how. In the past, we had to do that with letters or long-distance telephone calls. Now, a dear friend is only seconds away via a text, and seeing what loved ones at home are up to on Instagram or Facebook will quell the unease of feeling unattached. Any acting teacher in those first few months of training a new cohort will share how crucial it is to create a strong and healthy ensemble. But now, more than ever, it is vital that we nourish this belongingness early on. If we are asking our students to enter into this foreign arena of living life more fully present, less engaged with devices, they will need a safe and secure tribe to hold the space for the certain loneliness and anxiety that is approaching. That safe and secure tribe will come from nurturing a sense of belonging in all the individuals toward the greater good of the group. Ensemble exercises that promote inclusion, collaboration, and so on (Spolin, Boal, Johnstone come to mind) are fantastic for creating many skills an actor needs to thrive; and yet ultimately, most importantly, what their exercises are doing is creating the deepest foundation of belonging for all other work to be built upon.

Returning to our flame metaphor for a moment ... If we move through this life solely by the light of our own internal flame, our view is limited and we are isolated. But if we come together, our flames create a larger glow, illuminating more of our world, creating warmth, safety, and community. We look to banish shadows, darkness, and the cold. We connect and we belong. And by coming together with other flames, we learn what it takes to fuel our own flames, grow them, and protect them from being diminished or extinguished. Thanks to the Collaborative Gene and a positive nurturing process, aspiring actors have historically shown up to class with a solid set of basic social skills. These skills are an important foundation to acting training. We count on students to possess them.

But what if our students started showing up without these skills? What if the ability to collaborate, despite being hard-wired, hadn't been nourished? How could the need to belong be thwarted or otherwise satisfied? Unfortunately, there are factors that can impede the development of our collaborative behaviors: social isolation, neglect, and powerful distractions (addiction, etc.) among them. Imagine your first day of class: observing behaviors that are a far cry from the collaborative skills we have always expected. What would happen to actor training?

Bibliography

Boal, Augusto. *Games for Actors and Non-Actors*, 2nd ed. Routledge, 2002. Print.

Bonczek, Rose. B. and David Storck, *Ensemble Theatre Making: A Practical Guide*, Routledge, 2013. Print.

McConnell, Allen R. "Belongingness: Essential Bridges That Support the Self." *Psychology Today*. Sussex Publishers, 1 Aug. 2013. Web. 1 Jan 2018.

Spolin, Viola. *Improvisation for the Theater*, 3rd ed. Northwestern University Press, 1999. Print.

Chapter 2

The growing isolation of the Collaborative Gene

> We're filled with joy when we belong to an ensemble that works well together. We thrive on the reliability of it. We feel respected, liked, and loved – by the ensemble . . . We look forward to spending time with these playmates. It gives us a sense of security, a sense of belonging to a community. And without this we tend to hold ourselves back from the world.
>
> (Bonczek and Storck 9)

It would have never, ever occurred to any of us that collaborating, or the desire to collaborate, would be something that could be endangered. Sure, every student and teacher has times when they need a break from the work or from a group, but never a desire to stop the very act of playing and working together. Through our acting classes together, we've always worked with our students to realize the full potential of their collaborative skills and their humanity, but we've never had to teach them how to *be* human or how to *have* humanity.

Lucky us.
And then . . .

Something started happening. For some of us, it began as a "funny feeling"; students seemed to have less fun in exercises, we had multiple students who were chronically late, or we observed students ignoring each other for periods of time. For others, it was noticing how quiet it had suddenly gotten. For years, we had yelled "OK, quiet down and focus please. *Focus please?!?*" The ruckus became less ruckus-y; our classrooms of acting students that usually behaved like a giant pile of sprightly puppies felt a little more like a handful of weary, fat Labrador Retrievers snoozing on a porch. It went from being strange to feeling downright eerie. Who were *these* students? And what had they done with our frisky and playful ensembles? While we had always had introverts in our classes, we noticed a distinct change in behaviors. It was a sharp shift *away* from basic human social skills: empathy, listening, eye contact, and so on. There was a sense of students talking *at* each other instead of *to* each other. That is, when they *did* speak to one another.

Rose

I remember a new group of students who had seemed quiet during our early classes together. What struck me was that for the first time, no student stayed to ask me any questions at the end of class. Usually students had loads of questions – or they simply wanted to get to know me a little better to get a grip on expectations for the semester ("Is she a hard ass? Will she be relatively easy on us? Is she open to conversation outside of the lessons? What does she expect in those written assignments, really?"). No one stayed. At about class meeting number four, I noticed something even more peculiar. When class finished, and people were filing out, students weren't speaking very much to one another either. No exchanges about who was going where for lunch, who had time to rehearse a scene, it was pretty quiet. And bizarre.

We began compiling a list of those new patterns of behaviors that we were seeing; and what we saw gave us pause. We observed more students:

- Lacking empathy

  o   An inability to recognize social signals in others.
  o   More obliviousness to the feelings of others (lack of tact).
  o   Decreased ability to compromise or share.
  o   Decreased ability to work out problems with others.
  o   Not knowing how to apologize. "I'm sorry you took what I said the wrong way."
  o   Less awareness of how their actions affect others and how they make them feel.
  o   Quick to label discussion topics as offensive or inappropriate.

- Lacking ability to be present and in the moment

  o   Struggling to truly listen, engage and absorb information.
  o   Lacking patience; need for immediate success and satisfaction.
  o   Struggling to embrace silence and stillness with another (too awkward).
  o   Having less ability to manage time (organizing one's schedule, being on time, following deadlines, etc.).

- Having less willingness to be vulnerable

  o The inability to make sustained eye contact, particularly in moments of difficulty.

  o Refusing to engage in moments that require physical intimacy of the characters.

  o The repeated desire to get out of exercises that are challenging in favor of simply repeating favorite exercises.

  o Increase in students who value acting for its therapeutic value. Wanting to only play the roles, objectives, tactics, and so on, that makes them feel good.

- Lacking self-awareness and awareness of what surrounds them

  o Increased emotional immaturity.

  o The inability to handle failure to the point of having to leave the room.

  o The inability to articulate why they want to be an actor.

  o Disruptive or disrespectful behavior in classroom (yawning loudly without covering their mouths, rummaging loudly in their bags while someone is working, standing up and leaving while someone is working).

  o Less awareness of immediate environment; how to allow that to support choices.

- Struggling to be spontaneous and act on first impulses

  o Decrease in trusting their choices, or that of their partners.

  o Decrease in ability to recognize (or accept) what their impulsive responses *are*.

  o Struggle to commit to choices without "editing"; that is, wanting to correct a choice before it has even been responded to by a partner.

- Having less ability to take responsibility for one's actions

  o Increased citing of previous successes to fend off feelings of failure or inadequacy.

  o Increased blaming of others.

  o Not wanting notes, just affirmation that they're doing well.

  o Having less commitment to a work ethic of working hard to achieve goals.

- Having less desire and ability to play well with others

  o Preference for working on something important to them vs. something that the group creates together.

  o Lack of preparedness when scenes or group projects are due.

  o Increase in "blowing off" a scene partner or rehearsal outside of class.

- Lacking focus: mental and physical
  - o Lack of concentration.
  - o Suffering from insomnia.
  - o Choosing to stay up very late, then unable to fall sleep.
- Physical symptoms
  - o Lacking physical stamina.
  - o Fidgeting or bouncing their knees during class.
  - o Hunched shoulders, with neck (and eyes) downcast.
- Having poorer retention and memory (for text, reading, and rehearsal notes, for instructions given verbally in classes).
- Confusing the difference between actual memory and virtual memory (what they think they know vs. what they know they can access via a device).
- Having weak reading comprehension skills (struggling to synthesize ideas and readings).
- Having weak writing skills, including less ability to recognize errors or proofread written work.

David

I once had a freshman acting student who, despite all my best efforts to encourage her, gave minimal effort, and yet was quite satisfied with her work. She was displaying many of the symptoms that we have already described as being problematic: reluctance to separate from her phone, avoiding discomfort and vulnerability, a lack of empathy and stamina, and more. Gradually, I added to my encouragement a more direct and unsoftened critique of her work and her approach to the work. This did not go over well. She either couldn't grasp the truth of what I was telling her, or was refusing to acknowledge it. We've all had students in our classes who exhibit these behaviors and it's our job to continue to challenge them toward better work. I should tell you at this point, and you'll have to take my word for it, that I am not one of those "tough teachers"; I default to being encouraging and positive ("Yes and!"). But when the occasion calls for it, I can be tough and direct. And it tends to be quite effective for the very reason that it is out of the ordinary for me. Well, one day, I finally got tough and very direct with this student. In response, she simply threw her script to the floor, screamed in frustration, and left. Not just left the room, left the building entirely. After class, I sent her an email asking her to come meet with me in my office. The next day she was waiting outside my door when I arrived. I could feel the frustration practically vibrating from her body as she entered. At some point during the discussion that followed, she blurted out through her tears, "I have never worked so hard at anything in my life!" And it dawned on me: she was right. Despite the fact that I saw her work ethic as quite low, to her, it was a full 100 percent effort. In truth, she had always been passionate about acting and always contributed eagerly to class discussions. She saw herself as doing everything she possibly could to get better and couldn't understand why I thought so little of her efforts and her work. I told her that I believed her; that I had no doubt this was the hardest that she had ever worked. Then, as gently as I could, I told her that, through no fault of her own, she had been given unrealistic expectations. As I sat in my chair, I held my right hand out in front of me, palm downward, at about mid-chest level and indicated that this is how hard she's working. Then I held out my left hand, at the level of the top of my head, and told her that this is how hard you need to work as a professional. With my lap serving as the base, it created the impression that she was at about four or five out of ten (which was a generous rating). "This is how tough you have to be with yourself, how many hours you have to put in, how prepared you have to be, what the industry expects of you and needs from you," I said. She looked at me incredulously and kept crying. I once again assured her that this wasn't her fault, but that if she hoped to pursue a career as an actor, this is what it would take. Finally, I told her that I would help her to make this adjustment. She would have to do the work, but I would help her get there if she was willing to do it. In retrospect, this was an early warning sign of the behavioral shifts appearing in our students. I'm happy to report that after a weekend of thought, she returned to class and began the climb toward a more demanding approach.

We realize that many of these behaviors have been observed in our acting students before now; what we're talking about is a substantial increase in the consistency, frequency, and intensity of these behaviors. So of course we were compelled to ask, "*Why* are we seeing these shifts away from collaborative behavior, at this moment in time?" Finally, we asked ourselves, "What could possibly cause suppression of collaborative behavior if we are hard wired to do it?" *That* question led to this book; and we each remember the first time the answer hit us.

Rose

Louise's neck. Six years ago.

The new BFA Acting Program students in the Fall of 2011; improvisation class. The actors are always a little nervous; they think I'm going to force them to do "Whose Line is It Anyway?" Once they see how bad it isn't – the majority of them relax, follow impulses, listen, and then play play play . . .

We warmed up, and went into *Kitty Wants a Corner*. I noticed that the students were surprisingly disconnected. Now, there are few acting exercises on the planet that trigger one's Inner Kid more than *Kitty*. You get to play with a big group, you get to be sneaky, you're trying to "get home," and you get to run in a classroom. I think we'd have a better chance at World Peace if we had *Kitty Wants a Corner* gymnasiums . . . *Kitty* brings every acting element together; listening, awareness, focus, observation, objective, obstacles, tactics, stamina, specificity, and more. These new students were a bit more hesitant to let their Inner Kid out to play in their backyard. No worries, I thought, give it a little more time. We ended the exercise and sat down to a) catch our breath, and b) do our post-exercise discussion to talk about the acting elements in *Kitty*, and what their experiences were. They were a little quieter than last year's group. And then I saw it.

Louise's neck.

Louise's head was bent from her neck at an odd angle, with her eyes very firmly fixed into space at a point that was not quite the floor, but certainly not on any of the people in the room. My first thought was, "What the hell is she looking at?" My second was, "She isn't listening to what anyone is saying." I called her name, and she blinked her eyes and seemed to come out of a fog and turned toward me a beat or two later than one would expect. I asked, "What do you think of what Cristina just said?" She replied, "I don't know." She wasn't making eye contact with me, though she was trying to. My first thought was "Drugs? Insomnia?" and then chalked it up to how utterly overwhelming a new program can be. But when she looked away, I noticed one or two other students whose gazes were somewhere else – not on her or on me, simply somewhere else. OK, got it. This group needs more focus work. It'll get better.

But it didn't.

Louise – and a few others to a lesser extent – struggled to listen and make the kind of connections actors need to make. It was physically noticeable. At times, I would see that weird angle of the neck, their eyes seeming to stare at something specific in space, and their struggle to simply be in the moment. I had no clue what the hell I was seeing.

One day, I was walking across campus and I noticed several students with cell phones in hand – ah, there's that new smartphone thing, I thought – and the students weren't looking where they were going; they were looking at the device in their hand, texting or scrolling something with their fingers, occasionally bumping into one another. I realized their necks were at the same angle as Louise's. The following week I saw that, indeed, she had this newfangled smartphone thing, where other students had the old flip phones.

David

The most prominent behavioral change I noticed was in student inter-action immediately before and after class, and during the mid-class break. Most of the time, the room was silent. The students were all on their cell phones. Just a few years earlier, the room was abuzz with activity, not the least of which was a series of animated conversations. They were laughing, commiserating, arguing, supporting – they were sharing and interacting. This is what students had always done during free time. Now they were all looking down at their phones in silence.

I tried an experiment. I conducted an exercise that had consistently generated the most interest and discussion among the students in the past. As always, they were eager to share their thoughts afterwards. But this time, after only a few minutes of sharing, I cut the discussion off and announced it was break time. Some seemed genuinely disappointed. I moved to the corner of the room and waited. No one approached me to talk further. Only two students engaged in a conversation. Three left the room. Eleven out of 16 went straight to their cell phones.

I continued my observations for another week or so. I was fasci-nated (and admittedly, dismayed) by this behavior. Why weren't they talking to each other? Finally, I tried something radical: I shared my observations with them and asked them why they were going to their phones instead of talking to each other. I know, I'm no social scientist – after only one experiment I gave up and just asked them.

There was silence, as if I had asked them something forbidden. Then a few awkward mumblings and excuses, "I don't know," "I have to check my messages," and so on. Then someone said, "I wanted to see what's happening." This struck a note. "What's happening?" I asked, thinking there had been a big story on the news. "You know, see what people are posting." Ah hah! A light bulb moment. I inquired further. Eventually, I pushed for an answer to the question, "Why don't you talk to each other instead of going to your phones?" Finally, one student volunteered, "I don't know how to start a conversation with people I don't know." That wasn't too surprising; we all have introverts in our classrooms. But what followed shocked me. Nearly everyone agreed with him. A discussion quickly ensued. First, students wanted to admit and share their experiences about a seeming inability to make initial connections with others. The others watched intently and nodded as these stories unfolded. They grew bolder in their admissions as they realized how many others shared the same fears and difficulties. A pattern began to emerge: the fears and difficulties related to direct, face-to-face communications. As they explained, communication with people online was easier and safer. Dating apps, in particular, were popular. Every single student in that class had used one. It enabled them to prejudge people, eliminate undesirables, and establish some common ground with others, all before ever actually meeting face-to-face. It also gave them time to ponder responses and not be caught having to answer in the moment. This was another light bulb moment. The ability to avoid being in the moment. How devastating is that for an aspiring actor? Yet I empathized with their point of view. Who wouldn't be drawn to the avoidance, or at least minimalizing, of the downsides of direct interaction? Their choices made sense. It was the world as they knew it.

Roger

It was my first day of class at The New School in New York City. The course is called Performance Lab, a class I created to develop empathy, collaboration, and communication using methods from the performing arts. As I walked over to my studio, I noticed all my students were standing in a single file line outside the room. One would figure, it being the first day of classes, it would be cacophonous. The energy on the first day of classes is usually palpable. Not today. The hallway barely had a low hum of noise from the traffic of others finding their way. My students? Every single one of them was staring down at their smartphone. Every one. I paused, looking at them all. Fourteen. That's how many there were in line. Nobody noticed me there, still and staring. I wanted to take this sight in. There's awkwardness to first days, not knowing anyone. Instead of reaching out a hand to introduce themselves to the person in line with them, they were keeping themselves safe by engaging in their technology. Instead of dealing with another human being, and exchanging who they were, the students chose to remain safe from the "other." When I was an undergraduate and graduate student, I recall the excitement of meeting my peers on that first day. It would have felt strange to be sitting outside a studio with my classmates, being on my device, and not interacting with them. The shy students didn't have the protection of technology to keep them away from experiencing one another. We all had to engage with another, regardless if we were nervous or not. It was an acting class; a place where we were to explore stories through sharing deep interpersonal relationships. Yet these new students I was encountering on day one were from a different era than those who came before them.

The Digital Natives weren't doing anything wrong. They were making a choice to stay connected to their technology instead of connecting to their human classmates because of the conditioning they grew up with. This got me asking questions. In what condition are these natives arriving at our studios?

The common denominator was: smartphones. More specifically, *how* students were using smartphones: their use of Internet, texting, social media, and other spectacular creations of the digital age were squashing their Collaborative Genes. We're experiencing the first generation of students who have had smartphones, tablets, and unlimited Internet access in the home since early childhood. Education consultant Marc Prensky coined the term "Digital Native" back in 2001 to describe someone who has grown up with digital technology rather than learning those systems as an adult (he called those people Digital Immigrants) (Prensky). In a 2017 study, the Pew Research

Center reported that 92 percent of individuals between the ages of 18 and 29 owned smartphones; in 2011, that figure was just 35 percent (Smith). In a 2013 survey of over 2000 undergraduate students, women between the ages of 18 and 23 averaged ten hours of daily smartphone use (with the most popular activity being texting), and men in the same age group averaged eight hours daily (most popular activity being gaming) (Roberts et al.). A 2016 report titled *Kids and Tech: The Evolution of Today's Digital Natives* stated that the average age that a child gets a smartphone is ten, and their first online social media account at age 11. There's less need, and sometimes, less desire for, face-to-face interaction. Face-to-face has to compete with interface: social media, texting, sexting(!), computer gaming, email, and the allure of anonymity that's available through the Internet. As a result, our acting students are not reporting to their first day of freshman year with the same basic set of social skills that we used to rely on through the Collaborative Gene.

Rose

I had started the semester of September 2014 with a terrific group of new BFAs; so talented, smart, eager to learn. Two weeks into the semester, I was reeling from frustration. A significant number of students were late to our acting class, late to movement and voice classes, late turning in written assignments or they simply hadn't done them, were zoning out when called upon, and seemed unfocused. At week three, we were scheduled to start class with a discussion of the reading; I couldn't do it. I said, "Look. Something is clearly wrong here. You all worked incredibly hard to get into this program. You've all sacrificed a lot so that you can *have* an education. What the hell is going on? Truly – I need you to tell me what is happening in your lives – right now. What's interfering with your ability to meet even the most basic requirements? We can't support you and help you get what you need if we don't know what's going on!"

In seconds, several were in tears. They spoke of being up until all hours, unable to tear themselves away from social media and texts arriving from friends in the middle of the night. They spoke about starting homework on their computers, and then getting "sucked in" to something on YouTube and before they knew it, hours would have passed. They talked about how hard they would try to fall asleep after many hours on the computer, and being so exhausted and frustrated that their bodies wouldn't *let* them sleep. They spoke about their struggles with time management, or to simply be able to focus on a single task. And then Adama Jackson said, "I have a story that I must share. I'm embarrassed to say it, but I have to, because it is absolutely what we are talking about." And she proceeded to share what I consider a defining moment in my teaching career. The "Bug" story.

She said, "When I was in high school and living at home in Brooklyn, one day I was in my room, and I noticed this bug on my wall. It was one of those centipede things with a million legs; I hated that bug, and I squished him on my wall. I said, 'ha HA, got you!' And every time I would see the squish stain of that bug on my wall, I would think, again, 'ha HA, I got you!' I graduated high school, went away to SUNY Buffalo for one year, then decided to transfer to Brooklyn College last spring, and I moved back home last May. A few weeks ago, I was brushing my teeth, and I saw a little centipede in the sink. I killed it, and it made me think of My Bug who I hadn't looked at in a while; so I went to my room. I looked – I didn't see him – and I noticed that the walls of my room were a different color. I went to the kitchen and said, 'Mommy – when did you paint my room?' She said, 'Honey, we painted your room when you left for Buffalo last *year*.'" Adama paused for a moment, and with powerful emotion, said: "How can I possibly be an actor – how can I possibly expect to create truthful human behavior on stage – if I'm so unaware of everything around me that I didn't even notice that the walls of my own bedroom had been a different color for *months*? What does that say?"

And at this point, pretty much the entire class was weeping . . . with recognition. The discussion that followed – about their struggles to be present in their own lives and be in the moment – any moment – changed the course of my teaching. Those students' powerful and brave acknowledgments gave us all the courage to make changes in ourselves from that day forward.

What does a smartphone demand of its user that has the potential to interfere so significantly with an actor's abilities? Let's go back to the basics to find out.

It starts with the eyes

With a simple look, you can see or express love, hate, fear, regret, surprise, and a host of other emotions. You can give or deny permission. And you don't need to know someone's language or culture to understand the meaning of their eye contact. It is virtually a universal language.

We have strong associations with the quality of eye contact: personal integrity ("look me in the eye") and self-esteem or shame ("he just looks at the floor"). David was told as a boy that when meeting someone for the first time, he was to look them straight in the eye and give a firm handshake. He wasn't told what to say, just what kind of *contact* to make.

Eye contact is so potent that we have a hard time with it in concentrated doses. Ever have a staring contest? Or get a creepy feeling from too much eye contact? Or say, "I love you" before you *say*, "I love you."

Contact is remarkably intimate; it's direct. It's one of the most powerful tools that actors possess. It's also a powerful tool for teachers (although physical contact may be fraught with issues, there can be little doubt about eye contact). And when we can't get eye contact with an acting partner or a student, it makes the job harder.

Eye contact isn't easy. It's a social skill that requires practice through regular use. What has happened to eye contact in your classrooms? If it's anything like ours, eye contact has decreased as the use of personal devices has increased. As we began to express ourselves more and more through the filter of technology and devices (typing, emails, texting, etc.), the emphasis was placed on written words. Direct contact decreased. Our students developed fewer intimates in their lives and they grew more isolated. When words in texts didn't seem to fully satisfy, even after they were abbreviated (LOL), we came up with emoticons. Sure, they're fun, but a poor substitute for the human face. Emoticons acknowledged the need for physical expression, but they too, proved insufficient. Enter the selfie. "Here's some eye contact to show what I'm feeling. See how much fun I'm having?" So now we have the human face reintroduced, but with a single, frozen expression. You don't have to be a Mona Lisa scholar to know the intricacy of deciphering the inscrutable meaning behind an image. Yet the selfie proved insufficient for our technology-driven needs. Finally, FaceTime appears. "It's like I'm on TV!" True, living expressions are reintroduced, but reduced to a flat screen, usually much smaller than an actual face. Yet this is neither direct nor personal. If I'm falling in love with you, I want to fall in love with *you*, not a broadcast of you ("I can't see your pores, but your pixels look great"). And as much as it allows me to avoid emotional pain (breaking up by text message has become a thing), I shouldn't hide from difficult feelings if I want to be an actor or a fully realized human being. But, interacting through a device offers an enormous amount of control. It becomes so, so easy to hide behind a device.

The insidious quality of these machines is that they seem to make us closer. In many ways, they do contribute to communication, but they are not equivalent to direct contact. As we come to rely on them more and more, the slow erosion of direct contact goes unnoticed. The avoidance of pain is seen as an advance, not a double-edged sword. Our increased isolation is a confounding new environment specifically because it doesn't seem isolated.

Acting teacher Anya Saffir wisely said, "The job of the actor is to reveal themselves." So, if our students are hiding more, speaking less, truncating words essential to language and expression, spending more time online rather than in life, they have less awareness of the self they're being asked *to* reveal. We need to understand more fully why our students find it easier to communicate and share through electronic devices instead of having those discussions and negotiations with one another face-to-face. If they don't develop those skills and levels of understanding because they were raised with the omnipresence of devices, then they're not just avoiding an unpleasant situation; they will be lacking empathy, vulnerability, and the ability to be present and spontaneous. In short, they will struggle to collaborate and communicate effectively. If they're having difficulty living in the moment in their actual life, how can they live in the moment as an actor?

David

Improv w/eye contact

In my improv classes, I have always included exercises that focus on eye contact. Improv benefits from all the nuances that eye contact brings. In recent years, however, I find that it requires more work to get the same level of eye contact. It takes longer because some students are entering without the tolerance for sustained eye contact. And some even lack understanding of a full range of facial expressions. They can't tell me what the look on someone else's face means to them. They want me to tell them. This extreme is startling, and thankfully rare, but I don't remember it happening at all ten years ago. Each time this has happened, it was with a student who was chronically looking at their phone.

Empathy

Eye contact with non-interacting screens may feel real to our students, but without the live, intimate quality of direct eye contact, something valuable is lost. Viewing through screens allows us to distance ourselves emotionally from what we are seeing. Our sense of responsibility – and response ability – becomes diminished. When something is happening in front of us, so often now we pull out our phones, record it, then post it online as if to say, "Someone should do something about this." Apathy, and an unwillingness to get involved, has always existed in society. However, does the proliferation of cell phone videos give the illusion that the act of recording the event alone *is* "involvement"? Unless taking the video is followed by taking an action, then we might be creating a record that the event occurred, but we aren't actually responding to the event itself.

Albert Einstein said, "It has become appallingly obvious that our technology has exceeded our humanity" (Ann). The essential ingredient in humanity is our humaneness – our ability to be fully present and engaged with our fellow humans (and animals, of course). To share a compassionate bond with those around us, and allow our hearts to be affected by the experiences of mankind. Empathy is the essential building block to our humanity.

This empathy gap extends to how our students consider their actions toward one another. The phrase "the show must go on" is as cliché as it gets; but at the heart of it is a message of commitment to one another and to collaboration. If you don't show up, the show literally cannot go on. Increases in the lateness of students to classes and rehearsals may seem on the surface to be selfish carelessness (and of course it is that too!), but it really reflects a lack of empathy. If someone isn't considering what all those people who are waiting for them are doing or feeling, that's an empathy gap. This disconnect in our student's understanding (or caring) how their actions affect others seems to be growing each year, and that's bad news. In this collaborative profession, if they don't learn commitment and time management now, they won't have a future. As we often tell our students, your talent may get you your first job; but your terrible habits of lateness and your inconsiderate behavior will deny you your second. It's common human respect to understand that if someone is depending on you and you don't show up, you're affecting that person's ability to do their work, and possibly hurting them in the process. There is an assumption on the student's part that a simple text announcing their lateness absolves responsibility in showing up late. So why is lateness to classes and rehearsals becoming more common, despite talks with students, giving written guidelines, and consequences ranging from locked door policies to lower grades? Something deeper is at work, and that's a lessening of empathy.

Vulnerability, spontaneity   *Lateness ≠ lessening of empathy*

Communicating through a device also allows us to more carefully consider, plan, and edit our responses. Or to keep them secret altogether. We lose some of the honest, uncontrollable reactions that come from us in the moment and that are vital to communication. We're avoiding the consequences that come from direct contact. Of course, at first, that sounds like a good thing. Who wakes up in the morning and says, "I can't wait to see what consequences I get to face today?" But is avoiding consequences really altogether a good thing? What are the benefits of consequences? At the top of our list: learning. Pain is unfortunately necessary to human development. The more we enable ourselves to opt out of pain, the less connected we are to humanity. And that impact on our students is very real. If we had a nickel for every colleague who has bemoaned "The Entitlement Generation" of students, we could, well, let's just say we'd have a lot of nickels. Is it simply a coincidence that the "Entitlement Generation" is the same generation that has been able to avoid consequences through technology? The advent of trigger warnings is a result of an entire generation of students who don't have to suffer consequences, make regular eye contact, or feel necessary pain.

The sound of silence

As we each noted in our earlier stories, silence is fast replacing the sounds of animated conversations among our students. What are they literally doing instead? Texting, checking social media accounts (Facebook, Snapchat, Instagram, Twitter), checking email, swiping stories, clicking "Likes," scrolling for new posts, scrolling for a post newer than the ones they looked at two minutes ago . . . The smartphone allows us to carry a phone, computer, TV, and worldwide Internet access in our hand wherever we go. There is never *not* something new. The temptation to check and check and check again is beautifully summed up by Dr. Mari Swingle in her book *i-Minds* when she addresses her definition of "the anticipatory state":

> In an old world analogy, it is the brain state of the moment a person is presented with a wrapped gift, and the mini-high they get during the unwrapping. "Is it . . . ? Isn't it . . . ?" When multiple gifts are under the tree, the majority of children do not spend time on the unwrapped gift (no matter how much they begged for it and wanted it). They unwrap the gift, squeal with delight, and then jump immediately to the next. Most children will only go back to the gift collection once there are no more packages to be unwrapped. The million dollar question of the digital age is whether the expression of disappointment is due to the gift not received, or whether they just want more "highs" of the unwrapping process.
>
> (Swingle 13)

And this is why simply telling our students to "turn those things off" was not, and is not, enough; not even close. This is also why the argument "What are you worried about? Our generation watched too much TV; same thing" doesn't hold up. Our televisions never interacted with us, offered to personalize our programming, or could be pulled out of our pockets whenever we wanted to watch. This is why so many of our students look down at their device instead of up and into the eyes of their acting partner or teacher. There's an endless supply of wrapped presents in their hand. In fact, they have the whole world in their hand. They can control it, and get as many presents as they want: their device says, "Your wish is my command." But what about the person standing in front of them? "I don't know what presents they may have for me – if any. I can't make them do or say what I want. What if they don't like me? Too risky." We need to teach our students that the real present is their partner themselves; the gift is in the as-yet-unknown collaboration and joy in their moments together, and that they would do well to remember the adage "it's better to give than to receive."

Now, before any of us get too righteous, during the same years that we noticed our students' behavior changing, we saw faculty colleagues texting during shows (to the extent that students who had performed would come to us in tears, thinking that they had sucked so badly that even acting teachers didn't want to watch them). We noticed little by little that during faculty meetings, teachers went from sneaking peeks at their cell phones under the table while someone was talking, to outright having the phone in full view, scrolling and checking and texting while someone was talking or presenting. Look, no one *loves* faculty meetings, but it's the one day a month we can come together as educators. If acting teachers can't be present with one another for a brief time, then what the hell is happening in our classrooms?

Roger

Two of my high school students were up on their feet ready to present their first showing of their new scene. Greg had his script in hand, but Jackie informed me she forgot hers at home. I was irritated, and Jackie could tell. She begged, "I have the scene on my phone. Can I please work from it?" I caved, allowed her to turn her device on, and bring it in to the playing area. I should've trusted my instincts. I knew it was a bad idea, but I didn't want Greg to suffer the consequences of not working because of his partner's error. They began working. Greg picked up the words from his script, and married his impulses to the text in a way that was refreshing for a first run. Jackie? Not so much. Between the swiping to a new page, and the constant scrolling up and down to find her place, she had a deeper connection to her phone than Greg. Plus, the phone's screen wasn't very big, and she held it so close to her face I thought she would kiss it at one point! Jackie said things like, "Hold on, I lost my place," and, "Shit! The screen turned off for some reason. Hold on." There was absolutely no way she could be present for her partner when her phone was demanding all her *doing!* The class could sense my frustration, but I continued to remain quiet. I stopped them at a particularly unclear moment in the scene, and asked Jackie what she was doing. "I know what I'm doing, I swear. I wrote it down. But all my tactics are written on my script at home," she sheepishly confessed. I lost it. I stood up, exclaiming to the class, "Let's thank Jackie today for her beautiful example of why digital scripts are not allowed in my acting class!"

We have new competition in gaining and holding our students' attention; the smartphone is a new character in the story of education as we know it (and we'll get to know that character better in the next chapter). As theatre teachers and ensemble leaders, we need to analyze and learn as much as we can about it, because it isn't exiting the story anytime soon – if ever. It wields enormous power over our students and their ensembles in ways that we are only beginning to understand – so time is of the essence. In Chapter 3, we'll share what the current research has to say about the technology behind the smartphone, its design, and the role it plays in influencing human behaviors. In Chapter 4, we mainly turn the discussion over to our own acting students as we share the powerful (and sometimes heartbreaking) discoveries that they made as they embarked on a series of daily and 24-hour Digital Disconnects as part of their training. Their personal and artistic revelations, combined with what current research reveals, led us to make profound changes in our teaching and curriculum. With a broader understanding of the science behind the technology, and a deeper knowledge of the personal and societal reasons for our students' excessive tech reliance, we can create strong and effective strategies to teach them to maintain a balance between their screen time and direct human interaction. We can help them rekindle their Collaborative Genes, and guide them in developing a consistent practice to keep their acting and ensemble skills healthy and strong.

Bibliography

Ann, Jessica. "Will Technology Exceed our Humanity?" Jessica Ann Media, 30 Nov. 2011. Web. 5 Dec. 2017.

Bonczek, Rose B. and David Storck. *Ensemble Theatre Making: A Practical Guide.* Routledge, 2013. Print.

Influence Central, n.d. "Kids and Tech: The Evolution of Today's Digital Natives." Web. 4 July 2017.

Prensky, Marc. "Digital Natives, Digital Immigrants." *On the Horizon* 9.5 (2001): n.pag. Web. 4 July 2017.

Roberts, James A., Luc Honore Petnji Yaya and Chris Manolis. "The Invisible Addiction: Cell-phone Activities and Addiction Among Male and Female College Students." *Journal B.A.* 3.4 (2014): 254–265. Web. 12 Jan 2018.

Smith, Aaron. "Record Shares of Americans Now Own Smartphones, Have Home Broadband." Pew Research Center, 12 Jan. 2017. Web. 4 July 2017.

Swingle, Mari K. *i-Minds.* Inkwater Press, 2015. Print.

Chapter 3

Impact of technology on collaborative behaviors

This thing is a slot machine... every time I check my phone, I'm playing the slot machine to see, 'What did I get?' This is one way to hijack people's minds and create a habit, to form a habit. What you do is you make it so when someone pulls a lever, sometimes they get a reward, an exciting reward. And it turns out that this design technique can be embedded inside of all these products.

(Tristan Harris, former Design Ethicist at Google)

So far, we've focused on our students, and our observations as teachers, to identify the shifts in human behavior caused by the introduction of smartphone technology. As you read the quotes from the Digital Disconnects throughout the book, you may spot a recurring theme: students caught unaware of the changes that were happening to them. They all express their surprise at the realization of their behavioral shifts. How can this be? How can they largely fail to see what is happening to them? To help us understand, let's take a closer look at the evolution of our relationship to technology.

Meet Sam, a *Homo sapiens*. Sam is adaptable, a social animal. She has the benefit of 100,000 years of human development helping her negotiate the world around her. She belongs to a species that has learned to thrive by collaborating with others in order to survive. Archaeological evidence shows that ancient peoples suffered major injuries that healed; injuries that they wouldn't have survived without assistance from others (Schulting and Fibiger 14). Throughout the world, there are examples of early communal "stone villages" such as Skara Brae in Scotland dating back to 3100 BC (Orkneyjar: The Heritage of the Orkney Islands), and the Bronze Age settlement of Akrotiri in Ancient Greece (Santorini Web Portals); complexes with interconnecting homes and work places that illustrate tight-knit communities. Community gave us safe havens with supportive members, which aided survival. From those early days, all the way to today, an incredible device has allowed individuals to be productive members of their communities. Sam has the latest, upgraded model available. It's her brain. An incredibly intricate organ/machine that allows her to problem solve and execute highly complex functions. It is through this rather remarkable device that Sam is able to engage her Collaborative Gene and connect with those around her. It has been that way for tens of thousands of years.

Over time, the brain has been able to devise systems and methods to make its work easier; for instance, cave paintings. By painting the story of a successful hunt on the cave wall, Sam's forebear was able to download her knowledge using the medium of the day, allowing her to share her knowledge for the benefit of the community and succeeding generations. Plus, it freed up memory space in the brain, allowing her to reapply those gigabytes.

Let's fast forward all the way to the 1940s, when a significant development occurred. A new device that signaled a turning point in our world was born. It was as big as a cafeteria and called The Electronic Brain (Hally). It could compute, hold tons of data, and perform a task that would take Sam days to complete in only a few hours. The Electronic Brain allowed Sam to be much more efficient and productive. Computing power then advanced at an extraordinary rate. Within a few decades Sam could get one of these for her *home* – and while the computing power had increased, the room needed for it had shrunk – it could now fit right on her desk.

In the 1990s, this device that Sam had on her desk exploded into an endless matrix of social connectivity. Sam was able to chat with friends and family in real time without talking on a phone connected by a wire. She could carry her phone anywhere. Pictures of loved ones were shared through her email address. She connected with strangers who shared her passion for gardening and 19th-century American fiction. She could even find the occasional date on this thing.

Now let's jump to 2008. Sam is now efficient, productive, and successful. She has so much more than her ancestor in the cave: the ability to travel further, faster, and with greater ease, a longer life expectancy, and hunting for bison has been replaced with a trip to the market! And – exciting news – Sam has a special new companion in her life. Meet Nick, the smartphone. Nick does so much for Sam. He helps her with her job: he enables her to share her work with colleagues – from the office or at home or nearly anywhere. He lets her communicate with anyone, any time (and he never gets jealous). He saves her time, and with a gentle ping, lets her know she's got a message – from both her work and personal accounts. He holds so many addresses for her, Sam has an ever-expanding social group. He keeps her in touch with friends and family, sends and receives photos, posts and shares information on social media – oh, the connections, the friends she's made! As if that weren't enough, Nick is Sam's alarm clock, map, grocery store, library, calendar, music player, camera, bank and credit card, travel agent, AND he loves to have fun and play games. Hello Solitaire. Hello World of Warcraft. Amazing! And stop the presses (and they *have...*) – Sam can

write a script about "Nick" Sam's Companion that gives her everything but

bring Nick wherever she goes, even underwater. He's with her all the time. Plus, he's great in bed: providing a soft glow, comforting her, always keeping one eye open to alert her to the latest news or message. When she pushes his buttons, he responds just the way she wants, and he's right by her side when she wakes up, waiting for her. Nick is so useful and reliable, Sam knows she can depend on him. He's so cute, sleek and compact, and everyone knows how *smart* he is. Yes, Sam loves Nick. She loves him so much that she rushes headlong into their relationship, saying "I do" without stopping to think about it. After all, what is there to think about? Nick is *perfect*.

It's easy to relate to, isn't it? We all feel that way, or have, at some point. We all want to believe in love at first sight (it does happen), yet we've all made hasty decisions in relationships and regretted them later on. We can be so caught up in our heightened feelings that we don't stop to ask, "What do I really know about this person? Have I taken time to get to know their strengths, their flaws?" There's a reason there's a waiting period after obtaining a marriage license.

Sam is so smitten that Nick becomes her whole world. But as we know from Chapter 2, there are adverse effects, changes in her behavior. She stops hanging out with her friends, spends less time with her family, and even when they do sit down to dinner together, she's miles away with her beau. She's distracted when she's walking down the street, thinking about what she and Nick could be doing together. She's distracted when she's driving; she's dying to tell all her friends how great Nick is – through texts, of course. Sam's friends notice the difference, and they don't like it very much, but are loathe to say anything about it. Why? Because Sam *seems* so happy; who are they to judge?

Negative aspects of Nick

Unfortunately, Sam has no clue that Nick is having any adverse effects on her life. Why? Because Sam is so filled with happiness, that those good feelings completely preoccupy her attention. She feels terrific! She's convinced she's getting a lot accomplished, and that Nick has improved her productivity. Nick brings the whole world into the palm of her hand. He gives her limitless information, endless entertainment, constant validation, and the best part? He does whatever she asks him to do. This kind of swift effortlessness on Nick's part to accommodate Sam's every whim gives her a rush. Sam feels wonderful seeing a picture of her best pal's new baby, Jolie, getting 68 likes, or the selfie she took in her new sun dress getting smiling emojis, or cracking up over the video her mom sent her of a woman dancing on top of a coffee table and crashing right through it! Every time she asks Nick for anything, he provides it, no questions asked. No challenges, no arguments, no compromises. These good feelings she's getting are powerful and they make her *feel* powerful. Not only that, but she feels in control. She believes that she has a firm grasp on her relationship with Nick – she can put him down whenever she wants.

What Sam doesn't realize is that those feelings are *so* good, it makes her want even *more*. So she keeps coming up with more and more things for

Nick to do for her, and he never fails her. He always makes her feel as if she is the center of his universe, so Sam's rush of good feelings keeps coming. Nick has found the secret to making Sam feel good; he's found the place where her good feelings are stored, and he's got a master key to that room. Those feelings are coming from the pleasure center in Sam's brain; her original device!

Dopamine

We will return to Sam and Nick, but right now let's look at the science behind her predicament. Sam's good feelings are related to a naturally occurring chemical in our brains called dopamine. While the brain may use dopamine for a variety of purposes, one of its major contributions is toward reward-motivated behavior (Brookshire).

Think of it like this. You're walking down the street after a delicious meal, and you see an ad on the side of a bus for your favorite bakery that has your favorite German chocolate cake. Release the dopamine! Turn around and start walking toward the bakery to get your reward. Even thinking about how good that cake is going to taste gets you wanting it more and more as you get closer and closer (You kind of want cake right now, don't you?). You arrive, salivating at the thought of finally getting to eat a slice of the delicious chocolate cake. But, oh no! The gates have been pulled closed, and the lights are off. The bakery is closed for the night. And that German chocolate cake, *your* German chocolate cake, sits smack dab in the center of the window, practically mocking you. You want that cake, and the fact that you can't have it makes you want it even more. So what happens? Will you be denied your reward? Hell, no! Off you go to another bakery, deli, or to the supermarket in pursuit of your cake. We've all experienced when our cravings can't be fulfilled the way we want them to. It's even more disappointing when we have to settle for far less. Oftentimes that craving stays with us into the following day, building and building until we find ourselves saying, "I have to have it!"

Dr. Susan Weinschenk offers further insight on dopamine by contrasting it to "the opioid system":

> Instead of dopamine causing you to experience pleasure, the latest research shows that dopamine causes seeking behavior. Dopamine causes you to want, desire, seek out, and search. It increases your general level of arousal and your goal-directed behavior. From an evolutionary standpoint this is critical. The dopamine seeking system keeps you motivated to move through your world, learn, and survive. Dopamine makes you curious about ideas and fuels your searching for information. Research shows that it is the opioid system that makes us feel pleasure.

According to researcher Kent Berridge, the "wanting" (dopamine) and the "liking" (opioid) are complementary. The wanting system propels you to action and the liking system makes you feel satisfied and therefore pause your seeking. If your seeking isn't turned off at least for a little while, then you start to run in an endless loop. The dopamine system is stronger than the opioid system. You tend to seek more than you are satisfied.

It's easy to get in a dopamine-induced loop. Dopamine starts you seeking, then you get rewarded for the seeking which makes you seek more.

(Weinschenk)

Imagine how this is affecting Sam. She goes online to see if anyone has liked her latest post (dopamine). It has 59 likes – that feels great (opioid system). Therefore, she is propelled to look for something that will extend or increase that good feeling. Nick, of course, is happy to oblige. So Sam scrolls through other people's posts searching for that good feeling before trying a quick game of Candy Crush, texting with her bestie, checking for new emails, and watching the latest viral video featuring the world's cutest Yorkie puppy named Peanut. And on and on and on. It becomes very easy to go from one innocent check-in on her device to this constant seeking. She has no clue her behavior is keeping her in a dopamine-induced loop. And all the while, Nick happily supplies an endless stream of things to fuel her seeking.

"Brain hacking"

If you're thinking that "caught in a dopamine-induced loop" sounds scary, and "brain hacking" sounds like something out of *Invasion of the Body Snatchers* (1956), you may be right. But it's not science fiction. The reason for Sam's "seeking a reward" behavior lies inside Nick. "Brain hacking" is programming smartphones to compel you to *want* to check in constantly (*60 Minutes*). These "intentional designs" have the twin goals of making the user use as much as possible, and sell as many devices as possible. Brain hacking capitalizes on natural human brain chemistry and takes advantage of it to alter behavior. Yes, Sam is being "body-snatched" by Nick. He has hacked that wonderful machine in her head that comes with 100,000 years of finely honed abilities and seduced her into falling in love with him. What Sam doesn't realize is that Nick doesn't love her. He can't love her. Nick is programmed to make her *dependent* on him. Now he's got control of her and she's blind to it, blissfully clinging to him, her great love.

Scared yet? No? That's okay, because like all great horror stories, it gets worse.

Ramsay Brown is a co-founder of the start-up company, Dopamine Labs. He has a master's degree from The University of Southern California in

Neuroinformatics. In an interview, he shared how apps like Instagram withhold likes to keep users continuously checking their phones. It's called "intermittent rewards" (Bambenek). He described how our online experience is being monitored by companies through their apps so that they can determine the best time for a burst of responses to be released to keep us coming back (60 Minutes).

Poor Sam! Think about the endless array of apps she gets from Nick. He gives her Twitter so she can stay updated on the world's events, Instagram to see her friend's latest pictures while sharing her own, and Facebook to be in the know on her social network's comings and goings. Ebay will tell her when someone bids on the cookie jar she's watching, Hopper keeps her abreast of the flight she hopes to book for Paris this summer, and Yelp recommends the newest Thai restaurant in her neighborhood. Sam is constantly being pinged and buzzed by Nick. Every ping is another release of dopamine, and every release of dopamine makes her look forward to that next ping. This isn't coincidence or happenstance. That dopamine-induced loop is intentional on the part of the product designers to keep Sam tapping and swiping. She didn't have a chance.

And it's not just Sam. We are a nation of smartphone users/people who say, "I want to go steady" after the first date. A 2017 Pew Research Center report shows that among Americans, 92 percent of 18 to 29 year olds, 88 percent of 30 to 49 year olds, 74 percent of 50 to 64 year olds, and 42 percent of those over 64 own a smartphone (Pew Research Center). Nick (and his twin sister, Nicole) have found their way into many of our lives. So, like *Invasion of the Body Snatchers* (1956), it is taking over a population. And if most of us are like Sam, unaware of the impact it's having on us, then how can we spread awareness and regain control over our devices?

Scared yet? A little? Well, hold on. . .

Keep in mind that Sam is a mature "I can make my own decisions because I pay my own way" adult. But what happens when Sam isn't an adult, when Nick comes into her life at a younger age? As 85 percent of brain development happens in children between the ages of one and three years old (Lally), Nick's presence plays a prominent role in neural and social development.

Can you hear that? Listen closely. It's coming from your smartphone: muwahahahahahaha!

Technology and youth

Today, Sam is on her way to a party! It's a baby shower for her sister Melanie who is expecting a baby boy soon. Lots of friends and family will be there. With any luck, the cake will be German chocolate cake. Thanks to Nick, she shopped for a present online. The shopping was easy and convenient, except for the problem of so many choices! She thought it would be a good idea to get something for the baby that would make life a bit easier for Melanie and her husband Mike. Nick helped her narrow down the choices, pointing out the very latest in modern baby care items. It was delivered to her front door, already gift-wrapped. Melanie and Mike have recently moved into a new house to accommodate their growing family. That's no problem for Sam, who simply gives the address to Nick and he provides perfect directions. A few hours later, Melanie and Mike open Sam's gift. It's "The Fisher-Price iPad Apptivity Seat, Newborn to Toddler." The product description on Amazon describes the seat as follows: "It's a grow-with-me seat for baby that's soothing, entertaining, and has a touch of technology, too. . . It also has a large, 7" × 5" mirror to reflect baby's smiling face and promote facial recognition and a sense of self as baby develops. If you insert and lock your iPad into the mirror's case, the visual display provides another way to stimulate and engage baby while protecting your device from baby's sticky fingers and preventing unintentional navigating to other apps" ("Fisher Price iPad Apptivity Seat, Newborn-to-Toddler"). Out of the 204 customer reviews online, 62 percent gave it one star. One reviewer wrote:

> As an early childhood educator, I have to say that this is an absolutely terrible idea. Kids learn best by moving, exploring and doing things. Children under the age of two should not have ANY screen time according to the best educational authorities.
>
> (Fisher Price iPad Apptivity Seat, Newborn-to-Toddler)

The Campaign for a Commercial-Free Childhood named it the worst toy of the year, and began a campaign against the product (*Mail Online*).

We get it. Kids are lovable as heck, and yet they can drive us to pulling out our own hair. What parent wouldn't be tempted to buy an item like this? Something that redirects a tantrum? These smart devices (smartphones and tablets) are akin to a modern-day pacifier. And there's plenty of content to put on the screen – a whole industry built around supplying content for children. Parents might think, "Hey, how about those 'Baby Einstein' videos? They're great for babies." Well. . .

"Baby Einstein at the Farm" is only one of a myriad of choices within the Baby Einstein brand. A study conducted by renowned pediatrician Dr. Dmitri Christakis showed that within a 20-second clip of farm work, there was a scene change every three seconds. Babies aren't trying to piece together a linear narrative of the differing scene changes. They don't have that kind of cognitive ability yet. What's keeping them engaged are the flashy colors and quick shifts from scene to scene. If a baby is exposed to that kind of speedy stimulation during the formative years of early brain development, it's setting expectations for high levels of stimulation later in life, conditioning them for an inability to simply be in the moment (Christakis).

It's been just over six months since Melanie gave birth to her beautiful baby boy, Owen. Today, Sam has stopped by for a visit and is pleased to see that Owen is happily in his Apptivity Seat, watching "Baby Einstein at the Farm." Melanie is eager to show Sam that Owen can now crawl! She takes Owen out of the Apptivity seat and lays him on his belly in the middle of the carpeted living room. Sam asks Nick to record this event so she can post it on Facebook. Melanie joins Sam on the sofa and calls to Owen, urging him to crawl toward them. Owen has already pulled himself up onto all fours. Cooing excitedly, he begins to crawl. However, instead of crawling toward Melanie, he makes a turn and heads toward the Apptivity Seat. More specifically, he heads back to the tablet.

Okay, you may be thinking, "I get the point, but babies do all manner of cute, funny things. It doesn't mean that babies will choose tablets over their mothers." Or does it? ABC World News Tonight decided to find out. They performed a fascinating experiment. Just as in our story about Owen, they placed babies equidistant between their mothers and a tablet. The moms were calling to their children in a loving, excited tone, arms outstretched. In each instance, the baby crawled toward the tablet, sometimes going right past their toys. Not only that, the moms would often giggle at their baby's choice of the machine over them, finding it cute. One mom justified allowing her baby time on the tablet because it would ensure that he would eat dinner. Babies aren't immune to desire; in fact, in many ways, they're more pure about making their wants known (and heard!). They want the device more because it gives them pleasure, and they want it more because it seems to give their parents pleasure (Chang et al.).

Dr. Dan Siegal, a psychologist specializing in early childhood bonding, says, "You learn the world through your mother's face. Through mirroring, attachment to caregivers helps the immature brain use the mature functions of the parent's brain to organize its own processes. We learn to care, quite literally, by observing the caring behavior of our parents toward us" (Matousek). Babies need time staring into a mother's face. The deep neurological wiring that occurs in this mirroring is profound. When that opportunity is supplanted by staring at a screen, these connections can be diminished, if not lost outright, and the ability or desire to connect (the Collaborative Gene) is not developed. In the history of our existence, there has never been such an accessible and ubiquitous device that allows us more opportunities to disengage.

The American Academy of Pediatrics states the following:

> Some media can have educational value for children starting at around 18 months of age, but it's critically important that this be high-quality programming, such as the content offered by Sesame Workshop and PBS. Parents of young children should watch media with their child, to help children understand what they are seeing.

For school-aged children and adolescents, the idea is to balance media use with other healthy behaviors.

"Parents play an important role in helping children and teens navigate media, which can have both positive and negative effects," said Megan Moreno, MD, MSEd, MPH, FAAP, lead author of the policy statement on media use in school-aged children and teens. "Parents can set expectations and boundaries to make sure their children's media experience is a positive one. The key is mindful use of media within a family."

Problems begin when media use displaces physical activity, hands-on exploration and face-to-face social interaction in the real world, which is critical to learning. Too much screen time can also harm the amount and quality of sleep.

(American Academy of Pediatrics)

While these recommendations seem simple and straightforward, keep in mind that following them may not be as easy as it sounds. For parents to engage in quality, face-to-face family time, they may have to overcome their own dopamine-induced loops so that they can put down their devices too. A 2014 poll in American Pediatrics monitored 55 caregivers, 40 of whom used mobile devices during a meal with their children. Sixteen of those adults used their phone throughout the entire meal. When this happens, children begin to feel unimportant to their parents and this leads them to seek other connections, often through their own devices. In another study of 225 mother/child pairings (children six years of age or under), when mothers pulled out their cellphones at dinner, they had 20 percent fewer verbal and 39 percent fewer physical interactions with their child. Nonverbal interactions included eye contact, smiles, head nods, and hand gestures indicating that they were listening (Radesky, Miller et al. 241).

In our schools

It's been a few years now and Owen is growing up fast. He's in junior high school and was recently cast as John Proctor in the school's production of *The Crucible*. Today, his Aunt Sam is dropping him off on her way to work. Owen was up late, overslept, and missed the bus to school. Sam tries to strike up a conversation in the car, but Owen is distracted by Nicole, who is helping him post a selfie on Snapchat. Nicole is Owen's best friend. She has been with him since Christmas of fifth grade. Although he had an old tablet that Aunt Sam gave him when he was a baby, he was thrilled to meet Nicole – she goes with him everywhere, even to school. Now Owen fits right in with his friends at school who all have a Nicole of their own. But right now, he's annoyed by Aunt Sam's wanting to talk to him. She's old and boring, like most adults. And now she's pestering him, wanting to know how rehearsals are going. "Fine," he says with a grunt, and texts her a picture from a recent rehearsal without looking up. "She's even worse than Mr. Nickerson," he thinks to himself. Mr. Nickerson is the drama teacher and director of *The Crucible*. And for no good reason that Owen can discern, Mr. Nickerson hates Nicole.

What is happening to Owen is not uncommon. As reported by CNBC:

> In Influence Central's 2012 version of [their] survey, which collected data from about 1,000 women, children reportedly received their first cellphone between the ages of 10 and 12, according to a company spokeswoman.
>
> Some 50 percent of respondents to the most recent survey reported that their children created a social media account before the age of 12.
>
> Some 77 percent of kids with accounts use Facebook and Instagram, 49 percent are on Twitter and 47 percent are sharing photos and videos on Snapchat.
>
> While children's presence on social media is growing, adult supervision has dipped. In 2012, 49 percent of parents reported having strict limits on where and when their kids could use their electronics. This year [2016], about 41 percent have set limits.
>
> (Whitten)

This increased access to smartphones and social media has driven screen time higher and higher. In 2015, Common Sense Media reported:

> Teenagers (ages 13–18) use an average of nine hours of entertainment media per day and that tweens (ages 8–12) use an average of six hours a day, not including time spent using media for school or homework.
>
> The study finds that devices are finding their way into study time for teens and tweens. Notably, at least half of teens say they often or sometimes watch TV (51%), use social networking (50%), text (60%) and listen to music (76%) while doing homework.
>
> On average among teens, 39% of digital screen time (computers, tablets, and smartphones) is devoted to passive consumption (watching, listening, or reading), 25% to interactive content (playing games, browsing the web), 26% to communication (social media, video-chatting), and 3% to content creation (writing, coding, or making digital art or music).
>
> (Common Sense Media)

Listening

Sam again tries to start a conversation with Owen, but he doesn't respond. "Does he not even hear me?" she wonders. She calls out to him forcefully. "Huh?" he replies, startled. "Owen, are you listening?" "Yeah, I'm listening." "Can you put down your phone?" "I'm multi-tasking. Gotta finish this text." "Owen, talk to me!" Without lifting his eyes from Nicole he says, "I am talking to you." Sam lets out an exasperated sigh as she merges on to the highway.

Owen doesn't realize it, but "Are you listening?" is a question he has been asked a lot lately. By his Mom, his Dad, Mr. Nickerson and most of his teachers, and now his Aunt Sam. Not only is he not listening, he's not aware that he's not listening. Yet all of this time spent on devices tends to be viewed as healthy, or at least harmless, by students we know. "I'm multi-tasking," is a common refrain used to highlight how productive they think they are. For a while, it seemed that multi-tasking was a popular buzzword, a sought-after quality among employers. But as smartphone use began to spread, more articles and studies on the "myth" of multi-tasking began to appear. In 2014, *Psychology Today* stated:

> Much recent neuroscience research tells us that the brain doesn't really do tasks simultaneously, as we thought (hoped) it might. In fact, we just switch tasks quickly. Each time we move from hearing music to writing a text or talking to someone, there is a stop/start process that goes on in the brain.
>
> That start/stop/start process is rough on us: rather than saving time, it costs time (even very small micro seconds), it's less efficient, we make more mistakes, and over time it can be energy sapping.
>
> (Napier)

How often have you seen your students engaged in conversation, all while being on their smartphones at the same time? And how often are you participating in the same behavior? Rose doesn't have a cell phone at all. David and Roger joke about her still having a rotary phone at home attached to the wall. But Roger and David do have smartphones, and both admit to having conversations while using their devices. So many of us are splitting our time listening.

Psychologist and author Dr. Guy Winch offers great insights on how interruptions from mobile devices affect self-esteem and belonging. He uses the term "technoference," meaning when technology is interfering with our personal connections.

> When a conversation, meal, or romantic moment is disrupted because of a text, email, or any other task, the message is, "What I'm doing on my phone is more important than you right now," or, "I'm more

interested in my phone than in you," or, in some cases, "you're not worthy of my attention."

It is because the other person is likely to experience such moments as rejections that technoference can literally impact their psychological health. Rejections, even small ones, tend to be extremely painful, as your brain responds the same way it does to physical pain. Even mini-rejections, such as a partner turning to the phone in the middle of a conversation, can elicit the common reactions rejections cause—hurt feelings, a drop in mood and self-esteem, and a surge of anger and resentment. Over time, these small wounds can fester and increase conflict, lower relationship satisfaction, and lead to a drop in life satisfaction and an increase in symptoms of depression.

(Winch)

Sam pulls her car up to the curb in front of Washingtonville Junior High School as Owen continues to be enthralled by Nicole. "See ya," Owen barks as he gets out, never taking his eyes from Nicole. Sam watches him walk past a few other students, all on their phones, too. Owen doesn't acknowledge them. She's not sure if he even *saw* them. As she drives off, Sam is sad. She is upset that Owen didn't talk to her and didn't say "thank you," before he left.

Nobody likes rejection and actors are at the top of that list. In a career full of rejection, they train to be the very best at their craft in the hope of keeping rejection to a minimum. Yet, thanks to technoference, most of us are not only experiencing it every day, we are causing it too. Cloaked in the veil of "everyone has a phone and it's fine to use it mid-conversation," we aren't fully conscious of all the rejection that's been added to our lives or how socially acceptable this formerly rude behavior has become. For actors, it's an additional burden; one that may diminish their level of creative risk taking for the comfort of playing it safe.

Beyond the rejection lies the impact of repeated interruptions. When Owen is in school, and the notifications are turned on for his numerous apps, Nicole is bound to ping him throughout the day with multiple updates on all the events happening with friends, family, games, and more.

As Sam drove home, she thought about Owen's behavior. In the past two years, he'd grown increasingly inattentive, impulsive, and hyperactive. Melanie and Mike took him to see a doctor, who tested him for *attention deficit hyperactivity disorder* (ADHD), but the results were negative. "It's odd," Sam thought, "he has the symptoms. Maybe they should have him tested again."

Scientist Kostadin Kushlev at The University of Virginia partnered with colleagues at The University of British Columbia and conducted an experiment to uncover what these interrupting pings were doing to a student's attention (Kushlev et al.). They monitored 221 students over two weeks. During the first week, notifications were turned on, and the students were open to being interrupted by pings throughout the day. During the second week, notifications were turned off. When the students answered questionnaires, all of them reported higher levels of inattention and hyperactivity when the notifications were left on. The study also reported that students who had never been diagnosed with ADHD (see Maitre for an explanation of ADHD) were experiencing some of the same symptoms of that condition, such as not listening when spoken to directly and being easily distracted.

Roger

Two young women in my acting class were working on the sister scene from Carol Churchill's "Top Girls." After an in-class showing, I was surprised at how little they were listening to one another, or taking each other in. Of course, I had seen similar non-listening over the years, but this was extraordinary, unlike anything I had witnessed. As we began to work the scene, I stopped them regularly to ask, "Did you hear what she just said? Are you listening to her?" Often in hindsight, with my pointing it out, they could see the missed moments. And it's not only tone and behavior they were missing, but also literally what the other person had said. We ran the scene again, with my impressing on them to really listen. It wasn't much better. If you know the scene, you know it is heated. And yet they both felt disconnected from their partner's words and points of view. At the scene's end, one of the young actors offered in awe, "I know you asked me listen, and I'm trying, but for some reason I keep zoning out. It's like I actually can't listen."

Empathy

How might Owen's behavior affect his ability to do his job in the school play? Playing John Proctor is a tremendous challenge and he needs to be able to relate to Proctor's journey. He certainly can't know what it's like to live the circumstances of Proctor's life, but as a human being with 100,000 years of finely honed social skills working for him, he can imagine what it's like to wrestle with his conscience and struggle to do what is right. All actors need the ability to empathize so that they may open their souls to the characters they portray; to walk in someone else's shoes, fully open-hearted to experience the given circumstances and other characters in the world of the play. That is the actor's job.

Owen's teacher, Mr. Nickerson, has grown frustrated with his cast. They aren't able to empathize with their characters. They're simply not in the world of the play and not relating to each other. If he could only get them to put down their cell phones! He's been trying to, but in the past few years, that's become akin to a whack-a-mole game. As soon as he gets one student to put their phone away, he turns around to find another student on their phone. The school hasn't provided a clear policy on student phone use and he feels overwhelmed trying to combat this problem in addition to everything else on his plate. On top of that, he hasn't been able to reach Mr. Ryan, the production designer, who is a shop teacher at the school, and Mr. Nickerson's nemesis. If there's one person he *wished* would carry a cell phone, it's Mr. Ryan. Mr. Ryan is nearing retirement and does things "old school" as the students like to say. He checks his email (an AOL account!) once a day. Mr. Nickerson is watching Owen and Jennifer Perez, who is playing Abigail, in Act II, Scene 1 as Mr. Ryan strolls in with a rolled-up set of drawings under his arm. "Where have you been?" Mr. Nickerson practically screams, "I was trying to reach you all weekend." "Camping, Nickerson. No phones, no computers. It's like Salem in 1692. You should try it. And take these damn kids with you. Maybe they'll start to understand what the hell you've been saying."

In the publication *Computers in Human Behavior*, a study compared two groups of sixth graders. Group A spent five days at an outdoor camp without any technology. Group B was left to go about life as usual. Each student was given a pre- and post-test to read facial expressions in photographs and video. Those students on the technology fast, left only to interact with their peers and natural surroundings, had significant jumps in their ability to read non-verbal cues, versus the other group who stayed in their routine with their technology (Uhls et al. 391). The digital media was helpful in some areas of teaching and communication, but when dealing with human emotions, face-to-face time was the winner (Uhls et al. 391).

UCLA Psychology professor Patricia Greenfield, one of the authors of the camp study, was interviewed on NPR (Summers). She commented on early *Homo sapiens* evolving without technology, where the only option was interacting face-to-face. "Since we were adapted to that environment, it's likely that our skills depend on that environment. If we reduce face-to-face interaction drastically, it's not surprising that the social skills would also get reduced" (Summers).

Dr. Sherry Turkle expands on the summer camp experiment. When speaking about empathy in an interview with *The Atlantic*, she had this to say:

> The empathy that I'm talking about is a psychological capacity to put yourself in the place of another person and imagine what they are going through. It has neurological underpinnings—we know that we're "wired" to do it, because when you put young people in a summer camp where there are no devices, within five days their capacity to watch a scene, and then successfully identify what the people in the scene might be feeling, begins to go back up again from being depressed when they first arrived, armed with their devices. We suppress this capacity by

putting ourselves in environments where we're not looking at each other in the eye, not sticking with the other person long enough or hard enough to follow what they're feeling.

(Davis)

Remember, Owen is spending an average of nine hours a day actively involved with Nicole. If he's sleeping eight hours a night (and that's a big "if"), that leaves seven hours for everything else. The majority of Owen's day is with the screen. No wonder he's having trouble in the play! He's not empathetic toward his scene partners, he's not listening, not in the moment, not yet able to memorize his lines, and not fully present in the room during notes. The impact on actors undermines the very heart of what they need to do.

Relationships

Sam was still thinking about her ride with Owen. She was worried about him. The doctor hadn't been able to help, and she knew he'd been having difficulty getting along with Melanie and Mike, so she thought maybe a talk with Aunt Sam would help. She was waiting in front of the school when rehearsal ended and offered to take him for ice cream. As they settled into their booth, Sam felt strange. Where would she start? Impulsively, she reached for Nick, but he wasn't there. She'd left him in the car! "What is with me, today?" she thought. The waitress arrived and Owen managed to let go of Nicole long enough for them to order. As the waitress headed off to get their ice cream, Owen reached for Nicole, but Sam pulled her away. Before Owen could say anything, Sam spoke, "I'm silencing this. I want to talk to you." It was a halting, awkward conversation that seemed to pass more slowly than the ice cream could melt. Although Nicole couldn't ping, Owen's eyes kept darting down to her. Sam wondered if he was really listening to what she was trying to say. And there was something else. It was the way Owen kept looking toward Nicole. It was as if Owen would rather be with Nicole than having a conversation with her. And he *kept* doing it. Sam went from feeling Owen was distracted, to feeling annoyed by his preference for Nicole, to hurt by it, to finally feeling distracted herself. She was more engaged in noticing Owen's distraction than she was in the conversation. She knew it was silly, but she couldn't help but feel that Nicole was ruining her relationship with her nephew. She was really upset now and out of habit, reached for Nick. Then she remembered he was in the car. The next thought hit her like a bomb. Was her relationship with Nick having the same impact as Owen's relationship with Nicole? Was her behavior similarly affected? Her mind raced.

As we've learned, empathy is not gained by simply putting down your smartphone. You need to engage with other people. Now that awareness is beginning to dawn on Sam, there is hope that she might be able to break her dopamine-induced loop and get Owen to break his, but then what?

[With] every conversation we get a little bit better at reading people, at striking up a conversation, and at maintaining a conversation. Some people are becoming conversational cowards. They lack the willingness to have difficult face-to-face conversations, and they aren't cultivating those skills.

(Hill)

So says Dr. James Roberts, Professor of Marketing at Baylor University and author of *Too Much of a Good Thing: Are You Addicted to Your Smartphone?* (Hill).

Think about that in terms of acting. Is John Proctor having "a difficult, face-to-face conversation" with Abigail in the woods? How about Konstantin and Nina in *The Seagull*, Troy and Rose in *Fences*, or Mrs. Webb and Emily in *Our Town*? Or how about every piece of good drama ever written? "Difficult, face-to-face conversations" are the bedrock of all theatre. What Dr. Roberts suggests is that the prevalence of smartphones is conditioning our students away from navigating uncomfortable relationships. He further adds, "A lot of what used to be done face-to-face is now done via computer mediated communication and I think that's sad because what we've lost is the humanness of contact and conversation" (Hill).

An important component of intimacy is the exchange of spontaneous and unpredictable conversations, including the awkward, sometimes unpleasant moments that arise. The strong bonds of healthy relationships form by venturing through unscripted face-to-face conversations with one another. Dr. Sherry Turkle, in a speech at the Aspen Ideas Festival, spoke about the power of conversation amidst the digital landscape, and its impact on relationships. "Face-to-face conversation is the most human and the most humanizing thing we do. Conversation is there to reclaim for the failing connections of our digital age" (Turkle).

Dr. Andrew Przybylski is a social scientist at the University of Oxford. He conducted an experiment to see if the visible presence of a cell phone on a nearby table, while two strangers talked, affected their level of intimacy and connectedness. The British Psychological Society reported his findings in *Research Digest*.

34 pairs of strangers (were) asked to spend 10 minutes chatting with each other about "an interesting event that occurred to you over the past month." The participants sat on chairs in a private booth and for half of them, close by but out of their direct line of view, a mobile phone was placed on a tabletop. For the other pairs, there was a notebook in place of the phone.

After they'd finished chatting, the participants answered questions about the partner they'd met. The ones who'd chatted with a phone visible nearby, as opposed to a notebook, were less positive. For example, they were less likely to agree with the statement, "It is likely that my partner and I could become friends if we interacted a lot." They also reported feeling less closely related to their conversational partner.

A second study with a fresh set of participants was similar, but this time some of the pairs chatted about a mundane topic, whilst others chatted about "the most meaningful events of the past year." Again, some of them did this with a phone placed nearby, others with a notebook in the same position.

For participants with the notebook visible nearby, having a more meaningful conversation (as opposed to a casual one) boosted their feelings of closeness and their trust in their conversational partner. But this extra intimacy was missing for the participants for whom a mobile phone was visible. When the researchers debriefed the participants afterwards they seemed to be unaware of the effects of the mobile phone, suggesting its adverse effects were at a non-conscious level.

(Jarrett)

What is most fascinating about this research is the implication that the mobile phone's "adverse effects were at a non-conscious level." So now it's not only "turn that thing off," but we also need the "yes, and" to that statement. Turn it off, move it out of sight, and then, look at the person in front of you!

E-reading and retention

After a long silence, Sam looked up from her ice cream. "How's the play coming along?" she asked as she slid Nicole off the table and onto her lap. Nicole was now completely out of Owen's sight. "You're the lead, right?" "Yeah," Owen mumbled, glancing down as if he could see through the table and locate Nicole. "That's great," exclaimed Sam. "Except that it's a lot of lines and I can't remember them all," Owen continued. He looked dejected. "Mom downloaded the script to her Kindle for me. I work on my lines, I definitely know them, but then in rehearsal, I keep forgetting." Feeling helpless, he looked around for Nicole, then poked at his ice cream. "Go on," Sam said encouragingly. "I don't know. I thought I loved acting, but maybe I'm no good. I'm trying really hard and it's not working. I feel like I'm letting a lot of people down. Sometimes I think Mr. Nickerson is going to kick me out." Sam shifted in her seat. "I didn't tell you this before, but I played Elizabeth in *The Crucible* in high school. As I was listening to what you just said, I couldn't help but think your situation has some parallels with John Proctor's situation." Owen looked at her. He stopped wondering about Nicole. "Wow, I never thought of that. It makes sense. I guess I know a little of how he feels." "It's called 'empathy,'" Sam told him. "That's what Mr. Nickerson is always talking about! How come you never told me you were in *The Crucible*, Aunt Sam?" "I guess we haven't talked much lately." "Tell me more," Owen said. As they talked on, Sam realized that Owen seemed to be really listening to her, and was looking her in eye. And he had stopped searching for Nicole. They talked about their lives, and of course, they talked about *The Crucible*. They both felt connected to each other. Sam dropped Owen off at home and as she drove away, she thought about something that she held back from their conversation. She realized that just as Elizabeth had let her behavior towards John be motivated solely by his past infidelity, and not on reconnecting, she had been focused on Owen's relationship with Nicole, rather than the more positive choice of finding a way to reconnect. And for the first time, she began to question if Nick and Nicole were really as good as they seemed.

The *Guardian* reported a study on reading and retention led by researcher Anne Mangen of Norway's Stavanger University. Fifty readers received the same short story to read, half of them on a Kindle, the other half in paperback. Those who read the story on a Kindle across the board scored much worse than the paperback readers when asked to place 14 plot points in consecutive order (Flood). The researchers suggest, "The haptic and tactile feedback of a Kindle does not provide the same support for mental reconstruction of a story as a print pocket book does" (Flood).

Technology and writing

Sam isn't the only one concerned about Owen. Mr. Nickerson has noticed a shift in Owen's demeanor and his school work. As the director of the play, this is his third year working with Owen, so he's gotten to observe his habits over time. Mr. Nickerson requires his actors to keep a journal of their experiences on each production. The first year, Owen had a small part in *Twelve Angry Jurors*, but he wrote a detailed journal, investing far more into the character than was in the script, imagining his home life and a relationship with his son. He wrote eagerly about what he was observing and learning in rehearsals and filled at least two pages a week. Thus far on *The Crucible*, his journal entries had been no more than one page and were lacking the passion he exhibited two years ago. He seemed far more engaged then, with only a small character, than he does now with the lead. With very little to go on, Mr. Nickerson is finding it harder to help Owen. He's tried talking to Owen about empathy, told him he's not listening, and stressed to him the value of getting off-book early in the process. But that only seems to drive him further away.

Over the years, we have seen students' journals become weaker and weaker. Many of them are handing in less than a page, which covers three weeks' worth of classes. It's not just the length that has shrunk, but the quality too. So many journals offer generalizations rather than the specific analysis that comes from critical thinking. Much of the content is simply a retelling of what occurred in class that day. Instead, the students need to dig deep into their creative process, and develop the muscle of becoming an artist who can ask the questions needed to go further in their craft.

In a Pew Research Center study asking thousands of teachers if digital technologies were having an impact on the writing of students, "68% reported that digital tools make students more likely—as opposed to less likely or having no impact—to take shortcuts and not put effort into their writing, and 46% say these tools make students more likely to 'write too fast and be careless'" (Purcell et al.).

We couldn't agree more. When it comes to turning in assignments, Mr. Nickerson isn't the only one who has noticed a change. This kind of behavior has been on a steady increase since 2008. When it comes to turning in assignments, we are receiving entire sections missing, or the information is there, but it's presented incoherently. How many of us have had papers turned in with actual blank sheets? In the past, we three would try our hardest to make sense of their written work. We aren't doing this any longer, as it's a disservice to their education. Of course, we are not including the students who struggle with learning disabilities in this conversation. We have open discussions with those students early on, and develop a plan of action to meet their specific needs.

The body

Rose

Louise's Neck – Part Two:

After I'd noticed the proliferation of smartphones on campus, I asked my friend and colleague, Belinda Mello, if she had noticed anything unusual in students' collaborative behaviors in her movement class. Not only had she noticed similar things, she told me about a chiropractor friend who was treating more and more young people for bone spurs in their necks. So young people were using the new phones to the extent that not only were their listening and focus skills affected, but they were experiencing physical symptoms as well.

That same semester, I met with my first student who told me they struggled with insomnia. And then the following semester I met with a second, a third, and a fourth. Every single one said, "I'm up so late on my phone and on the computer." One student said, "My friend will get mad at me if I don't text her back." I asked, "At 2:00 in the morning?" She looked at me as if I was from Jupiter, and said "Yeah."

It's rehearsal time for *The Crucible*, and Mr. Nickerson can't seem to get Owen's eyes off the floor and onto his partners'. Repeatedly asking him to make eye contact hasn't worked. He's not getting that this is about *connection*. Owen's head is in a perpetual angle toward the ground. Mr. Nickerson knows the head is heavy, but this kind of ground gazing is a bit extreme. On its own, the average head weighs about 10 to 12 pounds. The neck, which sits atop the spine and supports much of that weight, is spending more time sloped at greater angles since the release of tablets and smartphones. Health professionals are experiencing an increase in the number of patients coming in for neck and spinal pain as a direct result of this new phenomenon, called "Text Neck." This is the name given to neck and spine pain that results from excessive time spent looking down at a tablet or mobile device ("Text Neck: Is Smartphone Use Causing Your Neck Pain?"). The British Chiropractic Association studied the relationship between technology use and neck or back pain. Here's what they reported:

> The survey of more than 2,000 UK adults who currently suffer from back or neck pain, or have in the past, found that almost three in five (56%) people experienced pain after using some form of technological device. Despite this, only 27% of people surveyed had either limited or stopped using their devices. The research showed that people were most likely to experience back or neck pain after using the following techno- logical devices: laptop computer (35%), desktop computer (33%), smartphone (22%), tablet (20%), games console (20%). The age group most likely to experience back or neck pain when using their smart phone were 16–24 year olds, while nearly half (45%) of young adults 25–34 years old admitted to experiencing back or neck pain after using a laptop.
>
> (British Chiropractic Association)

Dr. Kenneth Hansraj, Chief of Spine Surgery at New York Spine Surgery and Rehabilitation Medicine in New York, created a model of a cervical spine and changed the angles of the neck as if looking down at a device. He wanted to see how that change impacted the weight of the head on the spine. Dr. Hansraj describes good posture as "the ears aligned with the shoulders, and the 'angel wings,' or shoulder blades, retracted. In proper alignment, spinal stress is diminished. It is the most efficient position for the spine" (Hansraj 278). His research shows a large jump in weight as the head tilts forward.

> The weight seen by the spine dramatically increases when flexing the head forward at various degrees. As the head tilts forward, the forces seen by the neck surges to 27 pounds at 15 degrees, 40 pounds at 30 degrees, 49 pounds at 45 degrees, and 60 pounds at 60 degrees.

(And) Loss of the natural curve of the cervical spine leads to incrementally increased stresses about the cervical spine. These stresses may lead to early wear, tear, degeneration, and possible surgeries.

(Hansraj 278)

Sam has dropped by to talk with Melanie about Owen. She's been thinking about her observations at the ice cream shop and the possible impact Nicole is having on him. Owen will enter high school next year and the demands on him will only increase. Melanie listens and nods, but confides that she's concerned about something else. Owen has been complaining of neck and back pain. She can't figure out why someone so young would have such a problem without having suffered an injury. Melanie acknowledges that perhaps Owen is spending too much time on his phone, but says she's more focused on his physical pain right now. Sam gives her the number of her physical therapist, who is helping her with pain and numbness in her arms and hands.

As Owen and his friends are entering their teenage years, spending hours and hours on their phones, they're finding that they're asking their parents to make appointments with physical therapists for relief of neck and back pain. They don't realize that it's directly related to their relationship with Nick and Nicole (Healy). Physical therapist Megan Randich says, "We have teens experiencing the same shoulder, neck and back pain usually felt by people 30 years older. They shouldn't be experiencing those issues" (Healy).

And it's not only the head and neck that are being affected. Our hands and elbows are working in ways they never have before in the history of humans. Swiping and clicking are the new aerobic workout for our digits. "Text claw" is the medical term given to pain, numbness, and cramping and that occurs in the fingers, hands, arms, and shoulders as a result of excessive smartphone use (Wills). And all those selfies that Sam and Owen are taking ... guess what? Now add "selfie elbow" to the list of ailments from smartphone usage. It's like tennis elbow, but without the tennis. The angle of our arms required by all those selfies leads to inflammation and pain (Mirchandani).

In too deep

As Mr. Nickerson sits in his office going over rehearsal notes, Mr. Ryan walks in. "Nickerson, one of the actors just tore a flat. She was looking at her cellphone instead of where she was going and walked right into it. You have to do something about your actors. No cell phones on the set." "Damn it," Nickerson growled. "It's impossible, those things are driving me crazy. What do you do?" "I ban them in the shop. Safety." "If I ban cell phones, I'll have a revolt on my hands." Mr. Ryan sighed. "Look Nickerson, you have to teach them about these phones. Add it to your curriculum.

They don't know any different, and until you make it clear what these things are doing to them, why would they listen or put them down?" Mr. Nickerson sat stunned. The old curmudgeon seemed to have a point. "You're a good teacher, Nickerson. Teach them. Once they understand, they'll come around. I meant what I said about camping. You separate them from technology for a weekend and they get it. They don't like it, but they get it." Mr. Nickerson didn't say a word. "Tie it into acting, that's what they love. Hit 'em where they'll feel it most." Mr. Ryan turned for the door, "I've got a flat to fix. You want to have something to talk to them about on Monday? Turn off your cell phone and computer this weekend. It'll be good for you too." "Hey, uh, thanks," said Mr. Nickerson, surprised at seeing this new side of Mr. Ryan. "That was really helpful. You. . . You're a good teacher too." "Don't tell anybody," Mr. Ryan said with a smile as he closed the door behind him.

As Owen says goodbye to middle school and enters high school, he's maturing and making new friends. Unless someone intervenes and helps him, his bond with Nicole will only become stronger. A 2015 Pew Research Study of teens 13 to 17 years old reports that "twenty four percent go online 'almost constantly,' [and] fifty six percent of teens go online several times a day" (Lenhart).

PBS News Hour did a story on teenagers and their technology use. Teens were asked if they could live without their technology. Their responses included, "I really don't think I can imagine a world without technology," "I don't know what to do then," and the kicker, "Without that I really just don't know how I would, like, I don't know, see people or get to know people" (Wilcox).

The responses aren't always so candid. Dr. Delaney Ruston is a physician, mom, and filmmaker. Her documentary film, *Screenagers* (2016), delves deep into the relationship between technology and teenage development. Teenagers talk freely of lying about their technology use, sexting, excessive gaming, and not being able to focus. The film is an eye-opening experience, shedding light on the dependence that adolescents are developing for their devices. *Screenagers* has screenings all over the world, and upon request, the film can be made available for local screenings in your community.

From infancy on, young people are choosing to spend more and more time connected to their technology. This muscle of choosing grows stronger throughout their development, and then, voila! They wind up in our classrooms with a firmly entrenched reliance on technology to navigate their way through the world. It's not their fault, it simply harkens back to their origins with the technology. When we started to look at the issue through this very lens, we saw the unfair expectation we were placing on our students. We were expecting these Digital Natives to be fluent in the social-emotional language that we grew up developing without access to the current technology.

When too much is too much

Since that day at the ice cream shop, Sam had begun to see Nick differently. At first, she thought the relationship was suffering because Nick was smothering her. But as she continued to observe Owen's behavior with Nicole, she realized she wasn't being smothered. Rather, she kept going back for more. It was her choice, yet the pull was so strong, she wondered if she actually *had* a choice. It reminded her of something. When Melanie got pregnant, she began hounding Mike to quit smoking before Owen was born. He'd struggled with quitting for years. Sam knew smoking was an addiction and witnessed his compulsion to smoke, even though he was "choosing" to quit. She now saw parallels to her behavior toward Nick. But Nick couldn't be an addiction, could he? Sam wasn't sure, but she realized that she didn't really have control of her relationship with Nick. She decided it was time to do something about it. Not just for her, but for Owen too.

Across our research and discussions, the word addiction has come up many times, particularly in our student's journals and papers. We want to be very careful with our use of that word. We're not trained as doctors, addiction specialists, or therapists, but over the years, we all have seen our fair share of students struggling with an addiction problem, be it alcohol, drugs, sex, food, and so on. Delicately handling their situations, we usher them to the resources and professionals we feel are better equipped to handle their issue. In the same vein, we don't know many families whose lives have been left unscathed by addiction somewhere within their lineage. And perhaps there are those among us in our field struggling with their own addictions, or working with personal recovery. Addiction is insidious, affecting not only the addicted, but tearing through the lives of those closest to them like a powerful tornado.

What is addiction? Webster's offers the following definition. A "compulsive need for and use of a habit-forming substance (such as heroin, nicotine, or alcohol) characterized by tolerance and by well-defined physiological symptoms upon withdrawal." We saw that this definition lined up pretty well with what the students were describing in their own words in their Digital Disconnect papers. When the students wrote about feeling addicted, we asked "What does that mean to you?" Here were some of their responses:

"Addiction to me means someone feels required to use something to the point where it has nothing left to offer, while of course managing to enjoy it all the way through. Or maybe they aren't."

"Addiction is something that I spend my time, talent, and energy on while pushing the things I need to do on the back burner."

"An addiction is something you feel you have to constantly and consistently come back to. Whether consciously or subconsciously, without it you begin to feel you're missing something, incomplete."

"Addiction – a voluntary return to the substance/item/act that causes dopamine to release in the brain, creating such a burst of euphoria in a person's experience with that substance/item/act that eventually the return becomes involuntary; the person is now a slave to that substance/item/act where it affects that person's every move. It takes their time, their love, their attention, their money, and their energy. It consumes the person."

Notice the common thread of dependency in the students' descriptions, as well as putting off what they know to be the next best action on their to-do lists. They also add to their definition the idea of negative consequences; the notion that there is little, if any, time left for other activities outside the repetition of the technology use; often leaving them drained, exhausted, or sad.

In Matt Richtel's *New York Times* article "Are Teenagers Replacing Drugs with Smartphones," Mr. Richtel writes about the relationship between increasing smartphone usage and decreasing drug use in teenagers. Although the research linking the two is only preliminary, scholars aren't ruling out the possibility. James Anthony, a professor of epidemiology and biostatistics at Michigan State University and an expert on drug-use behavior, had this to say: "It would not take much in the way of displacement of adolescent time and experience in the direction of nondrug 'reinforcers' that have become increasingly available" (Richtel). The same article has David Greenfield, an assistant clinical professor of psychiatry at the University of Connecticut School of Medicine and founder of The Center for Internet and Technology Addiction, saying, "People are carrying around a portable dopamine pump, and kids have basically been carrying it around for the last 10 years" (Richtel).

This "dopamine pump" Dr. Greenfield coins is similar to the dopamine loop we described earlier. When we asked the students to go further in examining their behaviors with their smartphones, their comments highlighted their inability to get out of this dopamine loop.

"It was 1:00 a.m. and I was swiping through Instagram. I looked at the time and it'd been over 15 minutes and I couldn't stop. I didn't know when I would stop either. Was it 'til I saw something funny or disturbing?"

"Lately I have been finding myself refreshing over and over again to see new posts after I just saw the latest ones. And I feel it is not to see what people are doing or saying but rather to constantly see new information."

"I have a very real addiction to social media. There is an instant gratification that comes from posting a selfie and the stream of compliments that sometimes follow. It is like searching for validation for simply living your life. As if you need someone to validate that you are alive. When you post a picture on Snapchat it is like saying, 'Look at this awesome brunch I had. Someone please tell me how awesome it is that I eat

brunch. Wow, I want to create this image of my persona as someone who gets brunch on Sunday.' In the moment it may not feel like that is what is being done, but that is what happens when you post excessively on social media."

Internet addiction has become a global issue, affecting approximately 420 million people worldwide (Kosoff). Our Appendices offer helpful resources on Internet addiction (see Appendix X), including a checklist for cyber addiction as well as recovery programs.

The next step

Sam didn't know it yet, but she had put herself on the path toward reconnecting to real life. She was determined to work out her problems with Nick. She was sure they could remain friends, but knew that she wouldn't really be happy with anything more involved than that. She also knew that it wouldn't be easy; that there was work to be done to improve her habits.

Sam had spent more time with Owen over the past few weeks. In fact, they now had a weekly "ice cream date." Thanks to her encouragement, Owen had approached Mr. Nickerson and they were talking too. Sam and Mr. Nickerson both helped Owen see how his relationship with Nicole was affecting him and his acting.

Tonight is opening night of *The Crucible* at Washingtonville Junior High School and Sam is expectantly settling into her seat. She reaches for Nick, shuts him off, and places him in her bag next to Nicole. An hour earlier, before Owen had gone backstage to get ready, Sam told him, "Break a leg." Owen turned to her and held out Nicole in his hand. "Here, hold this for me until later. And thanks, Aunt Sam," he said as he gave her a hug. Sam smiled at the memory as the curtain began to rise.

As we noted earlier, we are theatre people, deeply rooted in community and ensemble. No doubt each of us of a certain age can recall what a relief it was to find our tribe in the school theatre. These Digital Natives, like Owen, have a similar craving to belong. They're also searching for their tribe. But because they are growing up in a digital world, some of their very first experiences of belonging may be happening in the digital realm. Knowing this, it makes perfect sense that when they come to our classrooms they may struggle to let go of their online community while we are ushering them to embrace a less virtual and more human community.

Our research led us to far more information than we can include in this book. If you have questions, there are answers to be found out there. We encourage you to do your own sleuthing. The best research we found came directly from our students. From all the Owens who are, for the first time, really examining their relationships with their Nicks and Nicoles. For us, that is truly the most eye-opening research we could have ever wished for.

Bibliography

American Academy of Pediatrics, 21 Oct. 2016. "American Academy of Pediatrics Announces New Recommendations for Children's Media Use." Web. 22 June 2017.

Bambenek, Cadence. "Ex-Googler Slams Designers for Making Apps Addictive Like 'Slot Machines.'" *Business Insider*. Business Insider Inc., 25 May 2016. Web. 22 June 2016.

60 Minutes. "Brain Hacking." CBS News, 9 April 2017. Web. 22 Nov. 2017.

Brookshire, Bethany. "Dopamine Is _____." *Slate*. The Slate Group, 3 July 2013. Web. 24 June 2017.

British Chiropractic Association. Roderick Pugh Marketing, 11 Apr. 2017. "People Point to Tech as Trigger for Their Pain." Web. 22 Nov. 2017.

Chang, Juju, Christine Rakowsky, and Daniel Clark. "Toddlers and Tablets: Way of the Future?" abcNews, 5 June 2013. Web. 22 June 2017.

Christakis, Dimitri. "TEDxRanier–Dimitri Christakis–Media and Children." YouTube, 28 Dec. 2011. Web. 22 June 2017.

Common Sense Media, 3 Nov. 2015. "Landmark Report: U.S. Teens Use an Average of Nine Hours of Media Per Day, Tweens Use Six Hours." Web. 24 June 2017.

Davis, Lauren Cassani. "The Flight From Conversation." *The Atlantic*. Atlantic Monthly Group, 7 Oct. 2015. Web. 22 Nov. 2017.

"Fisher Price iPad Apptivity Seat, Newborn-to-Toddler." Amazon. Web. 4 July 2017.

Flood, Alison. "Readers Absorb Less on Kindles Than on Paper, Study Finds." *The Guardian*. Guardian News and Media Ltd, 19 Aug. 2014. Web. 24 June 2017.

Hally, Mike. *Electric Brains: Stories from the Dawn of the Computer Age*. D.C.: Joseph Henry Press, 2005. Print.

Hansraj, Kenneth K. "Assessment of Stresses in the Cervical Spine Caused by Posture and Position of the Head." *Surgical Technology International* 25 (2014): 277–279. Web. 24 June 2016.

Healy, Vikki Ortiz. "Teens Showing Signs of 'Text Neck.'" *Chicago Tribune*, 2 Aug. 2016. Web. 24 June 2017.

Hill, Simon. "Are Smartphones Killing the Art of Face-to-Face Conversation? We Ask the Experts." *Digital Trends*. Designtechnica Corp., 5 Mar. 2017. Web. 24 June 2017.

Invasion of the Body Snatchers. Dir. Don Siegel. Perf. Kevin McCarthy, Dana Wynter, and Larry Gates. Allied Artist Pictures, 1956. Film.

Jarrett, Christian. "How the Mere Presence of a Mobile Phone Harms Face-to-Face Conversations." *Research Digest*. The British Psychological Society, 24 Sept. 2012. Web. 24 June 2017.

Kosoff, Maya. "Study: 420 Million People Around the World Are Addicted to the Internet." *Business Insider*. Business Insider Inc., 20 Dec. 2014. Web. 24 June 2017.

Kushlev, Konstadin, Jason D.E. Proulx, and Elizabeth Dunn. "'Silence Your Phones': Smartphone Notifications Increase Inattention and Hyperactivity Symptoms." ACM CHI 2016, San Jose, California. 7–12 May 2016.

Lally, Ron. "The Human Brain from Birth to Age 3." For Our Babies: A Call for Better Beginnings, 22 Feb. 2012. Web. 30 June 2017.

Lenhart, Amanda. "Teens, Social Media & Technology Overview 2015." Pew Research Center, 9 Apr. 2015. Web. 24 June 2017.

Mail Online. "Fisher Price Under Pressure to Pull the Plug on New iPad Baby Bouncy Seat Aimed at Newborns Over Claims It Is 'Unhealthy.'" Associated Newspapers Ltd, 10 Dec. 2013. Web. 22 June 2017.

Maitre, Sarah. "Attention Deficit Hyperactivity Disorder in Childhood; Overview, Diagnosis and Treatment." *AMA Journal of Ethics* 9.6 (2007): n.pag. Web. 24 June 2017.

Matousek, Mark. "The Meeting Eyes of Love: How Empathy is Born in Us." *Psychology Today*. Sussex Publishers, 8 Apr. 2011. Web. 22 June 2017.

Mirchandani, Raakhee. "'Selfie Elbow' is a Real Medical Thing Now." *Elle*. Hearst Digital Media, 30 June 2016. Web. 24 June 2016.

Napier, Nancy K. "The Myth of Multitasking." *Psychology Today*. Sussex Publishers, 12 May 2014. Web. 4 July 2017.

Pew Research Center, "Mobile Fact Sheet." 22 Jan. 2017. Web. June 2017.

Purcell, Kristen, Judy Buchanan, and Linda Friedrich. "The Impact of Digital Tools on Student Writing and How Writing is Taught in Schools." Pew Research Center, 16 July 2013. Web. 24 June 2017.

Radesky, Jenny, Caroline J. Kistin, Barry Zuckerman, Katie Nitzberg, Jamie Gross, Margot Kaplan-Sanoff, Marilyn Augustyn, and Michael Silverstein. "Patterns of Mobile Device Use by Caregivers and Children during Meals in Fast Food Restaurants." *Pediatrics* 133.4 (2014): e843–e849. Print.

Radesky, Jenny, Alison L. Miller, Katherine L. Rosenblum, Danielle Appugliese, Niko Kaciroti, and Julie C. Lumeng. "Maternal Mobile Device Use during a Structured Parent–Child Interaction Task." *Academic Pediatrics* 15.2 (2015): 238–244. Print.

Richtel, Matt. "Are Teenagers Replacing Drugs with Smartphones?" *The New York Times*. The New York Times Company, 13 Mar. 2017. Web. 24 June 2016.

Santorini Web Portals. "Santorini Archaeological Sites: Akrotiri Excavations." Web. 30 June 2017.

Schulting, Rick, and Linda Fibiger, eds. *Sticks, Stones, and Broken Bones: Neolithic Violence in European Perspectives*. Oxford University Press, 2012. Print.

Screenagers. Dir. Delaney Ruston. MyDoc Productions, 2016. Film.

Orkneyjar: The Heritage of the Orkney Islands. "Skara Brae." Web. 30 June 2017.

Summers, Juana. "Kids and Screen Time: What Does the Research Say?" *nprEd*. NPR, 28 Aug. 2014. Web. 24 June 2017.

Healthessentials. "Text Neck: Is Smartphone Use Causing Your Neck Pain?" Cleveland Clinic, 24 Mar. 2015. Web. 23 June 2017.

Turkle, Sherry. "We Are Having a Crisis of Empathy." The Aspen Institute. Aspen, Colorado, 29 June 2015. Lecture.

Uhls, Yalda T., Minas Michikyan, Jordan Morris, Debra Garcia, Gary W. Small, Eleni Zgourou, and Patricia M. Greenfielda. "Five Days at Outdoor Education Camp Without Screens Improves Preteen Skills With Nonverbal Emotion Cues." *Computers in Human Behavior* 39 (2014): 387–392. Print.

Walker, Amélie A. "Neolithic Surgery." Abstract. *Archaeology* 50.5 (1997): Archaeology-archive. Web. 12 Jan 2018.

Weinschenk, Susan. "Why We're All Addicted to Texts, Twitter, and Google." *Psychology Today*. Sussex Publishers, 11 Sept. 2012. Web. 22 June 2017.

Whitten, Sarah. "Study: Kids Are Getting Their First Cell Phone Before They Can Drive." CNBC, 20 May 2016. Web. 24 June 2017.

Wilcox, Amanda. "Lesson Plan: Are Teens Addicted to Technology?" *PBS Newshour*. NewsHour Productions, 4 June 2016. Web. 24 June 2016.

Wills, Kate. "Attack of the Phones: Selfie Elbow, Text Claw and the Other Surprising Ways Technology is Wrecking Your Body." *The Sun*. News Group Newspapers Ltd., 13 Nov. 2016. Web. 24 June 2017.

Winch, Guy. "How Cellphone Use Can Disconnect Your Relationship." *Psychology Today*. Sussex Publishers, 13 Jan. 2015. Web. 24 June 2017.

Chapter 4

Why are acting students choosing to isolate instead of collaborate?

I realized I had misplaced my phone. I was getting incredibly stressed out, worrying about my responsibilities to the people I had to stay connected with. I was verbally beating myself up, stomping the floor with frustration. About ten minutes later, I realized how childish I was acting and told myself to "Calm down... It's just a phone, you're still alive." It surprised me how desperate I got; how addicted I am to constant availability to other people. Since then I have thought more about who I am without my device, because that is the person who really matters to me.

Every performer has a vivid memory of what it was that kick-started their passion for acting. We played in the woods with our sisters and brothers to build tree forts, we made up stories about monsters and heroes, we performed skits and did impressions of aunts and uncles to the great delight (or great dismay) of our parents, or we corralled the other kids in the neighborhood to re-enact a great race (or a great escape). We played "pretend" with each other ("You be Wonder Woman and I'll be Batman," "Let's pretend that you're Mr. Solfanelli from the deli and I'm the bad kid coming to steal the candy."). We built ensembles and teams, felt accepted and loved, thrived on playing together in a safe group, and we had great, great fun. Something clicked in each one of us that – whatever we ended up doing in life – we didn't ever want to give up that beautiful feeling of playing and creating ensemble. Parents told us how impractical that idea was (it's their job to worry, so forgive them, folks). But we dreamed about finding a way to have that feeling of playing and belonging all the time. And somewhere along the way, a teacher or a friend said "Hey, we're doing this play... " A play is called a "play" for a reason – it's an invitation to gather others together to collaborate, create, and to play "pretend." All of our acting students had that epiphany at some point – and they've come to our colleges, conservatories, and universities to learn how to do it well so that they can make a lifelong career of it.

The ability to create authentic human behavior, and to collaborate together in that process, is the essential foundation of theatre and theatre training. Without it, we won't work, we won't thrive, and we won't be able to affect our audience, who, as we saw in Chapter 3, need to experience humanity and all its stories now more than ever. Our acting students know intellectually that they are choosing a collaborative profession, but there has been an observable drop in their understanding of what that truly means. In the previous chapter, we discussed how smartphones and apps are designed to "hook" people to use them as much as possible. (Potato chips are made to taste that good for a reason – you're *supposed* to buy more.) But why would an actor – someone who is so fulfilled by collaborative and imaginative play with others that they want to make a career of it – personally choose to disengage and avoid the very social interactions that feed and fuel them as an actor? You would think an actor would be immune to the negative influences that smartphones can have on social interaction. To the contrary; in many ways, actors are even *more* susceptible than others. Why might an actor possibly be more susceptible? A few possibilities:

- Actors are uniquely drawn to story; creating stories, telling stories, the thrill of playing a character in a story. Author Jonathan Gottschall writes "Humans are creatures of story, so story touches nearly every aspect of our lives (15)." With story already permeating every aspect of our existence, including our dreams, imagine that you love stories so much that you've chosen to make your living by telling stories. You spend your days looking for stories everywhere; for inspiration, fulfillment, and to seek that "high" that you get when you find a good story.

  Now consider smartphones, apps, and the Internet. How many millions of stories are told in a string of texts? In a series of linked articles? In a thread of comments in which people are responding to a posted story, and then a new story emerges from the responses to the responses? How often do you walk away from a book or a movie before you know how it ends? And what if the story never really ends? Social media is akin to old fashioned serials in which stories are told in installments – those were designed to hook us too. Now imagine someone who is already hooked on story having immediate and limitless access to a global library of millions of stories on social media and the Internet. It's hard to walk away without knowing who will have the last word and how it all ends.

- Actors must be vulnerable so they can be open and accessible to their partners, ensemble and audience. As we quoted acting teacher Anya Saffir in Chapter 2, "An actor's job is to reveal themselves." This is often easier said than done. If your job requires you to accept that you "are enough," to face your demons every day, to expose your heart, mind, and actions to the scrutiny and judgmental eyes of an audience (and colleagues) – that can be terrifying, and exhausting. Young actors already struggle, and sometimes want to run from the intensity of emotional and vulnerable work. If you have access to protection – that is, something that offers you a "filter" to the world, makes you feel less exposed, and gives you a respite from all of that revealing-of-self – it would be incredibly tempting to take advantage of that.

- Actors are trained to say, "yes and. . . " Recent studies have concluded that checking devices is contagious (Finkel and Kruger); when someone sees another person do it, they feel compelled to do it as well. Actors live, breathe, and work through agreement with one another. ("If you make that choice, I'll build on it and add something to it.") They are encouraged to "synch up" with ensembles and collaborators. So if your daily work requires you to say "yes and. . . " and to build upon what others around you are doing, that's going to permeate everything you do; including your use of smartphones.

"Technology is a blessing and a curse, and I fear for my generation that it's more of a curse than it will ever be a blessing. It literally consumes us in the worst way."

As teachers and leaders, we need to come to a compassionate understanding as to why this generation of acting students would choose activities that stunt their Collaborative Gene. It's not enough to tell them to turn that thing off; we need to know more about what's happening to them, why they may be more susceptible to excessive use, and then take actions to help them get back to a place of collaborative play.

Rose

Two months into the semester, I came to improv class and said, "I'm giving you a quiz." Gasps. "It's OK, it's an oral quiz." Cautious disbelief. Now, Brooklyn College has a massive clock tower on the top of its campus library; the clock chimes every quarter hour, and it goes "bong" on the hour. Loudly. The clock tower is on the college's logo, stationary, diplomas, everywhere; you can't miss the damn thing, and you can hear it no matter where you are on campus. I asked my students, "What color is the dome on the top of the clock tower?" Stunned silence. One person out of 12 got it. I asked, "What color is my office?" Again, one person out of 12. And so on. I continued to ask questions about obvious elements in the environment they had been living and studying in for two months. The most number of students who got a right answer at any given time was two. Two students out of 12. That quiz became a light bulb moment for us all, and opened the door for us to discover what it was that was being missed. The simplest observations.

> The things that surround you every day. We all got a bit emotional as I reflected on Emily's monologue from Thornton Wilder's *Our Town*: "Oh, earth, you're too wonderful for anybody to realize you. Do any human beings ever realize life while they live it? – every, every minute?" (108). Observation, awareness, sensory awareness, listening, and allowing the world to affect you; how can we hope to be storytellers if we are not involved in our own story?

Our first step to gaining insight into the personal "why" of our student's behaviors came in 2014 when we initiated weekly and monthly Digital Disconnects (also referred to as DD) into the BFA Acting Program at Brooklyn College. We required students to disconnect from all technology for one day per week (from 9:00 a.m. to 6:00 p.m.) as well as for a 24-hour disconnect period one day per month. (See Appendix R for a full description of how we did this, and how you might implement it yourself.) We hoped that by drawing their awareness to their use, they would be better able to recognize the effects that their smartphone habits had on their collaborative skills. What we discovered when we read their many hundreds of papers permanently altered our understanding of this phenomenon, and motivated us to make immediate changes in our curriculum and in the classroom. Our students themselves provided the answers we desperately needed as to why they were choosing to use their devices to excess.

"I need my phone so that I can be validated. I need to feel like I exist and that I have a means of connection to someone who understands what I'm going through."

One of the most disturbing sentiments we encountered from a great many students was they missed having their smartphone as a distraction from what was going on around them. That is, they specifically used it to distract them from the life that was actually happening right in front of them. Our students were consciously choosing to avoid the very thing they needed to nurture and develop collaborative skills; interacting with one another. Their smartphone had become their representation of ensemble and community; and many wrote that they felt a profound sense of loneliness when they were separated from their device. Not from their *ensemble*, but from their *device*. However, what was most heartening (and heartbreaking) was that their loneliness seemed amplified when they used their device right after their Digital Disconnect. Why? They had spent their DD in a panic, worrying about all the things they were missing. To their great sadness, when they got their devices back, they found they hadn't really missed anything at all.

"I made a scary discovery that I am dependent on getting texts or calls to feel important. I realized that I could have real conversations with people face-to-face all day long, but when I opened my phone at 6:30 p.m. (after the Digital Disconnect was complete) and saw that throughout the whole day not a single person tried to contact me, I was crushed. My feelings were genuinely hurt and I realized just how much more I value a text over a real conversation."

Over the course of three years of conducting Digital Disconnects (with roughly 100+ students), the students consistently cited the following personal reasons as to why they felt "I couldn't stop myself" and "it was no use resisting." Those are:

- Fear of missing out.
- Not wanting to be thought of as "weird" or "different" by not being seen using their device.
  - o   Fear of judgment and fear of rejection.
- Boredom.
- Avoiding: people, conversation, work.
- Loneliness.

Reading why these actors were choosing to create distance between themselves and other people, between themselves and their own feelings, and between themselves and life and nature itself, was alternately shocking and illuminating. Shocking because we'd always assumed our acting students had a wildly reliable preference for collaboration and interaction with others. We would never have thought that they would knowingly choose to isolate and remove themselves from the very situations and skills that were required for them to live their passion: acting. Illuminating, because – thanks to the honesty and courage of our students and what they bravely revealed about themselves – we finally had some insights that we could use to build solutions from. What did they reveal? We're going to let our students do most of the talking here.

"I HATE MY PHONE. I hate it so fucking much (excuse my French). I want to throw it out the window. I want to throw both of my brothers' phones out the window and also all of my friends' phones out the window and then stomp them into a million little pieces."

Fear of missing out

"I couldn't help but play on my phone on the bus ride home. I found myself looking at FB, checking my messages to see if I missed anything throughout the day. It's very upsetting in a way, sometimes we check our

social media because we don't want to miss out on anything, yet while
we're doing this we are missing out on what's going on in front of us."

FOMO – or fear of missing out – was added to the Oxford Dictionary in 2013. It literally means "anxiety that an exciting or interesting event may be currently happening elsewhere, often aroused by posts on social media" ("FOMO"). So, what's the "hook"? The promise of something else cool and new? A funny new video or photo, or an article or opinion that's just been posted? A new celebrity story or a big event in another part of the world? Perhaps even better, a friend may have posted something that has to do with *me*; the possibilities are endless. So, that can lead to endless use in order to try to keep up. Remember the dopamine loop we talked about in Chapter 3? And the endless stream of wrapped presents in Chapter 2? The promise of those limitless possibilities aimed directly at the pleasure centers in our brain is the hook that ensnares.

> *"I'm always feeling like I'm missing out on something during Digital Disconnect whether it's a text, phone call, or social media notifications. It's funny how I feel like I'm missing out on phone messages when I'm actually missing out on what's outside the phone; real life. It's almost like we have to choose or balance between two lives."*

> *"When I wake up in the morning the first thing I literally reach for is my cell phone. If I reach for my cell phone and I can't find it, I go into this little frenzy of excitement until I find it to see what I've missed while I was asleep. I use my phone as an alarm clock, but lately I've been waking up earlier than my alarm because my mind is telling me 'check your phone, someone is trying to reach you.' I don't know, it's weird."*

Quick note: Dr. Sherry Turkle recommends that everyone buy an actual alarm clock (Turkle). It removes the "I have to check the time" temptation to keep returning to the device.

> *"It's sad to see how much of a pull my phone has on me. It's like my mood shifted from being Happy Self to Moody Self. I hate to admit that there were times I wasn't doing anything and I would forget that I wasn't able to check my phone. I kept giving myself the excuse that anyone calling could possibly be an emergency, but by the end of the day nothing ended up being an emergency. Why did I need to know what was going on in the lives of people I rarely talk to? I have a phone, so why don't I use it to actually connect and communicate with friends and family? In my craft I need to be a great communicator."*

> *"Turning my phone on at the end of the day was a huge disappointment. I didn't want to turn it back on, but there was a little voice in my head telling me 'what if someone important texted me?' I couldn't fight the voice..."*

Not wanting to be seen as "weird" or "different": fear of being judged or rejected

"I began to work my way home and found myself in a vortex of electronics. . . I ended up on a bus filled with students. . . I had this sudden urge to take out my phone, which I did. I couldn't stop myself; I had this awkward feeling of being left out by people; students I don't even know. Was I afraid that these students around me would mock me?. . . I wanted to escape from this environment and the only way to do so was by going on my phone. I had other options however, I had books and plays I could read, I had homework I could begin working on. But my mind said, "NO. I MUST BE LIKE ONE OF THEM!" I had this urge to fit in. . . In relation to acting, I know there will be times in which I will want to escape from the environment. But I need to remember to breathe and keep moving forward. The only story I should worry about is my own, and this story must be a happy tale, not one of struggling to fit in with those around me."

"We constantly post things online with the expectation that other people will 'like' it. The more likes, the more gratified we become . . . the less likes, the more people seem to be passing an imaginary judgment on you, as if you aren't good enough. I think the judgments that accompany social media only increase the judgments we have of ourselves. If we are constantly judging ourselves then we will never be free to make bold choices or even obvious ones. And we will never challenge ourselves or grow as human beings."

Not wanting to be perceived as "different" or "weird" connects directly to fear of judgment, and fear of being rejected. "I'm not going to be accepted or included if I'm not doing the same thing as everyone." It's a story older than *The Crucible*. Actors are especially susceptible to these fears because they live their lives and create their work in front of the gaze of collaborators, directors, and audiences who are constantly assessing them. It's challenging enough for actors to separate what belongs to the character (sometimes unpleasant or morally corrupt personality traits) and what belongs to them. As we noted earlier, the desire to hide is strong among young actors, and their smartphone can serve as an escape, or even as a mask that protects them from judgment. So, if they can belong by doing what everyone else is doing, and be protected from the Judging Eyes of Scrutiny, that can feel like a pretty good deal.

Boredom

"I don't use technology for productive reasons at all. I am very accustomed to using it to merely distract and entertain myself from boredom.

This boredom is really me not wanting to be alone with my own thoughts."

"I check my phone as a way of taking a break from what is presently occurring. When I feel bored or I feel my attention wandering I check my phone out of habit."

Many students described they were willing to do almost anything to avoid feeling bored. They're not alone. A fascinating 2014 study focusing on the role of technology and solitude led by Timothy Wilson of the University of Virginia literally found shocking results. They conducted a series of experiments asking student participants to be alone with their thoughts in a room without any diversions (no technology, puzzles, or distractions) for a period of six to 15 minutes. After the early stages in which students ranked their discomfort with being left alone (a majority of them hated it), the research team then hooked them up to a device that would give them an electrical shock. They were given a buzzer that they controlled, and were told they could push a button and zap themselves during their "thinking time" if they wanted. Incredibly, 25 percent of the participating women opted to give themselves electric shocks during their alone time, but an amazing *66 percent* of the men chose to give themselves shocks during the six to 15-minute time period. These subjects were literally willing to do anything available to them to avoid being in solitude with their own thoughts. When asked for comment, Dr. Wilson said, "I'm still just puzzled by that." We're with you, Dr. Wilson (Cossier).

Unfortunately, by avoiding boredom an actor will miss the role that it plays in the creative process. Boredom allows us to sit in the moment, to be present, wishing for something to happen. It's that attempt to will something into being that nurtures imagination, sparks creativity, helps us get inspiration from the world around us, and to process our many thoughts from the day. If an actor can't allow themselves to be in a moment, or they condition themselves to avoid "empty" moments, that translates into a discomfort in their moment-to-moment work and can stunt their imagination. In an interview about her book *Reclaiming Conversation*, Turkle says, "If there's a lull in the conversation, let it be. Conversations, like life, have silences and boring bits. It is often in the moments that we stumble and fail that we discover." So, if an actor lets themselves stay with that boredom for just a little bit. . .

"Sure, I did all the looking around and noticing of people and nature. That was all well and good, but sometimes that gets boring. If you are looking at the same patch of land for an extended amount of time, you are going to find everything there is to find rather quickly. When these moments hit me, I entertain myself in a way I've been doing literally since I was a toddler. A desk would no longer be a desk. It would turn

into a battle arena. A battle arena where warriors from two opposing alien factions would battle it out. A tall tree was no longer a tall tree. It became a warzone. The leaf foliage wasn't foliage, it was the thickets of cannon fire, laser blasts and the movement of armor."

Avoiding: people and conversation

"There is a difference in social conversations when my phone is in my hand and when my phone is turned off in my bag. Most of the things people say would go through one ear and out the other because I'd be so interested in my own ideas without allowing myself to be touched by the thoughts and emotions of others."

Avoiding people. Avoiding people. *Avoiding people.* This phrase should send chills up all of our spines. How can we possibly be actors, or members of any ensemble or community for that matter, if we are consciously choosing to avoid one another? What happens to relationships? Listening? Empathy? Conversation?

"I want to avoid the harsh feelings that have a tendency to come with honesty. A lot of times it is so much easier to put yourself in a shell and feel comfortable. My phone has been a crutch that allowed me to do just that – take myself out of the moment. I relied on my phone to distance myself from anything that would have otherwise caused me to stretch and grow. I needed to trust myself that I was worthy of that process and that everything was truly okay – I did not need to hide."

"I noticed how much people were sucked into their digital devices. It was kind of like a force field, shielding them away from the world around them."

As we've written in previous chapters, lessening the amount of face-to-face interaction leads to more isolation, and a lessening of empathy. *Psychology Today* reported that since the year 2000, there had been a *40 percent* drop in empathy among college students. They cited several reasons for this, but particularly pointed to changes in how children have been growing up. Researchers noted the decrease in unstructured playtime in childhood (more on that in Chapter 6), and the increase of screen time (Szalavits). If children aren't getting to know one another when they're younger, it makes sense that our students will struggle more in their college years.

"[L]ooking all around me, people were either on their phones, tablets, or listening to music while reading something (strange). Looking around the subway car made me ashamed that I fit right in with those people on a daily

basis. Being open and vulnerable made me think of all the other times that I missed out meeting or having a conversation with someone. As humans, I feel that we thrive off of a good conversation. We're social animals and it's like technology is taking that away from us, one app at a time."

The very nature of conversation itself has been rapidly changing, from its frequency to its quality. We've noticed a difference in the amount of times students drop by during our office hours, and we note the shifts in the quality of conversation in group discussions. Rose pleads with her students to "phone, don't email" her if they have a question or concern. Quite a few of them ignore that request and email her anyway, while others get exasperated and ask, "why can't I just text you?" Conversation is a way for actors to practice communication and the expression of ideas, and it supports their collaborative skills in multiple ways. Those quieter classrooms that we've talked about are expressing only part of the problem. There's less conversation, but there's also less *quality* conversation. A 2014 study published in *Environment and Behavior* focused on the impact of smartphones on conversation. Researchers found that even the presence of a cell phone negatively impacted the quality and content of conversation. Participants reported that they experienced less of an empathic connection, and less fulfillment than in conversations without the presence of a cell phone. When a cell phone was visible, the content of the conversation also became more superficial. People were anticipating being interrupted by the cell phone to the point where the mere sight of it inhibited them from talking about matters of consequence (Misra et al.). Look, every talk we have with friends or colleagues doesn't have to be on the level of *War and Peace*, but it doesn't have to be about the latest celebrity scandal either. It also doesn't help that more and more, we refer to strings of texts or emails as "conversations" instead of "correspondence."

"Any conversation that we have via text or social media deprives us of the compassion or consideration we would feel if we were to have it in-person."

"I was more present in conversations because I didn't have the option to check my phone."

Hope springs eternal. When our students spent time disconnecting from their screens, they began making adjustments to their ways of thinking about conversing with others, and more importantly, to their actions.

"We finally got to the party and I came into a room of about ten people that I didn't know. So after introducing myself to the host I decided to go up to the others in the room and introduce myself one by one. After I did that a friend of mine came up to me and asked, 'why on earth did

you do that?' I just responded with 'because that's the right thing to do.'
He looked at me like I was crazy and that's when I realized that it's not
just about having technology that changes the way we communicate but
it's being born into a generation that has always had it. Things like
introducing yourself to others have become 'strange.' My friends made
me feel like I was doing something wrong when I knew better."

Avoiding: work

We have always had students who daydreamed when they were supposed to
be getting work done. They looked out the window or toward the door and
you knew they were simply somewhere else. But the door and the window
never pinged or offered them a cat video or anything other than a place for
them to direct their imaginations while they created their own momentary
fantasies. So, they always came back: to the discussion, to the class, to their
homework, to the rehearsal. What if the window literally offered them a
threshold into another place? One where they didn't have to engage, work
or think?

> *"As I began doing homework during my Digital Disconnect, it felt so*
> *weird because I always do my homework with my phone nearby so I can*
> *always check the time. Every 15 minutes or so I found myself checking*
> *if I had my phone. Everything felt so weird, like a piece of myself was*
> *missing. As I was doing homework I was too distracted since I kept wor-*
> *rying about my phone and who had texted me. So I had to stop doing*
> *homework."*

> *"I find myself in the middle of doing work reflexively wanting to go to*
> *Facebook. I observed how the unproductive things compounded on one*
> *another. I would go from Facebook to checking my email to Googling*
> *random things to checking my phone and the social media apps I have*
> *on it. Sometimes it was to the point where I was checking all of those*
> *things for longer than I was doing work. Even as I type these sentences,*
> *I think about if this thing I'm going to check is really that important.*
> *That puts me in the frame of mind to be able to say no, and keep doing*
> *what I'm doing. And it just happened again! Literally as I finished typ-*
> *ing the last sentence I moved my mouse and hovered it over my Google*
> *Chrome icon to click on it and got to FB to see if maybe something*
> *happened."*

Have we found a correlation between smartphone use and lower grades?
Absolutely. Researchers at Kent State University looked at the relationship
between cell phone use and academic performance in 500 undergraduate
students from 82 different majors (who knew there *were* that many majors?

Bless the scientists...). We know we've supplied a lot of data for you, but if you only have time to read one study all the way through, this is the one. Students who used their phones for an average of ten hours daily had a grade point average of (GPA) 2.84, while students who used their cell phones for an average of two hours a day had a GPA *of 3.15* (Lepp et al.). That's a significant difference. That's the difference between getting a particular scholarship or not (many have a 3.0 minimum requirement), or the difference between getting accepted into a college or university, or not.

> *"I have to do a journal and weekly reading for theatre history, and the previous week it took me about an hour and a half to complete it. This week because I didn't have my phone it only took forty-five minutes; that's about half the time. Thinking about it, it does make sense: (when I had my phone) for every couple of pages that I read, I would award myself time on my phone instead of powering through. That really opened my eyes to how attached I am to my phone."*

In theatre, we also grade our students on their ability to self-motivate, their timeliness and attendance, and their ability to be accountable with schedules they set with scene partners and teachers. Because these skills are also negatively impacted by excessive smartphone use, it's possible that theatre majors may be experiencing an even more significant drop in their GPAs than other students. We have no empirical evidence of this (yet!), but anecdotally, we're definitely seeing (and giving) lower grades among our acting students than in previous years. Not simply in theatre history classes (usually the hardest course for our acting majors), but in their "fun" classes, like acting, voice, improvisation, and movement. It's something we all need to be more mindful of as we address technology use with our students now and in the future.

Loneliness

> *"I tried to think why I was so susceptible to technology when I was home alone. I started to think that maybe I was lonely and I was looking for some interaction even if it was technological and not real. The interaction I did find with my device was not satisfying. It was empty, and in the end made me feel even more alone."*

Loneliness motivates us to seek love, friendship, and community. Loneliness can also paralyze us and make us set up camp in Lonelyville. Perversely, new devices and technology promise not only a solution to loneliness, but a "better" solution: they will get you *huge* amounts of community, thousands of friends, and many "likes," and you don't have to even look at another human being to do it. So if someone is shy by nature, which can lead to loneliness, the smartphone offers a tempting alternative. Recent studies have shown that someone who is lonely or shy (or has social phobias) is much more likely to use their smartphones to excess or become addicted to them (Bian and Leung). The more they use their smartphones, the more acute their loneliness actually becomes.

> *"It was such a hard week for me. I didn't want to do the Digital Disconnect because I knew I wouldn't have any distractions from my thoughts or feelings. I asked a friend of mine if she could ride the train with me so I wouldn't be alone. I feared if I didn't have anything to do or someone to distract me for too long, I would be left with myself and my problems to deal with."*

What shook our students the most? The discovery that none of it was real. That their loneliness had more truth than the virtual online community they had created in order to keep the loneliness and fear of rejection at bay. Just like when Dorothy and company go backstage after Toto unmasks the Wizard, there is a profound sadness to see and hear the booming image of Oz thundering overhead, while also seeing the puny, soft-spoken man at the controls. Nobody likes to be fooled; and we're doubly hard on ourselves when we're asked to look at the role we played in our own deception.

Progress and the good news

The good news is that all of our students experienced significant discoveries, and made outstanding progress in increasing awareness of their use, and of the world around them. They took positive steps in their collaborative skills of awareness, empathy, and listening, which, coupled with actions we took in the classroom (more on that in Chapter 5), led to stronger and healthier actors. They enthusiastically shared what they noticed, *how* they noticed things, conversations that they had, and things they felt they would not have seen or experienced had their smartphone been available to them. To our delight, they also now know what color the top of the clock tower on the library is.

The more time students spent with their devices turned off, the more they wanted to have the kinds of experiences they were having without their devices. They noted the differences in themselves, in their relationships, and in their acting skills. It has been an incredibly challenging process to select (and limit!) our students' observations and deep insights; we could easily create a Volume II with their words alone. We decided to create categories based on the acting traits we discussed in Chapter 1 and to include two or three points of view for each. We include family relationships at the end of our list for an important reason. Like us, you may have many students who live at home or with family. The impact of a family – and their support – can make a significant difference in their lives.

Awareness

"When I'm on my Digital Disconnect and I'm walking outside I notice more things and they resonate more with me. I still remember everything I observed during my DD more clearly than any other day when I'm on my phone. My awareness has definitely improved because even when I'm listening to music, I look around and observe things as if I'm on my DD. I have to say that my senses have definitely improved."

"The act of living life gives life it's meaning and as actors we live many different lives from different time periods, and other countries and cultures. So we have to experience as much of life as possible in order to take these journeys. Social media can show you the brownie someone ate, but it can't capture what it tasted like. It can tell you two people are now in a relationship, but it can never communicate what it was like for them to fall in love. We have to go out and do it for ourselves. We as human beings have to give life meaning."

Being present

"I have started being more present and actively listening to everyone around me. DD's rediscovered for me the meaning of being present. In order to be empathetic and actively listening, we need to be present. I have noticed a shift of energy from people around me."

"I only thought about the things happening in that very moment. After 22 years of living, my time was me just being; no music, no thinking, just be where I was physically, mentally and spiritually."

Risk taking

"I feel like I take more risks now that I'm 'looking up.' There's two different realities in front of me, one in which I'm glued to my phone 24/7 and not taking risks or being more involved, or the other side in which I put myself out there. This Digital Detox is not just breaking an addiction but it's shaping who I am and I'm becoming more aware of that true self inside me."

"It doesn't take much for me, both as a person and an actor, to become self-conscious, and I know from personal experience that self-consciousness is the death of risk taking. It wasn't until I began

Digital Disconnects that I realized how much of that self-consciousness came from my sub-conscious awareness that I was constantly being judged via social media. Taking a break from technology allowed me the freedom to fail, and therefore, make bolder choices in my life, and my acting work."

Productivity

"Usually it would take me about a week to get off-book for scenes after I have done the script analysis but in the past two directing scenes I have done, I was off book way ahead of schedule."

"Keeping technology out of the way allowed me to fully engage in the text, especially since I have been having the hardest time trusting that I know my lines. I do attribute that now, in part, to my investment in technology."

Conversation

"I found myself looking for more conversation. I felt myself drawing energy from the people I was around. There was an energy pull that I thought radiated from my eagerness to connect a little more than usual because I didn't have my cell phone to hide behind."

"I found myself way more talkative with my peers. I was joking around with my ensemble; usually I would be using my phone as a means to escape the conversation."

Memory and retention

"I'm remembering things way easier that I had before. After reading the scenes with my partners four or five times, I was already half memorized. It feels so good to not have to be on my phone every second! I feel like a new person."

"Cell phones and electronic tablets are not helping us remember things because everything we ever need to know is literally in the palm of our hand. We don't have to take notes anymore because we can always snap a picture of someone else's. I'm guilty of this myself. But today on my Digital Disconnect I went back to taking notes on what was needed. I had to read Waiting for Godot for today's history class and usually I'll have the play on my phone and look back at it if I need to. Today I re-read it before class and wrote as many notes as I could about the play and it helped me understand the play more and actually remember what happened."

Sensory awareness

"When I take my headphones off, not only do I notice sounds, but I also notice colors and the conversations of people around me. I find myself observing people and their interactions, and projecting my own idea of who they are, as if I were creating a character."

"As funny as it sounds, as I kept doing Digital Disconnects, I found that my hearing had gotten a lot better. I'm able to hear things from further away and I am much more attentive to things around me. I started to bump into friends throughout the day because I was not distracted. It's like I was afraid of eye contact before starting the Disconnects."

Connecting with scene partners

"I realize with each Disconnect I'm coming closer to being with the person I'm acting with or connecting with in an exercise. I noticed that the one muscle that has grown drastically through doing the DDs is connecting with my partner, and this goes back to listening skills. I feel like an infant that has just learned to let others speak and not interrupt others while speaking."

"A beautiful thing happened with my ensemble in the cafeteria. When one is without a phone you get curious about different things, things you might think are not important when you're glued to your phone. I found out everyone's real, full names. It was fascinating to know how many cultures are mixed in this ensemble. Some of their names are beautiful with a sense of pride attached to them; pride about their origin."

Connecting with family

"I woke up (on the day of my 24-hour Digital Disconnect) and helped my mom make breakfast. Again, all I am thinking about is trying to keep myself busy so I won't go running to my phone as a distraction or to keep me entertained. My father made a very funny comment, 'I am going to win the lottery. You're up early, you helped your mother cook, and you're not busy on the phone. Are you feeling OK?'"

"I am a Muslim by religion. . . I noticed today how my mother prays, which is beautiful to watch because she makes it so personal that it inspires me to have that kind of commitment to art. I also noticed her crying at the end of the prayer and I realized she has been doing this for as long as I can remember, and I never noticed her crying at the end of her prayers."

Empathy

> *"I was actually pretty worried about myself in the past because I wasn't able to put myself in other people's emotional shoes when they tried to talk to me, no matter how tragic or sad the incident was. I feel like these Disconnects have made me more human again."*

> *"To be better actors, we have to be better human beings. The best part of this soul work (the Disconnects) was to know that all that work is paying off. We start seeing changes in our work and our daily lives and it gives us permission to go deeper and dig deeper into whatever it is we are experiencing. As better humans, we have our empathy muscle being worked at the fullest which makes our acting abilities more available to go to."*

Final thoughts

As the Digital Disconnects continued over several months, we encouraged our students to consider more and more complex questions about their use and how it related to the skills needed for their art form. With each passing week, they took greater responsibility for their actions, and they took greater initiative in finding creative solutions to achieve a healthier balance of their device use. By the end of the semester, they had made profound connections about theatre, acting, and humanity itself. Their beautiful anthropological and artistic discoveries could serve as its own guidebook for their peers, as well as for teachers who work toward understanding this phenomenon better. If one of them ever does decide to write that guide, we hope they lead with these two beautiful quotes:

> *"I think the nature of human interaction has evolved because of technology. We can't fight it because technology will continue to advance and humans will continue to depend on it. I think as humans we have to remain conscious of what we lose through technological communication. Even though our dependence on technology might grow, we can still have the power to put down our phones and have a real conversation with someone. I also wonder what effects it has on this generation's artists. It is a challenge we actors face to maintain real, human interaction in order to tell truthful stories."*

> *"I finally discovered what this assignment was about. That the actor's job is to be connected to the sensual world around them. I need to experience the world, so that I can create it onstage in my work."*

Conclusion

We have never been more convinced of anything than that we initiated Digital Disconnects and made changes in our teaching in the nick of time. Seriously, *just* in the nick of time. What students describe in their first week of DDs is shocking at best, and terrifying at worst. Fortunately, the number of students who think the assignment is stupid or a joke averages about three or less (which, out of our roughly 40 students, is pretty good odds). Those "three-or-less" students take about two to three weeks before they also have their light bulbs go off. Even those who passionately love their devices and their gaming will grudgingly admit how much the Digital Disconnect has benefitted them, and that they see how their excessive use was negatively affecting their acting work. Those grudging admissions evolve into deeper and more beautiful insights about themselves, their art form, and the world around them.

However, Digital Disconnects are simply the first step in nurturing and empowering our acting students to gain insights about their choices and behaviors. That device will never stop offering its temptations and imagined protections against boredom, judgment, and people. It is up to us to offer our students something greater; to help develop the skills and practice they need to reconnect with their original passion for acting, collaborating, and playing. We literally need to help them rekindle their Collaborative Gene so they can consistently – and joyfully – be able to give all of their true selves over to their work with the empathy, listening, awareness, honesty, focus, and presence that is needed in every creative moment. Their re-ignited Collaborative Gene will instinctively help them know how to collaborate and how to create with one another; and we can get back that beautiful feeling of playing and of creating ensembles together.

Our students can do this. *You* can do this. We all can do this. The following chapter offers a series of processes and exercises that will support you in addressing the actor's unique vulnerabilities and needs, and gives you a supportive guide to help strengthen their collaborative abilities so they can consistently have their acting skills – and their dream of acting throughout their lives – available to them always.

Bibliography

Bian, Mengwei and Leung, Louis. "Linking Loneliness, Shyness, Smartphone Addiction Symptoms, and Patterns of Smartphone Use to Social Capital." *Social Science Computer Review*. 33.1 (2015): 61–79. Web. 12 Jan 2018.

Cosier, Susan. "People Prefer Electric Shocks to Tedium." *Scientific American*. Nature America, Inc., 1 Nov. 2014. Web. 4 July 2017.

Finkel, Julia A. and Daniel J. Kruger. "Is Cell Phone Use Socially Contagious?" Abstract. *Human Ethology Bulletin* 27.1–2 (2012): n.pag. Web. 4 July 2017.

"FOMO." *English: Oxford Living Dictionaries*. Oxford University Press, Web. 4 July 2017.

Gottschall, Jonathan. *The Storytelling Animal: How Stories Make Us Human*. Houghton Mifflin Harcourt, 2013. Print.

Grandoni, Dino. "Cell Phone Use is Contagious, Study Shows." *HuffPost*. Oath, Inc., 4 Dec. 2012. Web. 4 July 2017.

Lepp, Andrew, Jacob E. Barkley, and Aryn C. Karpinski. "The Relationship Between Cell Phone Use and Academic Performance in a Sample of U.S. College Students." *Sage Journals* 5.1 (2015): n.pag. Web. 22 Nov. 2017.

Misra, Shalini, Lulu Cheng, Jamie Genevie, and Miao Yuan. "The iPhone Effect: The Quality of In-Person Social Interactions in the Presence of Mobile Devices." *Environment and Behavior* 48.2 (2016): 275–298. Web. 12 Jan 2018.

Szalavits, Maia. "Shocker: Empathy Dropped 40% in College Students Since 2000." *Psychology Today*. Sussex Publishers, 28 May 2010. Web. 4 July 2017.

Turkle, Sherry. "3 Questions: Sherry Turkle on 'Reclaiming Conversation.'" Interview by Peter Dizikes. *MIT News*. Massachusetts Institute of Technology, 17 Nov. 2015. Web. 4 July 2017.

Wilder, Thorton. *Our Town: A Play in Three Acts*. New York: Harper Perennial Modern Classics, 2003. Print.

Chapter 5

Rekindling the Collaborative Gene

We instruct our new scouts that the first thing you need to collect is tinder, which is very small pieces of wood, balls of lint, pine needles or even bark. No tinder=no fire. The next step is kindling; once tinder has caught fire, its heat can get larger pieces burning. Finally, once your fire is burning, you can add fuel, which is the life of the fire. Fuel is usually pieces of wood that are the size of a forearm. Fuel can make the fire bigger, brighter and last longer. As long as you continue to feed fuel, the fire will continue to live.

(Patrick Delaney, actor and Eagle Scout)

So where does all of this research and change and tumult bring us to? Right here: to this moment in time where our choices and actions will impact the future of teaching acting and theatre forever. Clearly, we want things to be different and, as you see from their powerful words in Chapter 4, students want things to be different too. Colleagues and theatre practitioners from Montreal to Dublin, and from New York to New Zealand sought us out to have conversations about these new phenomena that they were trying to understand. We *all* want things to be different in this vital moment in the history of our art form where we need to change our pedagogy, methods, and approaches. Turning phones off, and experiencing Digital Disconnects (DD) are great steps to take – but they're not enough by themselves. We need to develop a clear process to help students regain the skills they need to move from self-involved actions to behaviors that support ensemble building and collaboration. Armed with the information and research, and the belief that it *can* be changed for the better, we can take actions to make sure that the next generation of acting students has the essential collaborative skills for their craft. It's a tall order, but as Cliona Dukes of Smock Alley Theatre in Dublin said, "We are the people to solve this problem." This chapter is one big recommendation for a series of processes, steps, and solutions that we've found successful in rekindling those struggling Collaborative Genes.

Starting the process

To rekindle something is to re-ignite a flame. Trust that when you see Collaborative Genes that have been tamped down, the embers are still burning under the ashes. How do you get a fire going again? Gather some tinder, place bits of wood or pine needles next to the hot coals, and then gently blow oxygen into those embers. If it doesn't catch right away, don't worry; it may simply need a bit more time, effort, or materials. Once you have a small flame, treat it with care; don't smother it. Don't blow *so* hard that you extinguish the flame; that is, try not to let your desire (or eagerness?) be the thing that actually puts it *out*. As actor and Eagle Scout Patrick Delaney wisely said, "If you throw a large piece of wood on top of a small flame, it will do nothing but put out the fire." Rekindling or starting a fire takes time, a careful selection of materials, a keen understanding of the nature of fire, air, and breath, as well as patience and faith. Have faith in your own abilities as well as in your students. Look, it took our students a long time to get to where they are now; and it will take time, care, and patience to create meaningful change.

Rekindling the Collaborative Gene is no different. Simply because one's collaborative traits have been dulled, doesn't mean they can't be revived. Each year, we adjusted the structure and content of our classes, and we saw the Collaborative Gene roar to life once again. There are still occasional flame outs, but any Eagle Scout will tell you there are several ways to get a fire going again – that all Scouts have their secret trick or method through their choices of fire starters. Rose, Roger, and David have successfully applied all of the suggestions in this chapter in their own classrooms – but that took time, trial, and a fair amount of error. What we include here are the methods and exercises we found most consistently valuable to the progress of our students. Hopefully, these will build on practices that you've already been trying yourself. So whether you choose pine bark or balls of lint, we're confident that the following recommendations will help you discover your own path to rekindling your students' Collaborative Genes.

How to build a fire (or five steps to healthy collaboration)

1) *Awareness*: Draw the actor's attention to his/her behaviors and to their tech use. Don't tell them *what* they will discover; allow them to discover it themselves.
2) *Discovery*: Awareness creates the sparks of *Discovery*. When students become more mindful of their tech use, they realize what it's been displacing in their lives: empathy, being present, awareness, and oh yes – other people.
3) *Acknowledgement*: Once you have the sparks of Discovery, they're fed by the twigs of *Acknowledgement*. When someone accepts the truth

about their actual tech use ("no, *really* Professor, I *have* to have my phone in class; what if I get an important text?") they're better able to understand what's happening to them and why.

4) *Understanding*: What forces of nature are the flame vulnerable to that might extinguish it? Rain? Heavy winds? Timing: feeding it too soon, too late? Guide your students to analyze their experiences, and help them understand the science behind their devices so they can recognize why their brains and behaviors are affected. Look, there's a reason we don't let little kids play with matches. . .

5) *Actions*: This is the oxygen. *Actions* are the breath that delivers the oxygen needed to turn a low flame to a roaring fire. And those Actions *must* come not only from the ensemble leader, but from every person in the group.

This five-step process leads to *Empowerment*. Once the flames are burning brightly, collaboration is fueled as it always has been: with consistent commitment, sacrifice, and trust that leads to strong ensembles. The ensemble itself becomes those pieces of wood that provide the fuel to keep the Collaborative Genes burning under their own power.

1) Awareness – the tinder (gather some pine needles. . .)

> *"It was really interesting how I didn't talk to my friends that I was having lunch with because we were all on our phones. I realized after opening an app what I was actually doing. It was weird to see that I was conscious of when I was going on my phone. Once I got off the app, I found myself more interested in the people around me."*

> *"I feel a little more confident that the world won't blow up if I'm not answering every text and call I get. This will be a struggle, but I think it is necessary as an actor (and human being) to be able to be a part of the world around you instead of the world inside your little hand-held machine."*

Awareness is the essential tinder you need to rekindle the fire. As we wrote in Chapter 3 about the impact of the dopamine loop, the temptation to unwrap the next and the next and the next present can lead to their consistently choosing screens over people. Our new generations of acting students aren't completely aware as to how they're being affected. They need the objectivity and support of Digital Immigrants – you know, *us* – to gain perspective and awareness into how they're using technology, and how their use is affecting their collaborative skills.

> *"As humans, it is in our blood to work together as a community. What technology is doing is trying to strip us from our very DNA and encode us with something entirely different."*

To gather our tinder, we begin by leading them toward awareness of their behaviors and use. *Telling* them "too much technology is bad for you" gets you nowhere. Think of it like directing: when we direct an actor, we *could* tell them "cross there, sit down on that line, say the line this way." Of course, that gives actors absolutely no role in the collaborative process, and no ownership in the outcome. And, actors *hate* it. Dictatorial directors who deny actors their own investment in the creative process usually wonder why the actors seem so unhappy. The most successful productions happen when ideas are shared, and actors are encouraged to make discoveries of their own. Similarly, no student will willingly stop using their device just because someone *says* it's bad for them. And if the problem is that they're excessively online instead of "in life," personal awareness is one of the first things to suffer.

This is why they must discover it for themselves.

> *"I never realized how attached I am to my phone or even how much I rely on it. It was an interesting thing not using my phone, I felt as if a part of me was missing? And that's terrible, I feel as if my phone is an extended part of me. . . "*

Gathering your tinder: **Actions to stimulate Awareness: the first class meeting**

Create a supportive atmosphere. Plan your opening remarks carefully; *how* you present your plan to explore their smartphone/tech use in their course work is as important as implementing the actual policy. Your goal is for them to become a bonded ensemble, and to do that, they need to address all aspects of their personal behaviors. Part of your goal is to help them understand the difference between the ensemble in the room with them, and the extended ensemble that they believe lives in their phones.

- When you arrive at the first class, take note of how they're behaving toward one another. Are they chatting? Are they on their phones? Is it quiet? Are people sitting in the back row, with no one in the front row?
- Introduce yourself, and give your opening welcome and remarks. Let them know that part of your work together will be exploring the role of their tech use in relation to their acting skills. Reassure them that the goal is not to condemn technology, but to examine how we use it.
- Ask students to turn their phones off and physically "check" them. Deposit them in a plastic tub that preferably shuts with a resounding "click" of a snap lock; then place it out of sight. Let them know that this will now be part of a permanent ritual for starting each class. After the first class, alternate student volunteers to gather the phones; it includes them more deeply in the activity and gives them an even greater sense of

ownership in the process. Early on, the ritual of a "barrier" between the person and their device is fascinating. Observe their physical responses; you'll see their hands fluttering toward their pockets and bags, heads turning to wherever the Phone Check box has been put. . . and if there's a clock in the room, they'll seem to excessively check the time; over and over. A majority of our students reported during their DDs that they were "constantly" checking the time on their phones – and, so long as they were on the phone already: "Let me see if I got a text? Did Frankie post that photo of me on Instagram?" "Checking for the time" was one of the most widely reported "acceptable" excuses that students cited for opening their phones before falling down the rabbit hole of social media.

"A funny little situation I had was when I showed up to my math class and saw that everyone was waiting outside of it. We stood there for a while and the heat was getting to me so I decided to check the time to see how long I had been standing there. I didn't want to turn on my phone so I searched the walls for a clock and when I couldn't find one I asked the person next to me what time it was. After he told me the time I remembered that I was wearing a watch. This was totally bizarre to me. I had been wearing watches as accessories for so long that I forgot that the initial purpose of them was to tell time!"

- Tell students that they won't be permitted to remove their phones during class breaks. Then brace for impact. Asking them to check their phones is usually greeted with surprise and some grumbling, but withholding them during break can cause real distress. Create your own policy as to how to receive any emergency messages that may arrive during your class. For example, theatre professor Valerie Clayman Pye does the following: for personal emergencies, family members call the main office and someone is sent to remove the student from class. This policy lets a student know that in case of a true emergency they can always be reached, and that allows them to give their full attention to the class.

"Electronics have a way of making us expect instant gratification. We are so used to everyone being right next to their phone that when we do not hear back, we think something bad happened to them or they must hate us. Both conclusions are a terrible way to think."

- Inform everyone that they'll be required to "unplug" for the duration of all theatre classes. Brace for the possibility of revolt; but prepare for relief too. When Rose asked a recent applicant to her program what they would say about our Digital Disconnect policy, the applicant smiled and said, "I would first say, 'thank you.' And then I might cry. And then I would be relieved. Then I would say 'thank you' again."

- You'll need to notice who is comfortable with eye contact, who isn't, and whose head might be turning toward wherever you placed that plastic tub with the phones. Place the chairs in a circle or a formation that maximizes everyone's ability to see one another, and ask everyone to introduce themselves. Then, ask them to share at least two non-theatre related details about their life. What they choose to reveal will be illuminating, and will give you a sense of where their comfort zone is in this first class session.

- Ask each actor: "Why are you in the room?" Not because David said you *had* to register for the class – but what specifically inspired them to pursue acting and be with this ensemble at *this* moment in time? Each person is invited to share – out loud – what acting actually means to them and how deeply they care about it. As you guide them in this process, you can support them by being the steward of their stated purpose. That is, you'll have the objectivity to remind them of their passion for wanting to be an actor.

- If a student uses a tablet to take notes, create a specific time during class for note taking and ask them to challenge themselves to listen, absorb, and *remember*. Ask them to use a good ole fashioned notebook and pen. Current research concludes that those taking notes longhand experience greater benefits than those typing notes; the processing that occurs in writing their thoughts in longhand strengthened memory and retention in those students (Mueller and Oppenheimer). If there's a physical reason why they must use their smartphone or tablet, of course, support that student.

- After finishing introductory discussions and reviewing the syllabus, leave time for a series of first day on-your-feet exercises. The following suggestions highlight the skills you'll be focusing on throughout the semester, and will also give you a great gauge as to where the students are starting from. A few ideas for first day (and beyond!) exercises are:

  o Going on a Picnic (see Appendix F): listening, staying in the moment, memory, awareness, and a great way to get to know each other's names.

  o Murder Mystery (see Appendix A): eye contact, vulnerability, trust, awareness, a willingness to work with others.

  o Syllables of Your Name with Gesture (see Appendix G): vulnerability, physical expression, willingness to look silly, memory, awareness, observation, and another way to explore learning each other's names (physical).

  o Kitty Wants a Corner (see Appendix L): empathy, eye contact, vulnerability, trust, awareness, risk taking.

  o Shepherd and Sheep (see Appendix B): vulnerability, trust, willingness to be truthful for the ensemble's sake, awareness.

- At the conclusion of these exercises, you'll have a clearer understanding of where the students are starting from, and what elements they most need to work on. If you're pulling exercises from your own collection, we strongly suggest you include ones that require as much eye contact as possible. Making eye contact, or the avoidance of it, becomes an excellent barometer to guide you in the weeks to come.

Activities to stimulate Awareness: second, third, and fourth week class meetings

After that first class, you'll have gathered plenty of information to inform the following suggested activities. Whether your acting class meets two to three times a week, or once a week, apply the following activities in a way that gives you – and them – time to absorb their growing awareness in between class meetings. Remember, slow and steady.

- When you arrive at your second class, notice the level of conversation and interaction. How many students are on their phones, and how many interacting? What is the back row versus front row ratio? Begin to tease apart how much behavior is part of the natural process of getting to know one another, and how much is inhibited because of using phones to avoid/displace interaction.
- At this second (and third class, etc.), did any student volunteer to take the Phone Check box around to help check phones? Did anyone ask to keep their phone out to charge it? ("I'm not using it! I'm just charging it for later!" Good luck keeping their attention when it's in view. . .).
- Give them an assignment to create a technology log reflecting a single day in their life. Ask them to write down the number of hours spent on texting, social media, Internet surfing, gaming, any use of tablet, computer, or smartphone. As we described in Chapter 2, research revealed that the average tech use of undergraduate college students was roughly 98 hours every week. That's nearly 80 percent of one's waking hours. And that's a lot of lifetime spent being disconnected from. . . well. . . *life*. There are apps available now that allow the user to track how many minutes they spend on their phone, how many times they unlock it, and how many times they check social media accounts. It's encouraging to note that there are multiple apps available that, in addition to tracking the user's time spent on the phone, permit the user to set daily limits on their use. They receive a warning that tells them they've reached their limit.
- Introduce the policy and concept of them conducting one daily Digital Disconnect each week (see Chapter 4, and Appendix R), one 24-hour DD every month, and require them to write about their experiences. Reinforce that this is not an exercise for them to determine if their tech

use is bad or good, but to examine how they use it, how often, and what they experience, notice, and observe when they are digitally disconnected. As you saw in Chapter 4, the writing process becomes a vital (and private) way for students to explore their revelations about their behaviors, and they will discover things that may be hard for them to speak about or admit.

"I usually use my phone for music when I shower and the truth is that it felt so quiet and weird to just hear the water falling from the pipes. Just the water. By the time I got dressed and left the house I was already feeling off. The walk to school felt lonely because I usually listen to music or talk on my phone. I felt little itches to reach for my phone. The thing is with social media is that it's so accessible that you can use it anywhere you have phone service. The things I see on FB are all things I've seen before, never anything new. So why do I feel the need to look at my phone so badly?"

- One of the most striking results to come out of our first round of DD papers was how few people were actually able to do it. In their first DD papers, Brooklyn College students poured their hearts out in a panic; they didn't make it past the first *hour*. They worried about being addicted to their phones, and suddenly became aware of how much control their device had over them. What scared them most though was – they had thought the *opposite* was true.

"My phone is almost always in my hands so the weirdest thing I felt during my Disconnect was how I constantly felt like I was missing something. Because my hands were empty I would have to remind myself that my phone was turned off and put away in my bag."

"As we were walking I had noticed a very young girl with headphones, you could tell she was talking to someone but she was also on her phone, probably checking her social media, just like I do. She was so into her phone that she passed by three people and she bumped into every single one. You would have thought she was drunk... but that wasn't it. She was so invested into her phone that she didn't even notice the people around her. And the worst part was that every time she bumped into someone she would get so mad, because she thought it was their fault."

- Around week three or four, ask the group to discuss their experiences in class. By this point, you'll have had the opportunity to share some private feedback with them in their weekly DD papers. Having a group discussion will help them realize that they're not alone, and they'll have support from their ensemble.

- Be mindful of when students aren't listening to others. Some students are so used to skipping past things that don't hold a high degree of interest for them, that they're not developing the ability to listen thoughtfully to everything that is being said. If you observe this, ask a student to repeat what was just said to illuminate the point. But, only do it when *you* are speaking, rather than another student. That reduces fear of fracturing peer relations; that is, it's easier to take responsibility for not listening to your teacher than it is to admit you're not listening to your ensemble.

- As you plan your practical work in these second, third, and fourth week classes, include exercises/activities that are group based, and focus on physical instead of verbal skills. Verbal work tends to ignite feelings of harsh self-judgment ("that wasn't clever enough... funny enough... original enough... ") which – if students are already isolating – only serves to isolate them more. Words can kick the analytical mind into high gear, and collaborative behaviors then take a back seat. Group play encourages a greater sense of *free* play, helping them to feel safer and more confident about collaborating. Adding group play to every class will help draw their awareness – in the safety of the ensemble – to making connections with themselves and with the group. A few recommendations of group exercises for these weeks:

  o Continue with Kitty Wants a Corner.
  o Mindfulness (see Appendix N): awareness, being present, listening.
  o Pass the Snap (see Appendix K): awareness, being present, clear communication, commitment, working as an ensemble.
  o Torpedoes (see Appendix M): eye contact, empathy, being present, listening, finding agreement, awareness, working as an ensemble.
  o Walk and Rename Objects (see Appendix J): awareness of one's immediate environment, being present, imagination, observation skills.

- Include improvisation as much as possible. All acting techniques have at least one thing in common among their goals: to put the actor truthfully into the moment. Improv is singularly about the moment; the immediate moment. If students are good listeners, then their actions in the moment will be informed by the previous moments, but ideally, their full awareness is on the here and now. Listening will pay off for them in the form of impulses that appear while they're squarely in that moment. When their mind drifts, they tend to miss something and that can have consequences. That's why students may sometimes hear improv teachers say, "don't think." A few improv exercises we recommend are:

  o The Mirror Series, Gibberish, and Contact (from Viola Spolin's *Improvisation for the Theater 3rd Edition)*. These exercises remove recognizable language, forcing actors to slow down and increase their focus on listening and observing. It's almost impossible to think – all you can do is act and react in the moment.

o   For the next level of work, we recommend "Understudies." Though this isn't in her book, it's based on Spolin's work. Two people begin improvising a scene, while two "understudies" watch offstage. When the teacher yells, "Freeze," the actors freeze in position. The understudies take their places and continue the scene as the original characters. They should mimic the original actors as much as possible. The original actors wait offstage for the next "Freeze," when they return to the roles. The series of switches continues with the teacher calling "Freeze" periodically until the scene is over.

David

I have been playing and leading improv games for over 25 years. For much of that time, I have also been teaching the basic elements of Stanislavski Technique: Objective, Obstacles, Tactics, and Stakes. At some point, I realized that they were essentially the same thing. Every game has an objective, obstacles, tactics, and stakes. Take Monopoly for instance. Objective: end up with all the assets or bankrupt everyone else. Tactics: should I buy those cheap properties and build houses/hotels right away, or hoard cash in the hopes of getting the more expensive properties? Obstacles: paying rent to fellow players, getting taxed, going to jail, and so on. Stakes: those who invest in the game fully, have more fun. Plus the interesting twists and turns of landing on Chance or Community Chest keep an element of risk in even the most cautious player's approach. Finally, players must be engaged with one another, aware of their moves, and planning counter strategies, perhaps even negotiating deals.

Armed with this knowledge and awareness, every scene may now be seen as a game to be played. Many young actors focus diligently on their objective without reacting and responding to what their partner is doing. When we introduce listening (to which I will add observing), the players are no longer in a vacuum, simply displaying their technique to another (and us); they are using that technique to play the game of the scene with each other. *The Upright Citizens Brigade* ("Besser"), incorporates this concept of "the game of the scene" as a central part of their improv technique. Their improvisers approach each scene looking to discover or create a game that can be played.

For actors in a scripted scene, the term "game," does not necessarily have to mean comedic, or even fun (as in "fun and games"). The game of a scene in a horror movie, for instance, could be a "sick" game. So while it may be fun for the actors to play the game of a horror scene, the scene itself is not viewed by the audience as fun, but may be sick, disturbing, tragic, and so on.

Nearly all students understand how to play a game and love to play games. Games are not only an effective teaching tool, but getting actors to see a scene as a game will help them engage more fully and fight harder to achieve their objective. Often, a young actor will find greater stakes playing a game than playing a scene.

The worlds of improvisational acting and Stanislavski-based acting are not far apart. They both remind us that, in the end, what we do is *play*. This is what Viola Spolin understood. Her improv-game-based approach to acting advanced upon the teachings of Stanislavski. You can see great examples of the synthesis of these approaches in the work of Mike Nichols and other artists who were equally at home in the worlds of improvised and scripted theatre.

The mainstream acceptance and use of improv has exploded in recent years. Today there are improv theatres and training programs in most major cities and even in smaller cities. Improvisers are regularly hired as writers and performers in the film and television industries, but for years it seemed as though those industries didn't quite know what to make of us. I daresay that in 20 years, an actor without improv training will be at a disadvantage when auditioning for film and television.

Why has improv exploded? It's because the timeline mirrors the explosion of cell phones and social media. The growth of improv is part of our response to the growth of technology in our lives. It's the Collaborative Gene fighting back; it's a cry for more play.

One of the biggest discoveries we've made is that the more we return in our acting classes to the foundational exercises that directly elevate the underdeveloped social skills needed to engage the Collaborative Gene, the more responsive our students are and the more discoveries they're able to make with one another. There's no better way than to return to the source of improv, Viola Spolin. In referencing Ms. Spolin's work we'll call them games (instead of exercises). Play is what nature uses as a teaching tool (ever see a mama bear teaching her cubs?); and games are structured play. Isolated, disconnected students can be brought together quickly and powerfully through structured play. Every game has a point, a lesson, and a skill or skills that are required. At no time can the point/lesson/skills overrun the fun for very long. The fun or "playing the game" removes self-consciousness and allows the freedom for creative expression and learning. Play is perhaps the most fundamental of all human behaviors after the satisfaction of survival needs. And, we survive when we work together.

The above recommendations for individual and group work, combined with reduced device use and individual written reflections, will provide a fertile and supportive environment for your students' awareness to flourish, and awareness will create the sparks of discovery.

2) Discovery – the sparks

> "I felt confident in my ability to let go of my phone for a mere eight hours. And then Prof. Zerfas in Voice class asked us to get our phones to record ourselves reciting the assigned text she gave us. This is when I started to panic. Having my phone, literally, in the palm of my hand and not scroll through Instagram, or send a quick text, or see who's doing what on Snapchat was too much for this recovering techno-addict to take. Before long I was scrolling Instagram and texting my mom about how I wasn't supposed to be texting."

After several weeks of group play, focused and uninterrupted work (with devices checked and out of sight), DDs and class discussions, the epiphanies the students have are exciting. This can be an emotional and confusing time for students, partly because they're discovering what they *think* their use is, instead of what it *actually* is. What they imagined their close online community to be was actually a surrogate that prevented them from actual time and communication with friends, family, and loved ones. During the activities outlined earlier, they'll start to discover the differences between being disconnected and being truly present and in the moment.

> "I was very panicky all day. It's sad to see how much of a pull my phone has on me. By the end of the day, I realized so many different things. I questioned why I was addicted to my phone. Why did I need to know what was going on in the lives of people I rarely talk to or my friends that I haven't heard from in a while? I have a phone, so why don't I use it to actually connect and communicate with friends and family? It's like my app addiction is a road block for actual communication."

Just as it took us time to discover the connections between what we were observing in the classroom and the power that these devices held, it takes time for your acting students to discover cause and effect in their actions too. Being present with more frequency also triggers discoveries about the five senses. Students may talk about sounds, smells, and sights as if they are discovering their senses for the first time.

> *"The meal I had... was delicious. I think it was because I was starving and the fact that I took my time to enjoy it instead of eating AND using the phone. I don't think I can recall the last time I ate at a proper set table without using my phone at all."*

> *"As I took off on my bike ride to school, I enjoyed having no music to listen to. I realize that the world's natural song (the wind, cars, conversations, and every other random thing that happens during the commute) is just as beautiful as music."*

It may be hard to believe, but some of them *are* experiencing those things for the first time. Others describe a feeling of "nostalgia" in being present in the world; as if somehow being present and listening is a distant memory. Being present reminds them of their childhood. It's a scary thought that some actors may have been plugged in to excess for *years,* and you may wonder, "How could they really not have noticed the color of their bedroom walls for the past year?" "How could they not have noticed a clock tower that they pass at least four times each day?" Try not to judge – *listen.* And as you would with any other acting discovery, ask them questions behind the questions to help them deepen their experience:

- What do you think you were focused on when you previously missed that tree/street sign/person/building? (they'll say, "my smartphone" – try to get them to be specific as to what application on their device is most used).
- When you've said that you have begun to feel more present, what have you noticed about experiencing the people/things around you? Try to recall as many details as possible.
- How would you have felt if you had missed these people/things?
- What does this have to do with acting? How do you feel the practice of being present with your immediate surroundings is impacting your skills of listening, observation, focus, awareness, memory, and retention in class or rehearsal?
- Why do you feel you've preferred being on your device instead of choosing to experience other people and the sounds/sights/smells of your immediate environment?

  o This question often leads to the most emotional conversations. Students open up about fears of loneliness, FOMO and being the only weirdo who *hasn't* seen or "liked" someone's post, fear of being thought of as a bad friend (for not responding quickly enough), and so on (see Chapter 4). Ironically, they fear loneliness, which can drive them to their phone instead of face-to-face contact with another person, and then they fear being alone and worry about being rejected by their peers or ensemble. Try to steer their revelations toward their acting work, and trust that they will connect the dots and realize that the simple but profound discoveries they've made are enough to get them on the road to reconnecting as an actor and as a human being. Remind them of this famous Viola Spolin quote:

> Everyone can act. Everyone can improvise. Anyone who wishes to can play in the theatre and learn to become "stage worthy." We learn through experience and experiencing, and no one teaches anyone anything. . . If the environment permits it, anyone can learn whatever he chooses to learn; and if the individual permits it, the environment will teach him everything it has to teach . . . It is highly possible that what is called talented behavior is simply a greater individual capacity for experiencing. From this point of view it is in the increasing of the individual capacity for experiencing that the untold potentiality of a personality can be evoked. Experiencing is penetration into the environment, total organic involvement with it. This means involvement on all levels: intellectual, physical and intuitive.
>
> (Spolin)

Essentially, you're guiding them to awareness and discoveries about their capacity for experiencing; in their acting work and in their lives. In their papers and in your class discussions, you'll see that the primary thing they're discovering is that they are simply *experiencing* more. They're experiencing more details about their own thoughts and feelings, about their environment, and of course, about other people. When they are fully able to experience another person, then they can truly begin to explore collaboration and ensemble building.

Rose

In a recent set of Digital Disconnect journals, I read a paper in which a student described her experience walking across campus without being "plugged in" to her phone for the first time since she had started school. She wrote that she saw an old friend from high school who she didn't know attended Brooklyn College. That woman was on *her* cell phone, and my student struggled to get her attention at first. They reconnected and made plans to get together, laughing that they had probably been walking past each other for many weeks. I stopped; I thought I had made a mistake. I had just read this paper – hadn't I? I went back into the stack. Sure enough, a *different* student wrote about nearly the exact same kind of experience. And before I got through all 12 papers, I encountered a *third* journal, describing the exact same thing; looking up at the world of Brooklyn College campus for the first time, and seeing an old friend they would have missed had they not been doing their Disconnect. And in every case, the old friend was deeply into what they were doing on their smartphone, and the actor struggled to get their attention.

During this next phase of the process, we encourage you to continue with some of the previous exercises and projects, and add exercises that focus on observation, sensory awareness, and agreement with partners.

- Initiate, Copy, Heighten (see Appendix E): observation, listening, agreement, awareness.
- It's Tuesday (see Appendix D): observation, eye contact, reading social signals and intent, physical connection, and awareness.
- Blindfold Series (see Appendix Q): this includes Hunter and Hunted or Augusto Boal's The Cobra (Boal). Blindfold work heightens senses of listening, touch, smell, and yes, sight. These are exercises to be done after the first four to five weeks of the semester. Vulnerability, being present, listening, sensory awareness, physical awareness, mind/body connection, commitment to actions, imagination.

By deepening their capacity for experiencing, your student's sensory discoveries will also increase. Once they begin to connect to their sensorial experiences, they will be more present, will listen, and respond more truthfully, and will begin to return to a more empathic relationship to those around them. Be mindful if the actors become impatient with their progress, and with their discoveries about their tech use. They may want to throw their phones into the Hudson River. Their smartphone becomes The Pod Creature from *Invasion of the Body Snatchers* that has possessed them – and their first response can sometimes be "all or nothing" (1956). This is a good sign that their awareness of their use (and that of others) is heightened, and they're discovering its impact on their relationship to the world and their community around them. This is a good thing; they're right where they need to be for the next step of acknowledgement.

3) Acknowledgement – the kindling: get your twigs together

This is the kindling that reignites the embers of the Collaborative Gene back into a flame. It's one thing to discover and become aware of an unhealthy habit; it's another thing to truly accept and acknowledge it. Taking responsibility is a major step toward doing something about it. So once awareness grows and discoveries are made, your acting students need to acknowledge and accept how their tech use has impacted their work (and possibly much more). Ownership of their personal discoveries will be strengthened and supported through their acknowledgement to their ensemble. Your best kindling will be how they share their common experiences with the group. Group sharing lessens the potential for "tech-shaming," and will encourage ideas for changes and adjustments to their tech use to better support one another, and to be stronger collaborators and storytellers.

Include/continue for classes in weeks five to eight: Activities *to stimulate* Acknowledgment

At this point in your semester, students already unplug in classes, do the DDs (and write about their experiences), write notes longhand where possible, create tech logs, do more physical work and improvisation, and participate in group discussions that include what they're observing about their use and their acting skills.

- Continue to have group discussions after each "set" of practical work that they complete (scenes, improv, theatre games/exercises). In the way that a key exercise in a rehearsal can unlock a scene and help you cover more ground than if you ran it five times in a row, taking the time to help actors acknowledge and integrate discoveries in the early weeks will serve to cover more ground. Ask them what they're noticing and experiencing in the class group activities, particularly in the areas of:
  - o Being present and allowing themselves to be affected by partners/ the ensemble.
  - o Listening.
  - o Empathy.
  - o Vulnerability.
  - o Focus and concentration.
  - o Awareness and observation.
  - o Physical stamina.
  - o Sensory awareness.
  - o Memory and retention.
- As ensemble members hear each individual express their struggles and perceived failures, it takes the fear factor out of publicly admitting it themselves. The support of the ensemble is essential in the Acknowledgment phase, building the foundation of belonging where the students can safely

explore. Many have been isolating and hiding behind their smartphones to avoid potential judgment and rejection; the antidote to this fear is the trust that is built when the entire ensemble acknowledges their behaviors with one another. The sting of shame is taken out when everyone experiences things together. And even though you may be the breath and the oxygen that directs their energy, the embers, tinder, and kindling are all found in the ensemble members themselves. To rekindle their Collaborative Genes, they need to practice mindful collaboration with one another.

- In addition to the class work you've already planned for your particular acting area of focus (scenes, monologues, etc.), choose a series of exercises that explore some of the skills listed above; exercises that can be repeated every week (see Appendices V and W for sample lists). What do you measurably observe in your students' progress with these collaborative skills each week? What are *they* noticing in themselves in the repetition of these exercises? What do you notice in the dynamics of the ensemble over the course of these repetitions? Draw attention to their progress. Exercises that are repeated weekly offer clear and undeniable proof of growth; or lack thereof. Either way, a student can't help but acknowledge their behaviors. You'll also have had the benefit of reading their DD papers and have an understanding of their perception of their skill levels in relation to their tech use. That is, you'll know who might be trying to fool you, or fool themselves. Have they written about being consistently "caught out" in Kitty Wants a Corner because their focus and observation skills are soft? Did they journal about their struggles with retention and have now brought in a scene for a third or fourth presentation and they're still not memorized? Have they noted that when they meet their scene partner on a DD day, they seem to connect more deeply to the text? Are you in week five of a basic movement class and they're running out of breath after just a few minutes of kinetics work?
- If you're teaching scene study, ask students to do their DD on a day when they have rehearsal with their scene partner. Students report that they notice powerful differences in their work when they rehearse on DD days.

"I noticed that the days my phone is off and away, I grasp the text much quicker."

"These Disconnects gave me the freedom to listen with ease. One of the most recent Disconnects made me aware of how my listening was not working in one rehearsal. I was so involved in how I was doing in terms of reaching my goal and objective, I was not listening. However, when we were on break, everyone went to their phones while I had ten minutes to reflect on what was going on and came up with the solution after we jumped back into the scene."

Again, like the actor/director relationship in rehearsal – it's always more valuable for the actor to acknowledge and share their observations themselves. Telling someone "I think you'll be more productive if you're on your phone for less than ten hours a day" is different from their own acknowledgement that ten hours without a phone can lead to enormous productivity. After one single DD period of eight hours, students in fall of 2016 wrote that they not only felt more productive, but a majority of them were able to complete projects that they had "been meaning to do for weeks and months."

> *"I noticed that when I did the Disconnect I felt less overwhelmed, over-scheduled, and less cluttered. I just got things done which was really great. I also noticed that when I did disconnect and I was a little less accessible to others, people seemed to follow through with prior set engagements because they couldn't call in and say they were running late. This was just an extra feature of the day that made things feel more grounded, planned out, straightforward and simplified."*

Acknowledgment *versus shame/blame: the role of "tech-shaming"*

Steer students away from both shame and "tech-shaming." Acknowledgment should lead to ownership and to healthier behavior; not to self-condemnation and pain. Young actors pride themselves on their perceived abilities to observe and create truthful human behavior; so it can be a real shock when they realize how much human behavior they've been missing: especially their *own*. Students can default to beating themselves up once they discover their truth. That feeling can deepen when they connect those realizations to acting notes they've been repeatedly getting in classes or rehearsals. ("Ashley, why do you keep looking at the floor throughout your scene?" "Tyler, you're not listening to what your partner is giving you. Again.") Further, they may be getting those "notes" from parents or loved ones in their *life*. ("Vanessa, I feel like I don't know you anymore ... where *is* my daughter?" "Dara, could you please put that down and really look at me when I'm trying to talk with you?")

Shame can be an exceptionally painful emotion, and isn't the same as embarrassment or guilt. It comes out of a harsh comparison of one's self to standards; sometimes an unrealistic or unattainable set of standards. It is self-judgment at its strongest, and it comes with the fear of being stigmatized, disgraced, or condemned because of the action (or inaction) that led to the sense of shame. Although it's far too big a subject to go into thoroughly here, we encourage you to explore this further in your own research. Author Andy Crouch writes about the links between social media and the "Shaming Culture." Briefly, he notes that the quest for online approval and "likes" is driven by fear of rejection by others. This leads to online members giving praise and multiple "likes" to better ensure their own acceptance by a group. Eventually, the group has "enforcers" who police what people are posting to make sure everyone is following the group's code, or else risk condemnation. If the group itself feels it's being disrespected, members are quick to "call out" the offending parties. A disagreeing opinion or point of view is interpreted as a threat, and action can be swift. On social media, those actions happen at lightning pace, and in the form of public shaming (Crouch).

> *"We constantly post things online with the expectation that other people will 'like' it. The more likes, the more gratified we become... the less likes, the more people seem to be passing an imaginary judgment on you, as if you aren't good enough. I think the judgments that accompany social media only increase the judgments we have of ourselves. If we are constantly judging ourselves then we will never be free to make bold choices or even obvious ones. And we will never challenge ourselves or grow as human beings."*

Some of our students shame themselves like a person who wakes up after a night of heavy drinking, realizing they uncharacteristically spent all night making out with someone who was *not* their significant other. You can't go back in time; but you can adjust your behavior to make sure you never drink to the point of not being able to control your actions. Just as we discourage young people from "body shaming" we need to discourage them from "tech shaming." You can't live without a body – and let's face it, we can't live without technology either. So we have to develop healthy practices with, and perspectives on, our tech use.

Shame drives a person deeper into their interior thoughts, separating themselves from the group or ensemble. The pain of shame is very real, and is exacerbated by the perception of judgment from others. Shame can make an actor retreat from the ensemble – and if the initial problem was "too much retreating from the ensemble" – shame only makes it worse. Group exercises and discussions have the combined benefit of actors making vital discoveries, and reinforcing that they're not alone. Most important, ensemble work reinforces that no one will be judged or rejected; that everyone needs to become stronger collaborators together in order to serve a collective goal. It's easier to shame yourself than to shame your ensemble... so if everyone is working together and publicly acknowledging their personal discoveries to the group, there's more support, more ideas for positive changes and adjustments, more collective ownership, and a robust rekindling of the Collaborative Genes.

4) Understanding – the nature of fire: be prepared

Understanding: *teaching students about the device*

Strengthening Awareness, making Discoveries, and Acknowledging what we've found is vital, but two big questions loom over every young actor after they've gotten their Collaborative Gene sparking again: "How the hell did this happen in the first place?" and "How do I make sure I don't let it happen to me again?" Understanding the phenomena will help them recognize that excessive use is one-part biochemical impact (Chapter 3) caused by the design of the device, and one-part personal and sociological choice (Chapter 4). Remember too that understanding is not something you're teaching them directly. It is something you are guiding them toward, so be on the lookout for it. There is no timetable; with every group, the timing of Understanding can be different. Keep watching, listening, and guiding – they'll get there. Introduce your students to some of the research and scientific data as to why it's not so easy to turn that thing off. What is the device literally designed to do to their brains that makes them want to clutch it for hours on end?

In Chapter 3, we've provided the most current available research and data, and in Appendix R you'll find a handout we've created that you can use with your students. We think of it like a "recommended daily allowance": vitamin C is an essential nutrient, but if you take mega doses of it, you could end up pretty sick. All comprehensive acting programs include movement classes and training on how to keep the body and mind healthy. Why wouldn't you include vital information about the potential harm of a device that nearly every acting student owns?

Understanding the science of smartphones should – and must – become part of an international curriculum for actors – and for all students. You don't have to be a neuroscientist to teach the basics about potential risks. Your acting students need this data just as much as their chart illustrating the larynx. Give particular focus to what happens physiologically in the brain and body during periods of excessive use (e.g., the role of dopamine release). Provide them with the research that illustrates the impact on their interpersonal skills from empathy to awareness, and include some of the sociological and psychological reasons why the excess begins in the first place. You can also provide topics to your students for additional research on the subject for them to share with the class. The ownership they'll have by discovering new information will deepen their investment in their process, and in the entire ensemble's progress.

Understanding the user

When working with young actors, it's common for personal issues to arise; vulnerability is part of the territory. They may struggle with a domestic scene because it's reminiscent of a fraught childhood; they might tell you about a fear of failure instilled by parents who were overachievers; they might admit to the ensemble that they're terrified of being touched because of a violent episode in their lives. Actors explore and acknowledge personal experiences all the time because of the intimate nature of the work. Similarly, they'll need to examine their personal reasons that led to their excessive use. Now, they may deny they use their device to excess, or they may have fabulous justifications as to why they need to use it as often as they do. ("I have the Complete Works of Shakespeare on my phone – I'm not texting, I'm doing homework!" [true story]). Ask them to simply see what happens if they don't use their phone as much. Here are a few questions to get started:

- What do they notice?
- Why would they choose to isolate instead of collaborate?
- Has their general use become habitual?
- Has habit turned into something they feel they can no longer control?

These are fair questions, and you're not overstepping as their teacher to ask them. Like anything in life, it may not be pretty at first; but if we're choosing the path of the storyteller, we need to intimately know and understand our own life, behaviors, and story before we can tell that of another.

Teaching your students about the nature of the device will also help them understand contributing factors that may have exacerbated their excessive use (Roberts et al.). Some potential discussion questions are:

- What behavior patterns contribute to them pulling their phone out when they're in a group of people instead of engaging in conversation?
- Why are they choosing to check (and re-check) multiple social media accounts, even if they checked them minutes before?
- If you were up all night playing games online, why did you choose not to go to sleep at a reasonable time?

Again, remember that you're a teacher and a detective; not a therapist or a doctor. If their discoveries lead to fairly straightforward cases of excessive use, the reasons will likely be straightforward as well. Not necessarily easy to change, but easy to understand and with patience and practice, the behaviors can be redirected to become collaborative once again. Not unlike the personal discoveries and connections they make in their acting work – understanding their behaviors related to tech use must now become a part of their education. In rare cases, there may be a student who needs professional help for tech addiction; refer them to your campus mental health facility. Educate yourself by going to sources that have the most current research and data available such as www.addiction.com, which reviews the basics of technology addiction, also referred to as Internet Addiction Disorder (not yet classified in the *Diagnostic and Statistical Manual of Mental Health Disorders*). See Chapter 3 and Appendix X for additional information on tech addiction.

It can feel a little dicey trying to teach young actors about the danger of tech addiction, though we don't think twice about doing that with recreational drugs and alcohol. The difference, though, is huge: if you're addicted to alcohol, your goal is to give it up, not learn to live with it in moderation. Yet that's what we're asking ourselves and our students to do with technology. It's unavoidable that we routinely use technology for everything from communication to work to entertainment. And as we wrote in Chapter 3, with more and more functions able to be executed by a single device, one that fits in our pocket, we can readily see the attraction and the temptation.

Try an experiment in class to help them understand this idea. Let's take the exercise, Kitty Wants a Corner (see Appendix L); it teaches invaluable lessons about acting: commitment, risk taking, trust, awareness, objectives, tactics, specificity in communication, and so much more. In this example though, let's focus on connecting it to a lesson in understanding a potentially slippery slope of excessive use of devices or tech addiction.

One person is "Kitty" in the middle of the circle; their goal is to take someone's spot while others are exchanging places. Begin by doing the "No" only version – that is, when the actor in the middle asks, "Kitty Wants a Corner?" the others can only respond with "No." So, the only hope that Kitty has is to take someone's spot while they're in the process of exchanging places. Usually, those folks are running. Not only running, but they're laughing, they're excited, and having a lot of fun with the thrill of "beating" Kitty. Kitty, however, often gets frustrated by their failed attempts to "get a spot," and they are most definitely not having the same kind of fun as those trading spots in the circle. Kitty is keenly aware of how long they have been "it." They also must continue to "ask for a corner" while experiencing being rejected each time. Kitty is also in the middle of that circle, with all eyes on them bearing witness to their repeated "failure." Do several rounds of this "No" version; you should end up with a majority of people having experienced being Kitty for a period of time.

In the post-exercise discussion, ask the Kittys to describe how they felt when they were in the middle. We've heard Kittys say the following:

- "I felt so alone, and lonely. Like no one wanted to play with me."
- "I felt like an outcast; as if no one wanted to include me in their group."
- "I felt rejected. Hearing that 'no' every time I asked, was hard."
- "I felt like the kid who gets picked last on a team, and somehow I had to prove myself by stealing a spot."
- "I felt everyone's eyes on me, judging me, and I was judging myself every time someone said 'no.'"
- "I hated it. I felt left out of all the fun."
- "I felt hopeless; like I would never get out of the middle."
- "I felt I had no power or control – that the people in the circle had all the power, and I wanted to be a part of *that*, not be the one who was 'it.'"

Now, ask the group what it would mean to them to never, ever have to feel that way again. What would happen if you could have the feeling of always being accepted by a community? What if you could consistently feel included instead of excluded? To be a part of a group that liked you, and consistently reinforced how much you are liked? What if you never had to worry about being judged? That you would always be able to find someone or something that supported how you felt or what you believed? How would it feel to gain a Friend with a single touch of your finger from anywhere in the world? What if you could have complete control over whether you would ever have to feel alone, or lonely, again?

What would you trade for all of that?
And what would you trade for *more* of that?

This conversation will help your students understand that no matter how good the control or the power of being online may feel – if they want to be actors and creators of human behavior, they can't avoid humans. It's that simple. The less time they spend interacting with others, the less they'll know *how* to create a truthful human being. Humans are messy, complicated, scary, loving, puzzling, and we can never ever have total control over what they do. As your students come to understand the fears or desires that lead to excessive use, they'll have a greater understanding of their own behaviors, and of the behaviors of others that they might be trying to avoid (judgment, rejection), or trying to experience more often (acceptance, love). This deeper understanding will support their path to healthier use, and will help them recognize the unhealthy behaviors when they arise so that they can prevent them from occurring again. Many will find that the reasons that drive their excessive use are more similar to one another than they might think.

> "In my 24 hour Disconnect I wrote 'We constantly post things online with the expectation that other people will "like" it. The more likes, the more gratified we become. . . The less likes the more people seem to be passing an imaginary judgment on you, as if you aren't good enough.' You asked me how this could be detrimental to the actor. I think the judgments that accompany social media only increase the judgments we have of ourselves. If we are constantly judging ourselves then we will never be free to make bold choices or even obvious ones. And we will never challenge ourselves or grow as humans. . . . Looking back I realized that during my Disconnect, for those nine hours I gave myself. . . the gift of being in the moment and present with who is around me and not being concerned with what isn't in front of me. It is a calm that is destroyed by having a device that connects you to everyone 24/7 at your fingertips. A calm that feels good, one that I need more often. And one that should exist in my acting. A calm that allows you to be present in the moment, and present with your partner on stage."

5)   Actions – oxygen: A consistent source of energy

The consistent and ongoing actions both you and your students take are the oxygen to help the flame of the Collaborative Gene burn brightly, becoming a roaring fire that will last. You've already taken action that reinforces the behaviors you want your students to embrace for their training. You might not need to add too much to what you're already doing; but you may need to do things with more frequency and consistency. You'll also want to develop a keener eye toward the students' progress with collaborative behaviors and bonding with the ensemble, not only for their individual progress as actors. We've broken this section down to principles and activities for the ensemble leader, and principles and activities for the actors/students.

Activities *for the ensemble leader*

Whether you teach improvisation, beginning acting, or advanced scene study:

- Assign and continue Digital Disconnects for the full semester. Some students will want to stop, saying "I get it already." Requiring it for several months will give them time to develop consistent practice that will take hold for their future.
- In all scene work, exercises, discussions, and written work, reinforce the idea that acting requires us to risk and fail. There's great power in making mistakes; it's how we learn what works and what doesn't. Students need to be free to fail; it's like riding a bike; how many times do we fall down before learning balance, coordination, the muscles that are needed to be good at it? Encouraging them to embrace mistakes and to risk relinquishing control allows them to be more present and vulnerable to their partners and to the ensemble.
- Continue to incorporate group improv exercises, either as warm-ups or as a primary focus. Consistent group play strengthens and develops empathy, vulnerability, listening, and awareness. Be careful not to use elimination exercises. Elimination creates insecurities that can be hard to untangle, and can further isolate those already struggling to make connections. Being free to fail, students learn that they have multiple opportunities to try, and try again, and that the ensemble will support them. The consequences of not doing something well are to simply do it again. Students who have conditioned themselves for immediate gratification via the Internet will also learn patience through their progress; patience with themselves and patience with others.
- Try to make sure that every student works in every class, every time. Don't allow them to sit out an exercise or a scene showing unless they're physically ill (in which case, they should be keeping their germs at

home). Those who are insecure about volunteering or participating will be encouraged by a structure that requires everyone to try everything. The ongoing ensemble group exercises will also create a safer space for them to face their insecurities.

- Continue to hold group discussions after each scene or exercise (even those that are part of your "Repetition Series"), allowing students an opportunity to share discoveries. Be mindful if they start to "review" themselves. "That was good." "That was terrible." Redirect their observations to the work itself and away from personal judgments. What choices seemed to work? Were the choices clear? As students become aware of their individual differences, remind them that those differences are what makes them uniquely the actor they are, and what they uniquely bring to the ensemble. Most importantly, the ensemble needs their unique contribution, and can't succeed without it. And that's collaboration, folks. If your students start to believe "I am needed. The ensemble needs me. The work needs me." – then you're on your way to rekindling the Collaborative Gene.

- For each class, set aside a few minutes toward the end of the period to give them time to write down personal notes (yes, even later in the semester when time is so crunched). You've been challenging them during the main body of the class to process feedback and class experiences without writing things down in the moment. Now, they think they'll remember, *you* think they'll remember, but memory is one of the skills compromised by excessive tech use. Setting aside that time for them to write will raise their awareness as to how strong their retention is, and will help them set goals for future classes. The time you invest now will pay dividends in their training and process in the future.

"I normally would read a scene a few times, and then be on my phone for five minutes, or if it went off I would fall out of the scene and be completely distracted. Technology creates a block in the middle of your mind that leads to the road of memory. It's numbing us to knowledge and to be able to do our job properly as storytellers."

- Include specific memory exercises in all classes, but especially in scene study classes. See Appendix W for suggestions. Simple exercises such as Multiple Pattern Juggling or Going on a Picnic stimulate and nurture memory and retention (which of course will help with text and memorization).

- Include observation exercises (see Appendix U) in all classes. Again, there are universal benefits, but particularly for scene partners; it helps them take each other in fully, supports listening and "yes, and." Deeper observations will also lead to stronger tactics, as noticing the smallest thing can provide clues to help someone achieve their objective. "Hmmm,

Charles just averted his eyes and folded his arms across his chest. He's protecting. Let me try an action to get him to open up to me more."

- You've spent weeks helping the students rekindle their Collaborative Genes. Some of that has been through the use of specific exercises to develop listening, observation, empathy, and so on. Now that you're moving on to "Action-Oxygen," you'll no doubt be moving on to other work in your class, but don't discard the work that got you this far. We recommend incorporating the early exercises into your warm-ups. You need not do each one every day, but rotate among them, revisit them, keep those newly recharged skills sharp. Revisiting exercises on either an "as needed" basis or as part of an ongoing "maintenance of skills" plan includes the added benefit of reinforcing healthier behavior through consistent practice.

- Encourage attention to their language, that is, point out if they use self-defeating phrases such as "I couldn't help myself"; "I had no control over it"; "I had to do it." They've worked hard to rekindle their collaboration skills and to gain greater control over their tech use. Remind them that they *do* have control, and that control lies in the power to make a choice, always.

- Continue to incorporate work that requires direct eye contact to encourage a broader comfort zone with vulnerability and intimacy. This will also nurture greater empathy. Strong choices for consistent inclusion would be status exercises, Meisner's Repetition (see Appendix O), exercises that require physical contact, and Spolin's "Change Three Things" – if you teach at college level, make this "Change Six Things." Six Things is played by pairing actors up, facing each other. They take a beat to observe as many details about the other person as possible, and then they both turn their backs. Actor A changes six things about him/herself. They face each other again, and Actor B attempts to identify the six changes. After students become familiar with the exercise, the length of time for the initial observation can decrease.

In recent years, we've changed class content and curriculum to address our students' challenges. To be absolutely honest, one of the most effective series of activities we found was bringing back basic exercises that we'd all relegated to the distant dust-bin-memory of our first acting classes. Remember "Mirrors"? Those fundamentals are sorely needed again to help our students develop foundational skills. Ultimately as ensemble leader, you're in the objective position to determine which collaborative skills you feel need the most attention in your classes. Here are some suggestions to help you create lesson plans for specific skill development:

- Being present/vulnerable/open (eye contact, listening, allowing one's self to be affected by their partner). See Appendix S.

- Empathy, responsibility (vulnerability, connections between actions and consequences). See Appendix T.
- Awareness/physical awareness (observation, physical expression, commitment, ownership, spatial awareness). See Appendix U.
- Risk taking, commitment (listening to impulses, relinquishing desire to edit choices, taking responsibility for one's choices and one's partner). See Appendix V.
- Memory, retention, processing of information (allowing one's self to truly experience and process the moment, allowing a person or event to leave a lasting impression). See Appendix W.

We have two other key recommendations that warrant their own section because of their benefits and the impact they have on countering the symptoms created by excessive tech use: mindfulness and movement work.

Mindfulness

To strengthen the growth of The Collaborative Gene, our students need a deeper examination into the unrest they were feeling from disconnecting. Excessive smartphone use contributes to stress, anxiety, distracted behaviors, and detachment; not the best states of mind to be in to try to learn. The practice of mindfulness is one tool that can counter those conditions, leading to a more present and focused experience of life, and has been applied in recent years to students from kindergarten to college. What is mindfulness? It is a practice of bringing oneself fully and completely into the present moment; to feel and experience what is occurring in your body and mind *right now* without judgment. It's an open, attentive awareness to the "now." It uses the practice of meditation to not only fully engage in the "now," but to also wholeheartedly be available to the present. There are many opportunities throughout the day that steal our attention from the moment. The proliferation of cell phone use has greatly increased this distraction. Author Geoffrey A. Fowler conducted one of our favorite studies in San Francisco called The Chewbacca Experiment. On a busy morning commute, he asked a colleague to dress up as Chewbacca, and then asked pedestrians who passed the Wookie if they had noticed. Many didn't. Ira Hyman Jr., a psychology professor at Western Washington University, coined a term for this phenomenon: "In-attentional blindness" (Fowler). Like the student who didn't notice the color of her newly painted room, or the students who were oblivious to the clock tower on campus, "In-attentional blindness" has found its way into the very lives of our acting ensembles.

As acting teachers, one of the skills we are honing in our students is to get them fully engaged in the present moment. Then they may be aware of the choices they are making (or not making), and have a better chance of seeing their own Wookie, or better yet, a gaggle of Wookies throughout their day.

Mindfulness Awareness Practice is a wonderful practice that students can incorporate into their warm-ups, practice at home, or even on the bus (see Appendix N). It is an excellent tool to bring the actor to a prepared place of readiness. Mindfulness Awareness Practice involves a conscious attention to the breath, and as oxygen is an essential component of breathing, it makes sense to introduce this practice during the Action phase of our five-step recommendation process. Mindfulness Awareness Practice will allow our students to experience in real time, and in a gentle way, their hyper-need to occupy themselves. What begins to reveal itself to the students is the clarity of their inability (at first) to simply be with themselves and their thoughts in stillness, without reaching for their phones to occupy their attention. It's a simple and potent exercise that can provide a powerful foundation for the awareness and presence of mind and self that's needed before one can begin to collaborate with others. Over time, and with sustained practice, Mindfulness Awareness Practice. Opens the student up to a richer experience of themselves and others in their world. By reinforcing their conscious choice to remain with their environment versus their unconscious choice of staying tethered to their device, students appreciate the technology-free moments of their day, and its contribution to their craft.

"I went to see Paul McCartney's soundcheck. I felt so weird standing in a sea of people holding up their phones and snapping photos. I wanted to take photos too. I wanted to record the memories, but when you are busy recording the memories, you actually miss the performance. You aren't present for any of it, because you watch the entirety of it through a small rectangular device and you miss the experience of Paul McCartney being literally right there in front of you... digital photography gives one the ability to instantly reminisce. In a way, it clearly defines the present moment from the past; however, you spend the present moment looking at what just happened."

Roger

Mindfulness is practiced everywhere right now, from elementary schools to Fortune 500 companies. Donna St. George, in her *Washington Post* article "How mindfulness practices are changing an inner city school," reports on uses of mindfulness at The Robert W. Coleman Elementary in West Baltimore, Maryland. "Principal Carlillian Thompson said the practices help the school's 378 students leave behind the stresses of their lives, including problems at home, violence on the streets and conflicts with friends, so they can get ready to learn." The Robert W. Coleman School has also implemented some new techniques in how they discipline. Instead of the regularly used practices of detention and suspension, the school has created The Mindful Moment Room. It's a beautiful sun-lit room decorated with bright furniture and comfy pillows where students are taken when they misbehave. "The third-grader who scuffled with a classmate broke into tears. Staff member Oriana Copeland held his hand as they talked. There were no harsh words. He came around slowly. 'Inhaling deep,' she guided him. 'Exhale and out.'" Principal Thompson shares that since incorporating mindfulness into their curriculum, the number of students sent to the principal is down, and there have been zero suspensions in the last two years. When beginning the school morning with breathing techniques, and using them throughout the day, teachers are seeing an increase in focus in the classroom. Not to mention The Mindful Moment Room now has students coming in throughout the day on their volition to simply sit and breathe.

Movement

At Brooklyn College, one of our first instinctual responses to counteract the symptoms we observed was, quite simply, to add more movement. It made sense to us: excessive tech use was making our students more sedentary with far less stamina, more passive and introverted, less willing to experience intimacy or physical contact, and less willing to experience discomfort in general. By the time we met them in our classrooms, they had already spent a number of years unconsciously training themselves to avoid discomfort. So when they felt challenged, they bailed out on the present moment with the distraction of technology. Those rescue behaviors they resorted to in their daily lives then manifested in their classes, rehearsals, and performances. To bring them into the present and face their avoidance patterns, we added more Alexander, more Laban, more kinetics work, more stage combat, and more yoga – specifically Kundalini yoga. It's a form of yoga that brings together poses, breath, and chanting to strengthen the nervous system. It's challenging, and not for the faint of heart; in the same way that being an actor is not for the faint of heart. The dynamism and immediate results of Kundalini makes it very appealing to actors. The physical work affects the glandular system and brings an instant presence to the actor. In addition to adding this and other new movement courses, we strengthened our focus on more athleticism throughout our movement sequence: more repetition, more time, nutritional guidance, personal body strength and training, guided visits to the campus gym, and more reading and research on physiology and body/mind connection.

Some of the first actors (circa 15,000 BC) expressed themselves through physical movement; the famous cave painting of The Sorcerer from the Cave of Trois-Freres in France shows a human figure wearing antlers, expressively posed, looking straight at the "audience" ("Trois Freres"). Physical storytelling is a primal instinct. Movement insists that we relate to and engage with our own body; and if we then share our movement with another, it creates an intimate communication without words. We can think of few things other than physical movement that can more quickly and naturally get someone out of their heads and into an incredibly personal and vulnerable place.

There are many pedagogies of movement training, all in pursuit of bringing the actor to a state of readiness and to fully experience the present moment. For our purposes, we'll simply choose one such pedagogy that accomplishes this: the aforementioned Kundalini yoga (we encourage you to explore many other forms, including dance). It brings the actor to directly confront and experience discomfort.

> *"The Digital Disconnect has raised my awareness of habits that have always been there unconsciously. I reach for my phone whenever I feel bored or afraid. This habit has conditioned me to disconnect from these feelings whenever they arise. If not for my phone, I would probably drown my emotions out in other ways. It is my awareness of this habit that has allowed me to repair it. Kundalini was the cure. In Kundalini, I trained to face whatever sensation may come up in my body. Whether it's boredom or fear or melancholy, in Kundalini I have no choice but to hold the pose and exist in the state that I'm in. This spills over into my acting in that it weakens whatever defense mechanisms I have in place to guard me from discomfort. In acting, we have to dare to go to the uncomfortable places. And through Kundalini and the Digital Disconnect, I am retraining myself to stay in the discomfort."*

For example, the "Balancing Head and Heart" series of exercises (see Appendix P) focuses on the challenges of the relationship between emotion and logic, which is one of the primary issues students struggle with because of their excessive tech use. There's a disconnect between what their feelings are telling them, and what their logic is telling them. Logic may tell them that they've spent far too many hours glued to a screen; emotions may give them a feeling of satisfaction. The first exercise in the series is hard. The students are often crying, moaning, yelling. After the first minute or two, a deep ache emerges in the arms and shoulders. It's not pain; it's discomfort. The difference between the two is when the arms go back down to rest, the "ouchy" feeling leaves. *That* is discomfort. Pain is when the arms go down, but the feeling stays and stays. More often than not, the students are coming directly in contact with some challenging discomfort. Their initial instinct? To put the arms down. "This doesn't feel good, I have to stop." It's exactly the same feeling they experience when they don't have their devices available. Some signs to look for that indicate a student is avoiding discomfort:

- Dropping the arms.
- Scratching the head, face, rest of the body.

- Thinking they need a drink, and reaching for their water.
- If there is a mirror in the studio, checking themselves out and possibly "fixing" their physical appearance.
- Rocking back and forth.
- Checking in with other students or the teacher.
- Saying "This is stupid. I'm not even doing this."

Guiding students to fan their own flames: Activities *beyond* the classroom

We've been focusing on what *you* can do as a teacher and ensemble leader to fan the flames of the Collaborative Gene. You've been nurturing your students' preference for direct face-to-face human contact, and they've now reconnected to the joys of their collaborative skills. Even those who may already employ healthy use of their devices will benefit from the discoveries of their ensemble, and the actions they take together.

Learning itself is as collaborative an experience as you can hope for. The strongest students have a deep investment, curiosity, and are self-motivated in their education and training. In short, they say "yes and" to all that you and the ensemble offer them in their learning. Actors can reinforce and strengthen healthy practices in their daily life to expand the discoveries they're making in the classroom. In the same way that we instruct our students to practice physical and vocal warm-ups, you can teach activities for inclusion in their daily practice to strengthen their Collaborative Gene. Even if a student has a healthy balance of tech use, these recommendations will still be of great value to their growth as an actor. Recommended activities:

- Encourage them to continue to keep a personal log/journal, as they might a nutritional or food journal.
- As students become increasingly aware of their own use and habits, they observe excessive use in others. Ask actors to mentor those in their lives who they feel are using technology to excess (to the exclusion of face-to-face conversation), by sharing their own discoveries (the power of identification here may be huge.). This will help them articulate what they are "missing," and what they've discovered. It also helps actors deepen their understanding of healthy and supportive uses of technology, as opposed to use that disconnects and isolates them.
- Daily observations: notice everyday things in their lives and in their daily routines:
  - People: notice a person on the bus or walking down the street. How would you recognize them if you saw them again? Eye color? Hair? Is their face lined or unlined? Posture? What are they wearing? Colors? Textures? Layers? Jewelry? Are they reading a book? Do they have ear buds in? What is their body language saying?

If you had to make up a story about that person, what would it be? If you had to create an animal based on them, what kind of animal would they be?

o   Environment: Open your eyes to a place you walk past every day, or one or more times a week. What organic things are in this environment? Trees? Flowers? Shrubs? How are they different from week to week? Season to season? Do they have bright buds? Are the leaves turning yellow at the edges? Does the tree have any new branches?

o   Animals: Try to notice birds, insects, dogs, anything in your environment. What do they look like? Sound like? Do you know what species of bird that is? How do they move? Is anything being communicated in their sound or movement? If you live in a city and walk past a dog park, what do you observe about the status interactions among the dogs as they play? Who's in charge? Who is submissive? Which one do members of the pack avoid? What's their relationship to their human owners?

"I've realized how much more observant I am without the influence of technology. I become so distracted that I literally ignore what's in front of me."

"After a song or two, I remembered I was supposed to be disconnected. I thought that it would be best to let myself be alone in my thoughts since it would be the first time throughout the day that I would have been able to. I got to reflect on the day and then I let my thoughts wander. Maybe I wandered a little too much because I ended up missing my exit back in the Bronx. Looking back and forth from the highway and my GPS, I ended up missing the same exact exit once again. This particular exit leads to Orchard Beach (less of a beach and more of a swampy bay area) and something inside me said to just accept that I was led to this place for a reason. I got out of my car, felt the evening breeze and listened to the light waves. I was at peace. After a little while, I was back on the road."

•   If they observe themselves multi-tasking, ask them to stop. They should try to do, and experience, one thing at a time. Multi-tasking gives the illusion that we are simultaneously performing tasks with an equal amount of attention and skill. Guy Winch is the author of *Emotional First Aid: Practical Strategies for Treating Failure, Rejection, Guilt and Other Everyday Psychological Injuries*. In an article for *Glassdoor for Employers*, he had this to say on multi-tasking. "When it comes to attention and productivity, our brains have a finite amount. It's like a pie chart, and whatever we're working on is going to take up the majority of that pie. There's not a lot left over for other things, with the exception of automatic behaviors like walking or chewing gum" (Robinson). We are actually *less* productive when we multi-task. And, multi-tasking can rekindle a student's desire to return to doing multiple functions/activities on their device in a reverse scenario of rekindling the Collaborative Gene.

- Limit screen time in the evening, and create a cut-off time; we suggest leaving a window of at least two to three hours prior to going to sleep to be free of computer screens of any kind. Research shows that the blue screens of computers, tablets, and so on, suppress the production of melatonin (the hormone that governs our sleep cycles) (Figueiro et al.). Also, the activity of doing work or conducting an Internet search is stimulating to the brain; it associates screen light with daylight, and it wants to keep going. So if you're giving your brain a signal to be alert right before you try to go to sleep, you're likely to be counting sheep for a long time. They should also keep their device out of the bedroom, period, or else the brain will associate the bedroom with a place "where you work" or where you "must be alert." Unless the smartphone is completely powered down, any sounds of incoming messages can send a person into response mode. There are available apps beyond "sleep mode" that offer to cut off all distractions and sounds; this feature is called "Bedtime." Greater rest will also improve memory and focus, and wellness and health in general. Visit www.sleephealthfoundation. org.au/public-information/fact-sheets-a-z/802-technology-sleep.html for additional information.

Rose

One of the earliest signs that something was wrong with our students was the uptick in insomnia. More and more of them were late – really late – to classes, more and more were tucking into back rows and nodding off. My wonderful team of teachers would ask me with alarming frequency, "Is Steve on medication? He keeps closing his eyes and falling asleep in my class." "Is Lynn alright? During warm-ups, she looked like she could fall asleep on her feet." Even our costume design professor gave me a heads up that students were nearly passing out during costume fittings. I started keeping a stock of granola bars, got a tea kettle (thank you Sergio!), and started stocking instant oatmeal in my office, thinking that maybe they simply weren't eating. Well, that turned out to be true too – but then something interesting happened. I often make myself a cup of tea and drink it while meeting with students – I grow my own herbs, and had created my own "Rosie's Relaxing Tea" blend of spearmint and lemon balm (relaxes digestive and nervous system). The bleary-eyed students who I would meet with – to talk about their droopy behavior and their sinking grades – would ask about the tea. "Does that help you sleep too?" "Sure," I said. "Why? Are you having trouble sleeping?" "I got about two hours last night." "I only got about three and a half hours of sleep." "I just can't seem to be able to turn my brain off... " I would ask "what are you doing right before bedtime?" And their responses ranged from "binging Netflix" to "texting all my friends." So along with noting this among the data we were already gathering, I advised them all to disconnect at least two hours before trying to go to sleep, instinctively told them to keep their laptops and smartphones out of their bedroom (this was before the research bore this out), and I was giving away many, many bags of my homegrown relaxing tea. I distinctly remember my student assistant coming in for work one day; he looked at a sizable Ziploc baggie on my desk that was filled with dried green herbs, and his eyes quickly darted away and he got flustered. It took me a moment to cop on as to why!

- Encourage students to increase the time they spend in nature, and combine that with physical activity. Taking a hike or long walk in nature, even in a public park, strengthens connection to our own biorhythms and increases relaxation. They can combine this with the observation exercises noted above.

  "The simple joy of finishing a play while lying on the grass came back to me in that very moment. I felt calm, relaxed, and one with the nature around me. This 24-hour Disconnect made me realize that the day is so much longer than I thought. I just waste huge amounts of it on social media."

- Perhaps most important, encourage them to participate in social and collaborative activities that don't involve technology. We know actors who play on local softball and kickball teams, who go dancing with friends every week, are members of hiking groups and yes, have joined bird watching groups. Ask them to challenge themselves to go to a party and not bring a device.

A side benefit – or, maybe a major benefit – is that adding all of these practices can help prepare students for encounters with acting partners who may *not* have ever practiced any sort of exploration into these phenomena. The processes you've guided them through have strengthened their awareness of disconnected behaviors and their ability to recognize those in themselves – and in their peers as well. The more they understand the behaviors and their causes, the less likely they are to simply dismiss someone who is disconnected or shutting them out as being a selfish jerk. Instead, they can consider "Wow, Louise isn't even looking at me; what might that be about? And what could we do about it together?" That is, because they've gotten better at self-diagnosis and being patient with themselves in their efforts to grow and change, they're far more likely to extend that understanding and patience to acting partners. Moreover, they're more inclined to take actions to improve their creative (and personal) relationships. We're not only talking about their fellow acting students; we're talking about those they encounter in professional jobs as well. This isn't only happening in schools, there seems to be a growing number of Digital Immigrants (you know, *older* people) who have fallen into particularly non-collaborative practices that affect professional productions too. It's a long life and (hopefully!) career for our acting students – and if the stories we've been gathering from professionals are any indication, then at some point we'll all work with artists whose tech-influenced behaviors can negatively impact everyone's creative process. We get it, there have always been selfish people in theatre (and any business really). However, there simply seems to be more *of* them, and they're expressing that selfishness in very specific ways related to their devices.

I was hired to direct an Off Broadway show, and I had some challenges with one actor in particular. He struggled with listening, being present, and the moment he would be finished in a rehearsal he would whip out his cell phone – which he kept in his pocket even when onstage. After our first stumble-through, we all sat down for notes. He had his phone out – but I gave him the benefit of the doubt that he was typing the notes electronically. Now – and these are all Equity actors, mind you – I had just given him a note, and I turned my head to the next actor. In the time it took me to turn my head and say, "Now Joanne, in Scene 4. . . " he jumped up and screamed. And I mean, screamed. We all were shocked, and then he followed the scream with "I just got tickets to *Hamilton*, I won the lottery!" Now, I have all joy for anyone getting in to see *Hamilton*. But he clearly had been checking social media while I was giving him notes. What would make an actor so selfish, so unfocused, so disconnected from the creative process, and so incredibly disrespectful to his ensemble and the collaborative process, that he would choose his smartphone and social media over our work together? I will never ever forget that scream. And I will never ever recommend that actor to any colleague.

(Joshua Chase Gold, director)

Conclusion: empowerment – the fuel

"It felt refreshing to not have to worry about taking care of something on my device while walking through the campus. We forget the simple joys of things when we are on our technology. I forgot how good it felt to just walk casually while enjoying the sun and observing people walking past me."

"Acting requires incredible concentration, patience, mindfulness and focus, and now I live in the moment and don't get distracted easily. Now I think a lot about time. I can almost feel time ticking away and I allow my mind to process what the most important elements of my life are. I notice things around me more than before. I even hear the wind rustling the leaves around me while I'm walking in a park or on the street. I feel I am more open to experience than before. Adventure awakens our senses and I feel I am bold enough to step into the unknown. Now I accept the moment I am in and try to feel whatever I feel without trying to resist, or control it, or even use my phone to help me not think about my problems. My phone can't hijack my attention anymore."

Throughout your process together, you've guided your students to healthier practices that nurture their collaborative skills, and helped them embrace the full benefits and joys of retaining those skills. They will have reclaimed control over their tech use, and in the process, discovered how utterly human it feels to reconnect with empathy, being present, and with each other in their ensembles and in their lives. Most important, they will find (or rediscover) the role their own humanity plays in their creativity and collaboration, and that they can never take that for granted again. That's empowerment, and that's how the fire stays alive once it's been rekindled; through the fuel of humanity, commitment, sacrifice, and the trust that is created when the ensemble collaborates together. Once the ensemble is strong and reliably working well together, it will continue to fuel each individual's empowerment. And that empowerment, combined with healthy personal practice, will provide the fuel to keep their Collaborative Genes burning for a lifetime.

Collaboration is alive and well, thriving inside each of us thanks to the strength and resilience of the Collaborative Gene. By responding to these new behaviors in our acting students, we ensure the full development and realization of The Collaborative Gene in all of its glory and power. We need to do this important work in our classrooms; being in the moment of their real lives will help our students be able to be in the moment on stage. We need to ignite, rekindle, and nurture each student – so that they can collaborate to create those characteristics that make them uniquely who they are as a collective. No more isolation: an ensemble. One that plays, creates, and grows together.

As long as you continue to feed fuel, the fire will continue to live.

(Patrick Delaney)

Bibliography

American Psychiatric Association. *Diagnostic and Statistical Manual of Mental Disorders*, 5th ed. American Psychiatric Association, 18 May 2013, Print.

Besser, Matt, Ian Roberts, and Matt Walsh. *Upright Citizens Brigade Comedy Improvisation Manual*. Comedy Council of Nicea, 2013. Print.

Boal, Augusto. *Games for Actors and Non-Actors*, 2nd ed. Routledge, 2002. Print.

Crouch, Andy. "Andy Crouch: The Return of Shame." *Christianity Today*, 10 Mar. 2015. Web. 4 July 2017.

Figueiro, M.G., Brittany Wood, Barbara Plitnick, and Mark S. Rea. "The Impact of Light From Computer Monitors on Melatonin Levels in College Students." *Neuro Endocrinology Letters* 32.2 (2011): 158–163. Web. 4 July 2017.

Fowler, Geoffrey A. "Distracted Texters Fail the Chewbacca Test." *Wall Street Journal*. 17 Feb. 2016. Web. 12 Jan. 2018.

Invasion of the Body Snatchers. Dir. Don Siegel. Perf. Kevin McCarthy, Dana Wynter, and Larry Gates. Allied Artist Pictures, 1956. Film.

Mueller, Pam. A., and Daniel M. Oppenheimer. "The Pen is Mightier than the Keyboard: Advantages of Longhand Over Laptop Note Taking." *Sage Journals* 25.6 (2014): 1159–1168. Web. 14 Jan. 2018.

Roberts, James A., Luc Honore Petnji Yaya, and Chris Manolis. "The Invisible Addiction: Cell-phone Activities and Addiction Among Male and Female College Students." *Journal of Behavioral Addiction* 3.4 (2014): 254–265. Print.

Robinson, Lewis. "The Science behind Multitasking and How It Slowly Erodes Productivity." *Glassdoor for Employers*, Glassdoor, Inc. 10 May 2017. Web. 14 Jan 2018.

St. George, Donna "How Mindfulness Practices are Changing an Inner-city School." *The Washington Post*. Washington Post Co., 13 Nov. 2016. Web. 4 July 2017.

Spolin, Viola. *Improvisation for the Theater*, 3rd ed. Northwestern University Press, 1999. Print.

The Editors of Encyclopaedia Britannica. "Trois Freres." *Encyclopaedia Britannica Online*. Encyclopaedia Britannica Inc., n.d. Web. 4 July 2017.

Chapter 6

We are the people to solve this problem

Rose

We were at the ATHE (Association for Theatre in Higher Education) Conference in Montreal in the summer of 2015. We'd been very nervous about our panel presentation on "The Impact of Excessive Technology Use on Collaborative Behaviors" because we weren't scientists and thought people wouldn't show up, and to our great relief it had gone really well. In fact, it went so well that we carried on talking with several terrific people who had attended. Everyone we met was clearly eager to have this conversation about tech use and acting – and our impression was that, like us, the attendees weren't finding enough people interested in (or willing to) examine the potential downside of this great new technology. As we talked, it became clear to us that we were not alone in the depth of our concerns. Moreover, as we listened to people from Florida to Montreal, from Tennessee to Dublin, what started as a scattered collection of people from all corners of the earth became a collaborative group of theatre folks saying "yes and" to each other's ideas. We realized that this issue was much bigger, and more widespread, than any of us had previously thought. Although it felt good to know we weren't crazy, the size and scope of the issue seemed to grow exponentially as we shared our experiences. "What have you tried? Oh, a technology-free camping trip with students? Ah, Digital Disconnects? Technology-free discussion groups? What changes have you noticed? Did things get better?" We grew more and more excited as we added to each other's ideas, but still felt rather daunted, until Cliona Dukes from Dublin's Smock Alley Theatre smiled widely, and confidently said "We are the people to solve this problem." In that moment, we knew we weren't overreaching, and that we would have colleagues and support in making positive changes in our classrooms and to theatre itself.

We've been down in the weeds getting to the taproot of this phenomenon for five chapters, and now it's time to pull back and open our focus to consider the worldview of what we've been wrestling with here. So let's (briefly) go back to the beginning of theatre to help fortify us for what comes next.

Theatre was borne out of ritual, and evidence of ritual can be traced back to more than 40,000 years ago (Insoll et al.). Ritual is defined as a set or fixed series of actions performed in a prescribed manner and/or as part of a ceremony. Rituals are found in the history and origins of every culture, and the more humans gathered to form tribes and communities, the more evidence of ritual we find. When humans moved from hunter/ gatherer societies to agricultural ones and put down community roots, there was more opportunity for evidence to accumulate. As fixed communities increased, so did ritual practice. One reason for this was that the more fixed a community became, the more vulnerable they became to their environment. A need emerged to communicate with the forces of nature, along with a desire to want to try to control them or encourage them to act favorably toward the community (Jones).

Another reason rituals emerged was, though living in communities provides benefits, living in larger groups also presents challenges. Not everyone is going to agree on the best hunting strategies now that there are more people to feed; someone's going to get testy about possessions, or territorial about another person or relationship. People had to develop a code of living to enable them to understand the world and how to behave with one another so that the tribe would thrive. Ritual teaches people models and rules of behavior so that the society can function and work together. Early rituals included stories about the best way to get those bison so the tribe could eat, and ceremonies about the sun and its life-giving light. Some rituals evolved so that the forces of nature were accorded human-like traits, but in supernatural form (you know, *gods*). Many rituals represented entities that the tribe was in conflict with, to try to affect a positive outcome. In the lessons embedded in rituals (along with ensuring good harvests and ways to bring down a mastodon or two), and in the group practice of the rituals themselves, people found codes to live by and learned to collaborate and become stronger together.

Rituals create a structured order, they commemorate great events, recognize stages of growth (initiation, coming of age), and the repetition of the rituals by members of the society teach the community about values they deem important. Perhaps most importantly, a ritual needs to be performed by the community, and for the community. Its repetitive nature demands commitment, asks for sacrifice (offer something of yourself for the greater good of the goal), and builds a bonded trust so the community is stronger and more cohesive as a result of having performed or experienced the ritual. Commitment, sacrifice, and support are the essence of ensemble building. Those key traits have taught us what a community needs from its members in order for it to thrive, but they also teach us how to behave in a moral and thoughtful way to be productive members of that society.

In the same way that ancient ritual taught people *how* to be human, theatre today *preserves* humanity, teaching us what it *means* to be human. And now we're back to technology (stay with us here): as technology can make us forget what we know about life and our humanity, theatre reminds us what it means to be human. When we began researching this subject four years ago, Rose created a file titled "Theatre Saves Humanity" for all the articles and research she encountered; and she took a lot of guff for the grandiose sound of that. It's not so funny now as it was a few years ago. As we love our devices more and more, forgetting about the people around us, what's happening to our human skills beyond theatre? And is there anybody else doing anything about this?

How is technology affecting collaboration in the business world, and how are they responding?

If you go to Google and type in "collaboration" and "corporation" together, one of the first search results you get is how to share and edit documents remotely. Articles about telecommuting, sharing technology, and working together long-distance also appear. One search result gives the word "Collaborate" as its company name; its stated purpose is to make it possible for customers and companies to "transact with each other for mutual benefit." (We don't exactly think of the purchase of a new lawnmower from somebody as "collaborating" with them, but hey . . .) Corporate leadership seems to be associating collaboration and "working together on the same project" as synonymous. They don't seem to be conceptually teasing apart face-to-face contact from the idea of people working simultaneously on a series of tasks.

There are changes in the field of business, however, and it's exciting to examine the growing role of theatre artists in companies that do value the skills we've discussed in this book. Corporations ranging from pharmaceuticals to banks are holding workshops for employees (and particularly, team leaders) to focus on listening, team building, and empathy. If corporate leaders are recognizing the role of empathy in the success of their company, that's heartening. Perhaps more exciting is that they're hiring experts to come and teach these "soft skills" to their employees; yup, they're hiring actors and theatre artists. "Soft skills" range from creativity and communication to persistence and resilience, and companies are finding the value in applying improvisation and theatre games to teach their employees about effective face-to-face collaboration and ensemble building.

Roger

After hearing about the work I was doing with students centered on the development of "soft skills" through play, The New School for Social Research hired me to lead multiple Professional Development workshops. The goal was to introduce the faculty to techniques in somatic learning that they in turn could bring into their classrooms to inspire new levels of learning and engagement.

One session had about 16 full- and part-time faculty. Most of the participants were curious to explore the work, smiling and fully willing to explore the exercises. Except one, a woman named Anne. And boy oh boy, I could see she hated the work, thinking it was silly and frivolous. We started playing Kitty Wants a Corner. The room was buzzing with giggles and screams as grown men and women took bigger and bigger risks. They were eagerly looking across the circle for partners to give them the okay to run! Not Anne. Her eyes were down, and when she did catch eyes with someone who wanted to exchange places with her, she looked away as if she never saw them. She did not leave her spot once throughout the duration of the game.

During the discussion that followed, everyone shared how much fun they had and the skills that Kitty was developing. Anne told the group that if the purpose of the game was to never be Kitty, then why would anyone ever leave their spot? She shared that the risk to exchange spots and possibly become Kitty was too big to take. To which another faculty member said, "What's the risk? You become Kitty?!" Anne's whole demeanor suddenly changed, and she started laughing. She said she thought the goal of the game was to win – and winning meant NEVER be Kitty. In actuality, she strategized how to *defeat* the game, missing the point altogether: the inherent joy in taking a risk. She didn't see that in any process of creativity, we must move outside of our comfort zone. Most importantly, she shared how she was robbing her colleagues, and herself, of the opportunity to collaborate together. Empathy is a big one with Kitty Wants a Corner, and Anne regretted not sharing in the joys and failures of her peers. To this day, Anne describes that moment as one of the two most profound teaching moments in her career. That Professional Development workshop was the first time I met Anne, and shortly afterward she invited me to co-teach a graduate course in the MFA Transdisciplinary Design Program called "Transforming Mindsets." In the course, the non-theatre students were exposed to games that develop soft-skills, as well as solve real-world problems that incorporate game playing.

Many companies have recently realized that though they had hired people with outstanding tech skills, their people skills were sorely lacking. They seemed to try to employ the "language" without fully understanding it; that is, "collaborate" became corporate speak for "playing nicely with others." But, it didn't necessarily mean you had to be in the same room while you played nicely. Some businesses were so focused on the processes of their particular line of work that the actual human skills needed for collaboration were neglected, or simply not valued. When the results began to show up in their financial success – or lack thereof – some heads began to turn. In an article titled "Why Personal Interaction Drives Innovation and Collaboration" in *Forbes* Magazine, author Harbrinder Kang writes:

> Recently Cisco [a multi-national corporation that designs and sells networking equipment] undertook a study of human behavior and the barriers to effective collaboration: how it affects productivity, workplace efficiency, and business results. This study showed without question that collaboration is grounded in human interaction and relationships. One participant even said: "We need to get back to the intimacy." We learned that people were more engaged when they could see and hear each other well, basically interacting the way humans have interacted for thousands of years: face-to-face.
>
> (Kang)

Additionally, blogger Adam Grant reported on a terrific study led by Harvard Business School Professor Boris Groysberg. In the study, 1000 security analysts found that when they moved to a new company along with their established team, they had a much greater chance of continued success than those analysts who moved to a new company by themselves. Grant writes that the value of shared experience has grown to where top experts in the field of team leadership argue that the ability for people to effectively work together be included as a standard measure in defining a team's effectiveness (Grant). Fortunately, these experts are turning to theatre practitioners and teaching artists to help them rekindle these skills.

Roger

In 2014, a pharmaceutical company hired me to develop a workshop for their upcoming leadership meeting. They asked me how they could augment their leadership's ability to communicate and empathize, to which I replied, "Have them play games!" They loved the idea and were great partners to collaborate with. I was to do eight 30-minute sessions each day over the course of several days. At the very first workshop, I had eight people. I estimated a thousand people total at this meeting, so I was bummed with such a small number. My gut told me because the sessions were voluntary, and mine was described as improv/play, there was a lot of eye rolling.

Those eight participants had a blast laughing, failing, succeeding, and supporting each other! The "aha's" they had between the exercises and their day-to-day lives both professionally and personally were a gift to be in the presence of. Every single one of them left with a joy, vigor, and a new way of seeing the world that they had not entered the session with.

I had a fifteen-minute break in between sessions. I heard a lot of ruckus outside my room. I peeked outside and there were about 50 people already lined up for the next session! Those in line shared how their colleagues had just told them they had one of the best and most profound learning experiences in quite some time; all while playing, and in only 30 minutes! My sessions were planned to hold about 20 people maximum, and I then had to go up to 27 people. We had to find someone to work outside my door to control the crowds, giving wristbands out that were numbered one through to 27. No wristband? No entrance. We actually got a huge velvet rope to put outside my room for people to wait behind as if they were going to a club! All the joy happening inside my room was spilling out to the whole area, and it was the best advertising I could hope for. The employees digitally scored all the workshops at the event, and the play sessions received the highest scores and most positive reviews. People like to play; they just forget.

What about the medical profession?

At a 2016 conference, Roger and Rose met several people from Australia, New York, and New Zealand who worked with nurses and doctors on skills of empathy, listening, and collaborating with the patient on their health care. Their colleague from New Zealand spoke about the role of ego in training young surgeons, and the challenges she faced in the classroom of "getting their faces out of their smartphones." She was tough and resolute about bringing these young doctors into collaborative relationships with the medical teams they worked with, and she was equally resolute about the benefits she felt collaborative behaviors offered to patients. Researchers Robert Huckman and Gary Pisano recently studied over 200 cardiac surgeons over the course of 38,000 procedures (Huckman and Pisano). They found that the sheer volume of procedures didn't guarantee success;

mortality rates didn't change with the amount of surgeries. However, when the surgeons worked with an established team of nurses and anesthesiologists for each procedure, mortality rates *did* improve. Blogger Adam Grant said it best: "The best groups aren't necessarily the ones with the most stars, but rather the teams that have collaborated in the past."

What's happening in education?

The wonder of technology and its potential to enhance education inspired new hope to educators. And with good reason. The Internet and smaller, cheaper devices made it possible for students in all grades, and in all locations, to have access to a world library, information and resources that would have been impossible for them to obtain at an earlier time. But some schools got a little swept up with the notion that "more technology means smarter kids" instead of "teaching kids how to effectively use tools that enhance their learning will make smarter kids." Online learning swept the industry, and colleges scrambled to offer online courses to be competitive with one another. There were, and are, big profits to be made in online courses. In elementary, middle, and high school, companies like Apple and Microsoft donate software and devices to enhance learning (e.g., Kolodny, Microsoft). Coincidentally(!), they also fund studies that focus on how *well* their products work in the classroom (Singer). Free equipment, free software, unlimited potential – but every new thing displaces something. So what's one of the primary things being displaced in classrooms?

We're seeing a systematic diminution of *group* play. It's disappearing from our schools; recess is no longer a guaranteed staple of the school day (Strauss). When more time is needed to teach the skills necessary to be proficient with newest technologies, or when budget problems (from obtaining all the newest models of technology) force cuts, which programs are the most frequently affected? Athletics, music, and theatre: all vital sources of group play. Dr. E. Paul Roetert, the CEO of SHAPE America, says, "Daily recess, monitored by well-trained staff or volunteers, can optimize a child's social, emotional, physical, and cognitive development" (Jenco). The story that flabbergasted us the most came several years ago from a school on Long Island, NY. It was reported that the elementary school administrators cancelled the annual kindergarten play and sent a letter to parents stating that they took that action because "we are responsible for preparing children for college and career with valuable lifelong skills" (Pawlowski). So, do we assume that they don't value communication skills, problem solving, creativity, the ability to work in cooperation with others, time management, the ability to work within a structure, and so much more? We strongly recommend that you visit (or revisit) the terrific essay written by Professor

Louis Catron titled "What Theater Majors Learn: The Advantages Theater Majors Have for All Jobs" (Catron). He cites no less than 25 skills that theatre majors/artists have in abundance. Do schools have to choose between activities that teach foundational human skills and activities that teach technology skills? Including "play" with lesson plans offers exciting possibilities.

David

Early in my teaching career, I was offered a course at Brooklyn College teaching Intro to Theatre to high school students. These students were among the best and brightest in their schools, yet came from some of the worst schools in Brooklyn. The program was designed to give them a step up on the ladder of their education. Most of them had never seen a theatre production in their lives. I was shocked. Not even a school play. They loved film and television, but to them, theatre was old and boring. Part of the curriculum required me to teach theatre history. The students met my efforts with a complete lack of interest. No matter how entertaining I tried to be, no matter how exciting I tried to make the material, the students were uninterested and unengaged. I asked myself, "What would Viola Spolin do?" I came up with a theatre history version of the game show *Jeopardy*. It worked. Most of the students were eagerly absorbing facts to score points. And I had more fun pretending to be Alex Trebek than I did trying to lecture the students on theatre history. I'm sure I'm not the first or only teacher to come up with this idea, but I have gone on to invent many games that serve my teaching.

Schools around the world at all levels are beginning to develop policies for responsible use of technology. Digital Citizenship, and acceptable use policies are becoming part of the lexicon in education.

Andrew Marcinek is Director of Technology and co-founder of Educator U.org, and he serves as Director of Technology at Grafton Public Schools in Massachusetts. He's been teaching on the topic of digital citizenship for years, and believes students must act the same way online as they would offline; with kindness, courtesy, and respect. Mr. Marcinek and his colleagues have come up with specific activities for elementary school students to develop the skills needed for a healthy online presence (Marcinek). For example: write a letter to a classmate, and then write a second letter to a person outside school (with pen and paper!). This forces students to slow down, use actual words (no "LOLs" or emojis), and adhere to the rules of syntax and grammar. It's a precursor to introducing email. Another example: set up easels with large pieces of paper around the classroom and have each student create something, anything, on the paper. The class then walks around the classroom, as if in a museum, taking time with each person's creation to offer positive feedback. A precursor to being on social media, the exercise is a metaphor for publicly offering your opinion without hurting someone's feelings.

What about play itself in our lives?

A generation ago, people played board games at home with friends and family, and in many households, kids were told to organize outdoor games with their friends and "don't come back until dinnertime." If we don't teach (or even allow for) group play, how can we learn to collaborate? Without a healthy dose of group play in our lives, especially in childhood, our sense of self in relation to others is transformed. We are more likely to be focused on ourselves as individuals, fueled toward individual success, rather than group success. We are no longer playmates, we're competitors. Even if we're on the same team, we're competing (who is first string on the team, who is lead role in the play, etc.). The team isn't a "team," it's a collection of individuals wearing the same uniform. The major point of playing a game and the benefits to be derived from it are lost because concern for the rewards and stigmas attached to the individuals overrun the shared experience. In the long run, we lose our sense of how to work together. We learn to be isolated while surrounded by people we're interacting with.

Author and play researcher Dr. Stuart Brown writes about the connections between play, socialization, and neural and cognitive development in his book *Play: How it Shapes the Brain, Opens the Imagination and Invigorates the Soul*. Quite literally, play and social interaction create new neural connections and are a "driving force helping to sculpt how the brain continues to grow and develop." Dr. Brown also cites intriguing research that shows (in rats anyway) that "the same areas of the brain stem that initiate sleep initiate play behavior" (Brown and Vaughn 42). The evidence seems to indicate that play deficit is akin to sleep deficit – creating darker emotional states, and an inability to feel pleasure. When you think of insomnia, you think of being in a bad mood, an inability to focus or truly listen, and feeling uncoordinated. Imagine now that lack of play and socialization creates something similar in our waking state – *and* contributes to insomnia itself? Though Dr. Brown writes that the sleep/play connections in humans are still anecdotal at this point, we feel we've heard enough to want to take action before we prove that the rats were right.

Dr. Brown and the National Institute for Play don't limit their research to young people; adults can gain profound benefits from continuing play throughout their lives. His research emphasizes that children learn empathy, communication, problem solving, and resilience through play, but that those same skills are cultivated in adults when they play in groups. In a 2014 interview with NPR, Dr. Brown points out the benefits of adults playing "German style games" where everyone is included as opposed to American style games (like Monopoly) where people are eliminated and then excluded (Yenigen). He cites two major reasons for adults to continue playing throughout their lives: 1) playing is how people connect and create community, and 2) studies have shown that playing helps adults remain mentally sharp, and strengthen memory and thinking skills. In the same interview, Dr. Brown states:

> What you begin to see when there's major play deprivation in an otherwise competent adult is that they're not much fun to be around. You begin to see that the perseverance and joy in work is lessened and that life is much more laborious.

(Yenigen)

Does absence of group play, plus increased social isolation, play a role in a rise in bullying?

As we referenced earlier in Chapter 2, young people who isolate more with their devices get to avoid eye contact. If they're not looking someone in the face when they say or do something cruel, they don't experience the consequences of their actions. If they take an action that parents and society have told them *not* to do because "there'll be consequences" – and then there *are* none – well, that can lead to a sense of power and a belief that they "beat the system." That is, the system of human values we've tried to live by for tens of thousands of years. Look at the rise in bullying awareness – doesn't it correlate to the advent of digital devices? The National Center for Educational Statistics reported in 2016 that one in five students reported having been bullied, with only 36 percent reporting their abuse. Additionally, the percentage of students who have experienced being cyber-bullied has doubled since 2007, from 18 percent to 36 percent (Patchin and Hindula). Interesting note: the iPhone was introduced in 2007 with the mass proliferation of smartphones following soon after. Available technology makes it easier to be cruel; it's easier to be vicious in a text message or on Twitter than being face-to-face. There is a sense of power when someone literally has the universe in their hands; and a person has ultimate control over that universe like a demi-god. They can be magnanimous and "like" their subjects, they can mete out justice, and they can punish someone they feel has wronged them, or hurt someone simply on a whim. When that power and control is coupled with a lack of consequences (at worst someone is un-friended), it can feed the bullying, and the un-punished bullying can lead to an even greater sense of power. That unlimited power can lead to a sense of privilege and feeling entitled to doing what the person wants, whenever they want it.

Rose

A few weeks ago I was walking to work and overheard a conversation between two parents and their roughly seven-year-old child. The child was on the far end of a tantrum, and still seemed unwilling to let go of the horror, the horror that he couldn't have a particular toy that moment of that day (these are the kinds of moments I slow down for to eavesdrop on . . .). "But I want it! I WANT it NOW! Why can't I have it?" The mom very patiently gripped her son and said, "We can't have everything we want honey. We need to work hard for the things we want, we need to be patient, and we need to think about all the people who help us get what we need." The father said, "When Mommy and I were little, we didn't have the Internet; there was no such thing as ordering things online." The kid was incredulous. "No Internet?" Mom said, "That's right. We went to a store – a real store like these here on our street – and if they didn't have what we needed, we had to place a special order with the nice shopkeeper, and it would sometimes take weeks and weeks for it to arrive. Then we would go to the store to pick it up. And it was so exciting, after waiting for weeks, to finally take that trip. Do you see what we mean? You need to see that not getting what you want right away is not really a bad thing." The kid was quiet for a moment, then said "I'm sorry I yelled mom." Then he paused and said, "What were you and dad like when you were little?" Here's to great parents, everywhere.

Perhaps it's no surprise that Millennials have picked up the nickname "The Entitlement Generation." All generations tend to bemoan those who succeed them, but let's take a closer look. They want out of anything uncomfortable and they're serious about it. They digitally curate their day for a tailor-made experience of endless positive stimulation through videos, pictures, texts, music, and so on. Technology has damaged these people as much as it has helped them. They're shaped by their reliance on devices, and really, it's not their fault, yet we tend to blame them (or perhaps their parents). The effects had to be discovered over time, and these effects have proven to include less compassion and less empathy, hence, an increase in bullying. Now that we can more clearly identify and separate the upsides from the downsides, we can begin to take positive action, rather than complain and blame. Stopbullying.gov is funded by the federal government. The website offers solutions for the identification and prevention of bullying, as well as updates on state and local lawmaking as it pertains to policies on bullying.

The Trevor Project is an excellent resource for young LGBTQ persons who might be contemplating suicide as a result of bullying. The CyberBully Hotline is another resource schools can use for students to report tips on bullying and remain anonymous.

What about the role of parents in a young person's technology use?

A story from a Brooklyn College student who works in an after school program:

> "At the end of dismissal there were some kids still waiting to be picked up by their parents, one of them being a first grader who now had been waiting for 20 minutes. As the other late students started to get picked up, this one first grader was still waiting for his parents. When his mother finally arrived to pick her son up (mind you it's been 30 minutes now since dismissal) she got out of the car, and she was looking at her phone, checking messages as she came up the sidewalk. She was not looking up. The young boy ran to his mother and gave her a big hug. This in turn knocked the mother's phone onto the ground. The mother scolded her child, pushed him away, and gave him the most terrifying look a mother could give. I felt so bad for the young boy – I wanted to say, "Is your phone more important than the child you forgot to pick up?" The reaction she gave was as if someone had hurt the electronic child in her hand. How can such an insignificant device hold such a dear place in our hearts? I saw a mother whose priority was her phone's condition, not her own living child."

We visited some of the issues of parenting and technology in Chapter 3, but let's take one more moment here to consider this. Those of you who are parents, or teachers for that matter, before you ask your child/student to consider healthier behaviors with their technology, examine your own use. Forget the harsh reaction to the dropped phone; could you have been that woman checking messages as she walked up to the school entrance? Do you give your children (of any age) guidelines about use in the home, or at bedtime? Do you find yourself saying "it's a losing battle, and they seem to like it and it keeps them quiet and and and ... " Consider some simple recommendations (and tailor them based on your specific lifestyle):

- Get your child an alarm clock so they won't be tempted to put the phone next to their bed.
- Don't permit the phone to be used in the dining room (family dinners), the living room (family activities), or the car. These are the primary places where you and your family have conversations; eliminating the

phone from these areas nurtures engagement, and allows your child to designate a room where they do use it. It's not forbidden for them to use it, simply regulate where they use it. And, be the first person in your family to enforce it for yourself.

- Depending on your child's age, have them keep their phone out of their bedroom, beginning two hours before bedtime, and until after breakfast. If they're older, we still recommend the phone not be stored in the room where they sleep. If they generally have balanced use with only the occasional "binge," make sure the phone is on airplane mode and kept five to ten feet away from their beds so they're not tempted to check messages during the night.

- Plan family activities and group family time; activities such as a weekly board game night, bowling, movies, or the theatre. To empower the family with healthy decisions, allow a different family member to choose the non-tech event each week. We particularly encourage you to consider outdoor activities.

"I'm usually exhausted when I come home from school or work and will dive into either homework or if I have some free time into YouTube or Facebook. I was always physically there with my family, but never mentally and it makes me feel disappointed in myself. Sunday was an eye opener as to how I being fully present impacted the whole household. We were all more connected as a unit and in sync with each other that entire day. The funny thing was that after my 24 hours was over and I turned on my phone and checked social media, I wasn't really interested in what was there. The connection I had with my family on my day of Digital Disconnect was a thousand times stronger than my connection to my phone."

Roger

I'm a child of the 1980s, and I loved video games! I will never forget that Christmas when Santa (aka mom) gave me Atari (sorry mom, I looked under the bed two days before Christmas and found it)! My favorite game at that time was Pac-Man, and I was great at it! I knew all the patterns for each level to keep on winning without getting eaten by those shifty ghosts Inky, Blinky, Pinky, and Sue. My mom had strict rules about when I was allowed to use the console. Cut to 1982, and for that Christmas, I got a hand-held portable knock-off of Pac-Man called Pakri Monster. Wait, now I can take the game anywhere I go and play anytime I want?! Heaven!

Every Friday night my mom took my two sisters and me out to dinner to a restaurant called Friendly's. It had basic diner fare, but what it was known for was its huge selection of ice creams and killer sundaes. We would get into our 1972 Chevrolet Caprice around 5:30, and off we'd go. My mom loved disco, and without fail all of us would be singing away to Donna Summer or Diana Ross while my mom drove us all toward ice cream heaven.

One Friday night, mom didn't know that I brought Pakri Monster with me. I sat in the backseat, head down, immersed with my chomping yellow guy while my sisters and mom sang away. Mom noticed I wasn't singing. She looked back in her rear-view mirror, discovered the glow on my face from the game, and had something to say. "That game is never to be played in the car, understand?" Whoa, I was mad. I put it away, and sulked and sulked. The following Friday, I was in the car, no game, and we started our drive to Friendly's. I still had a little residual "How can you do this to me and ruin my life mom" attitude, until she put on the radio. I saw my sisters light up, recognizing the latest disco tune, and off they went singing away with mom. I kept quiet. There was no way I was going to lose my bad mood! But then I saw how much fun they were having, and within seconds I was singing "backup" to the three most important ladies in my life. I forgot about my video game, because I was connected to my family having a great time. I didn't realize it at the time, but bringing that video game with me on our drive was disconnecting me from our Friday night ritual. There was such spontaneity involved in that drive because we had no clue what song would surprise us on the radio. It was a great time for my family to come together and play. Thanks mom!

- Have ongoing discussions with your children about the role of these new devices and apps in life, and the differences between reality and virtual reality. Too often people think it's all self-explanatory; it isn't. We can trick ourselves into thinking we have fantastic memories by being able to look things up instantly on the Internet, but that's not actually developing and strengthening memory (Wegner and Ward). People talk to Siri – but that's not conversation. We've heard people curse Siri out when she tells them she's "recalculating" – as if she actually could experience being punished because of her incompetence. Artificial intelligence like IBM's Watson can seem utterly lifelike (especially if they get picked to be on *Jeopardy!*). Robots like Paro the baby seal are being utilized as companions for older adults with dementia (Moskowitz); but they aren't offering real human emotion or feelings (Markoff). But let's face it – they do a pretty mean job of offering the *illusion* of reality. Part of our job as parents and mentors is to help Digital Natives experience the difference.

David

As I write this in early 2017, my six-year-old daughter, Maddie, is fascinated with a reality TV show called "Face Off." It is the second "grownup" TV show she has followed with any interest (the first was "America Ninja Warrior," which spurred her to embrace more physical activity). If you're not familiar, "Face Off" is a competition among movie special effects makeup artists. They are offered challenges and rush to create elaborate creatures, most of them grotesque. The show has helped Maddie deal with her fear of monsters and all things scary. And it speaks to her curiosity ("How do they DO that?").

Coincidentally, I recently directed a comedy show that featured an over-the-top horror moment in which a character "melted." Her face peeled off, her eye popped out, her guts spilled, and so on. It was a remarkable combination of effects, done before a live studio audience. Given Maddie's interest in special effects makeup, my wife and I thought she might want to see this piece performed. (You can watch the monitor to see what the camera is catching, but you can also see the actors and technicians [just out of camera range] working together to make it all happen.) Maddie watched very closely, transfixed. Afterward, we asked her what she thought. She said, "It's scarier than on TV."

The last thought we offer about your relationship with your child, no matter their age, is to support them in nurturing their ability to be in solitude. As we've written about our acting students, that ability to be present in a moment of boredom, or fear, or questioning is vital not only to the creative process, but to the process of being human. Too often, young people are alone with a feeling and they panic; they text a friend to say, "I'm sad! What do I do?" or post a message on Facebook saying "Hey hive mind: I'm having a bad day. Cheer me up." Then, their feelings about the feeling become contingent on the responses they get to their message. They haven't allowed themselves to be alone with their feelings. They immediately want to connect, and that constant connectivity interferes with their ability to simply "be" with what they're feeling so they can develop an awareness of emotions and fears. To quote Dr. Sherry Turkle once more:

> I have a feeling, I want to make a call. Now it's: I want to have a feeling, I need to send a text. The problem with this new regime of "I share therefore I am" is that, if we don't have connection, we don't feel like ourselves. We almost don't feel ourselves. So what do we do? We connect more and more. But in the process, we set ourselves up to be isolated. How do you get from connection to isolation? You end up isolated if you don't cultivate the capacity for solitude, the ability to be separate, to gather yourself. Solitude is where you find yourself so that you can reach out to other people and form real attachments. When we don't have the capacity for solitude, we turn to other people in order to feel less anxious or in order to feel alive. When this happens, we're not able to appreciate who they are. It's as though we're using them as spare parts to support our fragile sense of self. We slip into thinking that always being connected is going to make us feel less alone. But we're at risk, because actually it's the opposite that's true. If we're not able to be alone, we're going to be more lonely. And if we don't teach our children to be alone, they're only going to know how to be lonely.
>
> (Turkle)

Conclusion

Though we've focused this book on acting and actions for us to take in our classrooms and rehearsal studios, we shouldn't limit our scope. We have a powerful opportunity to apply the discoveries we're making, and this conversation that we're having, to areas beyond the realm of theatre and training. Our collaborative skills, and our efforts to rekindle and reclaim them, will play a vital role in our society's future. What we're doing in the classroom has the potential to impact the world; by adding the information and actions embedded in this book to your pedagogy, you're offering so much more than acting skills. And that's why "Theatre Saves Humanity" has become a true call to action.

Theatre and ritual are both self-reflective by nature. The stories we tell and the rituals we perform teach us how to be human, what it means to be human, and how to take action to become better people and better members of our community. If technology makes us forget what we know about life – and life is pretty wonderful – then theatre and collaboration make us remember who we are and how to truly live.

If we are the people to solve this problem, then the next groups of people, who will follow us in solving this problem, are our children and students. We're not just theatre people, we're also teachers and parents. Not only do we know how to save humanity, we also know how to teach others how to do it too. Theatre educators and practitioners: you are the new superheroes. The world needs you – go save it.

Bibliography

Brown, Stuart and Christopher Vaughan. *Play: How it Shapes the Brain, Opens the Imagination, and Invigorates the Soul.* Penguin Group, 2009. Print.

Catron, Louis E. "What Theater Majors Learn: The Advantages Theater Majors Have for All Jobs." Web. 24 Jan. 2018.

Cosier, Susan. "People Prefer Electric Shocks to Tedium." *Scientific American.* Nature America, Inc., 1 Nov. 2014. Web. 4 July 2017.

Grant, Adam. "What's the Common Ingredient for Team Success in Surgery, Banking, Software, Airlines, and Basketball?" *Granted.* 6 May 2013. Web. 4 July 2017.

Huckman, Robert S., and Gary P. Pisano. "The Firm Specificity of Individual Performance: Evidence from Cardiac Surgery." *Management Science* 52.4 (April 2006): 473–488. Web. 12 Jan 2018.

Insoll, Timothy, ed. *The Oxford Handbook of the Archaeology of Ritual and Religion,* Oxford University Press, 2011. Print.

Jenco, Melissa. "Toolkit Helps School Recess Provide Physical, Cognitive, Social Benefits." *AAP News.* American Academy of Pediatrics, 10 Jan. 2017. Web. 4 July 2017.

Jones, Dan. "Social Evolution: The Ritual Animal." *Nature: International Weekly Journal of Science.* 493.7433 (2013): n.pag. Web. 12 Jan. 2018.

Kang, Harbrinder. "Why Personal Interaction Drives Innovation and Collaboration." *Forbes.* Forbes Media, 9 April 2013. Web. 4 July 2017.

Kolodny, Lara. "Apple Stays in School, Donating 54,500 iPads to Students and Teachers." *TechCrunch.* Oath Inc., 7 Sept. 2016. Web. 4 July 2017.

Marcinek, Andrew. "The Path to Digital Citizenship." *Edutopia.* George Lucas Educational Foundation, 26 Nov. 2013. Web. 4 July 2017.

Markoff, John. "Computer Wins on 'Jeopardy!': Trivial, It's Not." *The New York Times.* The New York Times Company, 16 Feb 2011. Web. 15 Jan 2018.

Microsoft, 20 Oct. 2010. "Microsoft Makes Its Largest Technology Donation Ever to a Single Los Angeles School to Help Prepare Students for Their Future." Web. 4 July 2017.

Moskowitz, Clara. "Human–Robot Relations: Why We Should Worry." *LiveScience.* Purch. 18 Feb. 2014. Web. 12 Jan. 2018.

Patchin, Justin W., and Sameer Hinduja. "Summary of Our Cyberbulling Research (2004–2016)." Cyberbulling Research Center, 26 Nov. 2016. Web. 4 July 2017.

Pawlowski, A. "School Cancels Kindergarten Show So Kids Can Focus on 'College and Career.'" *Today.* 30 Apr. 2014. Web. 4 July 2017.

Singer, Natasha. "How Google Took Over the Classroom." *The New York Times.* The New York Times Company, 13 May 2017. Web. 15 Jan. 2018.

Strauss, Valerie. "The Decline of Play in Preschoolers – and the Rise of Sensory Issues." *The Washington Post.* Washington Post Co., 1 Sept. 2015. Web. 12 Jan. 2018.

Turkle, Sherry. "Connected, But Alone?" TED. February 2012. Lecture.

Wegner, Daniel M., and Andrew Ward. "The Internet Has Become the External Hard Drive for Our Memories." *Scientific American.* Nature America, Inc., 1 Dec. 2013. Web. 15 Jan. 2018.

Yenigun, Sami. "Play Doesn't End With Childhood: Why Adults Need Recess Too." *All Things Considered.* Natl. Public Radio, 6 Aug. 2014. Web. 7 July 2017.

Appendices

Appendix A

Murder Mystery

All participants sit in a circle. One person is secretly designated "The Murderer," and "kills" by winking at someone. Once the secret selection has been made, the participants start moving silently throughout the room. Whoever is winked at must silently count to five before dying an elaborate (i.e., fun, theatrical) death. The rest of the group must guess who the Murderer is, trying to "save" as many in the group as possible. To make a guess, the player raises their hand, the game is paused by the teacher/leader, and the player announces who they believe the murderer to be. If they're wrong, then *they* must die an elaborate death and remain lying on the floor until the game is complete. If they are correct, the Murderer has been captured, and a new game begins. Murderer can be played silently, or with the participants engaged in imagined circumstances (they're at a dinner party, etc.). We suggest starting with the silent version. One absolutely essential rule: no one is allowed to avoid eye contact (and thus avoid being "murdered"). Insist that taking the risk of being "murdered" is part of the fun of the game and is to be embraced. Encourage the players to have fun when it becomes their turn to "die," and to make creative choices. Also encourage them to explore tactics (a good tie-in to acting technique). For example, one of the best tactics David has seen was a "murderer" who faked his own death and slyly winked at fellow students from the floor as they walked by. Each "death" was done with a jolt of surprise and everyone knew something was up, but couldn't put their fingers on it. The stakes of the game rose to an unprecedented level. Eventually, only two players were left, and each accused the other of being the "murderer." Of course, both had to "die" as a result of their incorrect guesses. The "murderer" then sprang up in triumph and a long discussion ensued. Another time, a student winked at David and he performed a dramatic death, much to the surprise and enjoyment of the students. (Note: some players don't have the ability to wink, so having a backup method is helpful. We recommend the "murderer" sticking their tongue out at their intended victim, briefly, in a quick, darting motion. Silly, fun, and effective.)

For young people who are increasingly uncomfortable making eye contact, or simply having their faces off the floor, period – Murderer provides a structure that nurtures:

- Direct eye contact – vulnerability, trust, risk taking.
- Stronger visual awareness and alertness – looking at others, trying to make eye contact to see who might be "guilty" without getting "murdered" yourself.
- A willingness to work together through eye contact and silent communication only in order to collaborate on finding who The Murderer is.
- A focus on an objective that requires a person to think beyond their own "safety," and work to try to "save" the group.

Discussion:

- How comfortable were they making eye contact with one another? Especially sitting on the floor in a circle so close to one another?
- Did they use "not wanting to be killed" (playing the obstacle vs. the objective) as a reason they may have avoided eye contact with people all together? Remind them that their objective was to reveal the Murderer ". . .to save us *all*."
- What strategies did they employ to try to determine who the Murderer was? Were they individual or collaborative?

Appendix B

Shepherd and Sheep

Create a circle of chairs, with one less chair than there are actual people. Have one person stand in the middle: they must say one thing that is true about themselves. For everyone else for whom that is true *for*, they must stand and switch chairs. But – they have to sit on a chair different from the one they're currently sitting on. If the person in the middle gets to a vacant chair first, the one without a chair is the new "shepherd." True statements can be as simple as "My favorite color is blue." Or "I am a student at Brooklyn College" (if they want *everyone* to stand up!). This nurtures:

- Vulnerability, willingness to be open to others, honesty.
- Willingness to be truthful for the sake of the ensemble, even if it costs the individual their "seat."
- Making connections: seeing who else shares that truth with me, feeling less isolated, finding more common ground.

- Awareness: what is happening physically, spatially, where there is an opportunity to "gain a seat"?
- Risk taking: with each piece of information that is shared, students reveal more and more about themselves; each reveal leads to a bigger risk.

Discussion:

- How did it feel to reveal a personal truth, no matter how small a fact?
- How did the person in the middle feel when they observed one or more people standing up and sharing their truth?
- Did the person in the middle find themselves wanting to select a very general truth so that they wouldn't feel different, and could connect more to the ensemble?
- Did someone vacating a chair struggle with admitting what was/wasn't true about themselves ("I like *Gilmore Girls*")? What did the truth cost them? What did admitting the truth *gain* them?
- Did anyone hold back from admitting a truth? If so, why?

Appendix C

Dinner Party (as taught by Anastasia Bell)

The goal is to ensure that *everyone* in the group gets to "go in" to the dinner party. Students are instructed to walk about in the space as if they are in the foyer of a restaurant, and that across a specified line or threshold is where the dinner party is being held. At some point, you will ask them to start shaking hands with someone and introduce themselves, first names only. In each exchange however, the partners take on each other's name. For example: "Hello, my name is Miles." "Nice to meet you Miles, I'm Sergio." After they part, Miles now has Sergio's name, and Sergio has taken Miles' name. When they introduce themselves to the next person they encounter, they will use the names they received from their last encounter. But of course, once they meet a new person, they take on *that* person's name, and vice versa. *At some point,* everyone should have their own name given *back* to them. When someone receives their own name back, they are then free to go on in to dinner. Everyone should be given their names back by the end of the exercise.

However – invariably, we end up with three Monica's, or two Harrison's – with the *real* Monica or Harrison already having gone on in to dinner! After the group masters the first name version – you can have them do first and last names, and then graduate to using aliases. Instruct the group to try not to avoid someone who they know has their name in order to prolong things, nor should they run to whoever they think has their name in order to "get out quick." If your group is especially struggling with this deceptively simple exercise, have them try the "library" version. That is, they're in the library, and in order to leave, must get their name given back to them. In this version of course, everyone must whisper their introductions to one another. The whispering can help with focus, attentiveness, and, of course, listening. Dinner Party nurtures:

- Listening, and truly taking in another person.
- Focus and concentration. Were they so focused on remembering who they were that they missed the name they were given?
- Commitment to the ensemble: "My actions affect everyone, not just *me*."
- Being present, and being generous with each other. Was someone rushing ahead to try to find their name, and forgot to give a name to a partner?
- Objectives, obstacles, and tactics: the objective is to get the whole group in to the dinner party. Most obstacles are obvious ("I keep hearing my name over in that part of the room – what's happening?"). Tactics: how can they adjust their behavior to ensure that they successfully receive and give names in order for everyone to have dinner? Do they repeat a name being given to them? Do they find a physical gesture to connect with that name?

Discussion:

- Where was their focus? Was it on finding their name, or trying to ensure that everyone was able to go in to dinner?
- Were they truly taking one another in? Making eye contact? Listening?
- Were they taking their time with each introduction? If not, what made them want to rush?
- What did they do in order to embody each new name they had? What skills did they try to employ to help them to remember each name?
- What did they discover about their memory and focus in general?
- Perhaps most important, what happened in the moment when everyone succeeded? Why did it feel like such a huge accomplishment and celebration? We've never seen a round of this exercise where, upon the last two people exchanging the correct names, the entire group didn't erupt in cheers accompanied by ecstatic jumping up and down. That response comes from something very deeply connected to The Collaborative Gene.

Appendix D

It's Tuesday

The players stand in a circle. The first player makes a choice. It could be a character adjustment (an old man, a mad scientist, etc.) or an "as if" (*as if* they just won the lottery, *as if* they are lost in the woods, etc.). The player then crosses the circle embodying this choice, approaches another player and says, "It's Tuesday" in a manner befitting their choice. If, for instance, the player has chosen to play a mad scientist, he might get wide-eyed, raise his hands in the air, offer his best maniacal laugh, and then say, "It's Tuesday" as if he were Dr. Frankenstein saying, "It's alive!" Or, if he has chosen "as if I just won the lottery," he might skip and sing across the circle, offer a big smile, and happily exclaim, "It's Tuesday." The only two words the player may say are "It's Tuesday." Some students will want to change the words. Don't let them. The entirety of their choice must be reflected in *who* they are, and *how* they are saying those two words. The player who has received this news must react and reply. The response may be to copy the choice or complement the choice. If the player has received the mad scientist choice, she might respond by adopting the same choice (copying, also playing a mad scientist) and exclaiming, "Yes, it's Tuesday, the day our creature will come to life! Muwahahahaha!" Or she might adopt a complementary choice, for instance, Igor, the hunchbacked, eager assistant. She then embodies the physicality of the choice and might say, "Master – you've done it – you finally remembered my birthday!" The key for the responding player is to respond in a way that agrees with the choice made by the first player and offers some statement of explanation or support as to why Tuesday is important.

At this point, the responder becomes the initiator. She adopts a new choice (say, a superhero), crosses the circle, and says, "It's Tuesday" as if she were Wonder Woman. This process can repeat until every player has had the opportunity to do it three or four times. Starting with big, broad choices or familiar archetypes makes the exercise fun and easy. Over time, the choices will naturally settle into including more subtle and sophisticated explorations. *It's Tuesday* nurtures:

- Listening and observation – ability to take in a partner.
- Reading signals, facial expressions, tones, and intent.
- Communicating ideas clearly.
- Physical connection and awareness.

Discussion:

- Did your partner understand and reflect your choice in their response? That is, did you communicate your idea clearly so that it was understood accurately?
- What signals did you pick up on? Were you aware of physicality?
- Were you able to find agreement?

Note: David finds it helpful to remind students when playing this game (usually in improv class) that making a strong choice in acting is not as simple as playing an archetype or an emotional state. These choices are acceptable in improv, where the goal isn't building layered, complex characters over time, but rather, making bold, instantaneous choices. Back in acting class, leave these choices behind, in favor of the richer, fully motivated choices that acting requires.

Appendix E

Initiate, Copy, Heighten

Have the group stand in a line, side by side. One person steps forward and begins a simple, repeatable activity. For instance, lifting an imaginary spoon from an imaginary bowl to their mouth, as if eating a bowl of soup (sounds may be included, but no language should be used). They simply repeat the activity over and over without adding anything to it. (Simple choices are best. They need not be funny, clever, or even interesting; actually a seemingly "dull" choice like eating soup works well.) Another possibility is to initiate with an unrecognizable activity such as waving your hand rapidly in front of your face or hopping on one leg while squawking. The important thing is that ANY choice is valid, so long as it is repeatable.

Once the choice has been established, a second person steps forward and joins in by copying the activity. The goal for this person is to mimic (not mock) the first person as closely as possible. We now have two people doing the same thing.

A third person steps forward and joins in by performing a heightened version of the existing activity. Simple ways to heighten the activity include doing it bigger, louder, faster, and so on. Another way to heighten is by raising the emotional stakes. For instance, if the third soup eater eats her soup while sobbing, an interesting scenario has been established.

The whole thing is completed in a matter of seconds. Once the "heighten" choice is apparent, you may call out, "Next." Those three students return to the line while someone else begins a brand new initiation. Make sure students are eventually contributing to each of the three phases (i.e., not always supplying the heightening).

The first player takes a risk, the second player supports that choice, and the third player adds to it. Through repetition, agreement (copying), and adding to what has been established (heightening), three players build something *together*, sharing the responsibility. This exercise nurtures:

- Agreement.
- Listening and observation – the ability to take in a partner and build upon their choice.
- Working as an ensemble toward a group goal.

Discussion:

- Did you tend to initiate, copy, or heighten? Or did you do all three equally?
- Were you able to step out to initiate without a preconceived idea, trusting that your partners would support whatever choice came to you in the moment?
- Would you have supported any of the initiations, or did you find yourself judging some as more worthy than others?

Appendix F

Going on a Picnic

The group sits in a circle; they're all going on a picnic. The first person states their name, and then what item they're bringing to the picnic – the item must start with the first letter of the person's name, for example, "I'm going on a picnic and I'm bringing Sofiya and her strawberries." The next person must repeat what the person(s) before them have stated they're bringing, and then add themselves and their item to the list, and so on. For example, if two people have gone and we're up to Catleen, she might say, "I'm going on a picnic and I'm bringing Sofiya and her strawberries, Marisela and her marshmallows, and Catleen and her cashews." Picnic nurtures:

- Listening and staying in the moment, which promotes actually experiencing an event instead of skipping ahead to a "goal."
- Memory: if I'm truly listening and experiencing a partner's offer fully, I'm more likely to remember. If, however, I'm pre-planning and thinking ahead, I'll miss the offer, create anxiety, and be disconnected from my partners. And I'm certainly not present, nor am I in the moment.
- Collaboration: the entire group needs what I have to offer at this moment.

Discussion:

- If someone forgot what a person was bringing, why? What was blocking them?
- Did people tend to forget the person/item that came directly before them? This can be a sign of pre-planning when it was nearly their turn, making them disconnect from the listening process.
- What memory skills did they employ that helped them to remember? Having a specific image for each food item, or. . . ?
- Was anyone so focused on getting it right that they forgot that everyone was there for them, wanting to offer collaborative support?

Appendix G

Syllables of Your Name with Gesture

Each student creates a specific physical action that is meaningful to them for each syllable of their name, and then practices saying their name with those physical actions. For example: Julie might become "Ju (with hands pressed together, and crouched position) – lie (rising up with arms spread wide)." Have the group stand in a circle, and follow a similar structure as "Picnic." The first person introduces themselves with their name and gestures; the second person repeats that, then adds their own. The third person repeats the previous two, and then adds their own, and so forth. "Syllables" nurtures:

- Vulnerability: expressing one's name in a physical context can ignite worries about looking "silly." It also reveals feelings about self and identity.
- Physical connection and awareness; relationship of the body to memory and self.
- Visual memory: how is remembering what you see different from what you hear (if at all?)?
- Observation: how accurate is the representation of your partner's offer?
- Communication: sharing one's personal perspective of one's identity through physical and vocal dynamics.

Discussion:

- How did you feel when you created your physical and vocal expression? Were you censoring yourself? What helped you to be free?
- What specifically helped you to remember someone's physical expression?
- What got in your way of taking in your partner's offer? Were you observing and listening to those around you, or were you pre-planning what choice you would make?

Appendix H

Why Were You Late?

This is a simple improvisation. Have two people stand together before the group. Supply them with the premise that they have arrived late to class and that they are to jointly make up a lie explaining why they were late. Students love this premise because it is one they all have experience with. Doing it jointly, on the spot, gives it an element of fun by heightening the likelihood that they will be "caught." Tell them to always agree with each other and to take turns speaking, building upon what the other says. They are never to throw their partner "under the bus" by blaming them; stick together. You may also suggest this tip: no matter how odd, elaborate, or unlikely your lie, tell it convincingly. Then you begin by asking them, "Why were you late?" The replies usually have a natural life of a minute or two before wrapping up on their own. If they're too short or too long, you can prompt the players to offer more or to wrap it up. If the students are struggling, you can prompt them with more specific questions based on what they've already established. Why Were You Late focuses on:

- Not thinking ahead, but listening to your partner and picking up their signals.
- Agreement.
- Being generous to your partner.
- Sharing focus, taking turns.
- Trust.
- Risk taking.

Discussion:

- Were you able to stay with your partner or did you think ahead and miss something they said?
- Were you generous in supporting the offers from your partner, or did you push your ideas?
- Did you share the focus, taking turns?

Appendix I

Multiple Pattern Juggling

This exercise provides a healthy mental challenge and forces individuals to look beyond their own agenda. Everyone must share an equal responsibility for the patterns continuing or one or more will be dropped.

Participants stand in a circle. One person initiates by looking at another person and saying a word to that person, for example, "banana." The receiver of "banana" free associates on that word and says a new word, perhaps "apple," to a new person. This continues until the last remaining participant says their word to the person who initiated the sequence; the cycle is complete. Once a word is chosen, that word may not be selected by anyone else. For instance, if the first player says, "banana," then no one else may choose that word. This is true for additional layers of the game as well. Now have them repeat this pattern several times. They'll say the exact same word to the exact same person each time.

Once they have this pattern memorized through repetition, have them create a brand new pattern using completely different words. A different person should initiate the second pattern and everyone should avoid sending their new word to the same person they sent it to in the first pattern. Again, have them repeat this pattern, exactly, until they have it memorized. Let's say the second pattern begins with "Honda," followed by "BMW," and so on.

At this point, we have established two patterns: a fruit pattern and an auto manufacturer pattern. Now challenge them to keep both patterns going at the same time. Start with the fruit pattern and once it has gone all the way around, have them continue repeating it while the auto manufacturer pattern is added.

To ensure that neither pattern is dropped, every time a member says one of their words, they must watch and listen to make sure that the receiver received it and continued the pattern. For instance, if Matt says "banana" to Vanessa and he doesn't see or hear her say "apple" to Monica, then Matt keeps repeating "banana" to Vanessa until he sees and hears her say "apple" to Monica. He doesn't merely say his word and go back to waiting for his next word. Matt stays fully vested in making sure the patterns continue beyond him. The key to success is in the members seeing beyond their obvious individual responsibilities (which is to wait for the two words coming at them, and say the words that follow to the next person in each pattern). Matt will likely worry that if he's busy repeating "banana" to Vanessa, he will miss Maretta saying "Toyota" to him in the other pattern. He must learn to trust that Maretta will repeat "Toyota" until he is able to receive it. Repeating a word essentially puts the pattern into an active "hold," so that nothing is ever dropped.

Additional variations:

After some practice, groups become quite proficient. Here is a list of ways to keep increasing the challenge:

- Add additional patterns.
- Add a pattern that uses sounds instead of words.
- Add a physical pattern such as throwing a ball instead of saying words.
- Once several patterns are being successfully juggled, have the members mix up their order on the circle and see if they can still do it.
- Once several patterns are being successfully juggled, have the members face outward from the circle so they can't see each other and must rely on listening alone.

Multiple Pattern Juggling nurtures:

- Communication skills.
- Support: it compels each member not only to send a clear message, but to make sure that it was received and passed along.

- The ability to monitor several shifting points of focus at one time, a boost to listening skills.
- Memory itself, and how it works.

Discussion:

- How did you remember words? What associations did you make? Were they physical/visual, intellectual, or. . . ?
- What happened if your partner wasn't ready to receive your word from you? How did you strengthen your offer and support in that moment?
- What did you notice as far as relaxation, anxiety, trust? Did you have confidence in your ability to remember the pattern, or did worry intercede?
- What if anything blocked your ability to remember your words in the pattern?

Appendix J

Walk and Rename Objects (Keith Johnstone)

Have the class walk (silently) about the room; encourage them to take up as much space as possible. Note who is looking at the floor, who is walking with hunched shoulders, who seems to doubt that they know *how* to walk (shuffling, stopping frequently), who is sending their energy out to others, and so on. Observe how they fill the room with their energy – or do they? Give them a few moments to find their centers and for you to observe before giving them instructions. Then ask them to point to any object in the room and rename it out loud – they can call it anything except what that object *literally* is, for example, a chair is a "flower," a backpack is a "sofa," and so on. They can point to light switches and fixtures and other physical elements of the room. Side-coach them to rename as many objects as possible. At some point, have them pause from renaming, but continue to walk in the room. Ask if they notice anything about the room itself. Has anything grown smaller, larger? Then have them begin the renaming process again, with new names even for objects they've already "christened." Eventually call to go to neutral.

This is particularly useful for students who lack focus, are easily distracted, struggle to move beyond literal ideas, and lack awareness of their environment and the space around them. Renaming nurtures:

- Awareness of one's physical environment. What surrounds them? What are the things they walk past every day? How do those surroundings present opportunities to play?

- Observation skills. Everything that surrounds an actor is an opportunity: Renaming broadens awareness and compels them to take ownership of everything they encounter.
- Imagination, and commitment to one's imaginative choices. It helps those who have spent less time with their own imaginations because of limited group play in their lives.
- Trust. It develops the unfiltered instinct for actors to share their first choices without judgment or criticism.

Discussion:

- What did they notice about the environment and its contents when the exercise was over? It's not uncommon to hear a student say, "I've been in this room countless times – but I've never noticed that blue chair/light switch/dent in that door. Where have I been?" This leads to great discussions about awareness, observation, looking vs. seeing, focus, concentration, and how the lack of these things can lead to missed opportunities.
- How do they relate to those physical items? How comfortable were they in taking ownership of their relationship to the "new" objects and to the space itself?
- How did renaming objects, in effect proclaiming its new identity, make them feel about the space itself? Did the space feel larger? Smaller? Did they simply "notice" more of their surroundings?
- Did they struggle to let go of what the object literally was? Did their literal mind block their imaginative impulses? If they're struggling with believing that a chair can be a tulip, what will they do when creating a character whose personality traits and actions are different from who they are? How can they commit to transformation?

Appendix K

Pass the Snap (Viola Spolin)

Have the players move about the space in a silent, neutral manner. You also move throughout the space while continually snapping your fingers on one hand. As you do so, explain that the snap represents where the focus is and that this exercise is about sharing the focus. Tell them that you will make eye contact with someone and initiate a pass of the snap. In that exchange, you will stop snapping and the person you've connected with through eye contact will take over the snapping, without missing a beat in the snapping rhythm. This person now continues to walk and snap, thereby holding the focus, until they choose to pass it. Make it clear to those who do not have the focus that their job is to *support* the focus, not look to claim it. Have them continue moving, silently, passing the snap to each other until each person has held the focus a couple of times. Then institute a "three second rule" in which no player may hold the focus for more than three seconds. This begins a round of fast passes where the players must work together to keep the focus clear and create clear, distinct, crisp passes.

Once this has been satisfactorily explored, take a break to allow them to discuss the experience. Then start again, but announce that the focus will no longer be defined by snapping. Choose someone and say, "Madison will begin with the focus and make a choice as to how she will communicate that. When she's ready, she will pass it. Each player may explore their own way of communicating that they have the focus." Once it begins, stop it periodically to see if everyone agrees on who has the focus at that moment. Snap nurtures:

- Making connections.
- Awareness: what is happening physically, spatially, where there is an opportunity.
- Being present and being generous with each other.
- Working as an ensemble toward a group goal.
- Communicating clearly.

Discussion:

- Were you able to follow the focus? If not, why not? What obstacles did you observe?
- When you chose your own way to communicate the focus, did people seem to understand your intent? If not, what could you have done differently?
- How does this apply to your work as an actor?

Appendix L

Kitty Wants a Corner

Participants stand in a circle with one member in the center as Kitty. Kitty approaches someone asking, "Kitty wants a corner?" seeking to exchange places with them. The participant responds by saying "No," and Kitty moves on to the next person asking, "Kitty wants a corner?" and so on. While this is happening, other members of the circle are trying to find someone to switch places with them. They do this by making eye contact, using it to establish silent agreement (without gestures or head nods), then they swiftly exchange places. As each player leaves their space, heading toward the other's space, they temporarily leave a vacancy on the circle. If Kitty gets to one of the vacancies before the other person does, then the person who lost their spot becomes the new Kitty, and they begin asking for a corner, and so on.

In early rounds, require that the person Kitty is asking to give up their spot must always say "No." After you've done several rounds, then allow those in the circle to say "Yes" to Kitty if they choose. Kitty nurtures:

- Empathy and vulnerability. Eye contact is required, and then a silent agreement must be made. What was communicated in those exchanges? How intimate was it? How did they feel if they "left someone out to dry" because they committed, and then reneged on the commitment and your partner became the new Kitty? Did they experience the frustrations and victories of another Kitty's journey, as well as the journeys of those around the circle?
- Communication and connection.
- Trust. Partners silently communicate a willingness to commit and support their partner. If they fail, the consequence is to become Kitty – if that's the worst part of your day, it's not so bad, is it? Students start to tease apart imagined consequences from actual ones, and within that, trust themselves and each other more.
- Physical, psychic, and visual awareness.
- Risk taking. It's risky to look into someone else's eyes, risky to make an agreement without words, risky when you must rely on another person, and trust that person to honor their commitment to you and to the moment.
- Confidence. Was Kitty so prepared for rejection that they missed a "Yes" during that round? Were they muttering under their breath "I'll never find a corner," thereby missing an opportunity that happened immediately to their side? Kitty encourages following through on commitments, and taking risks via committing builds confidence.

Discussion:

- What communication skills did they have to employ? Did they struggle with making eye contact? What did the term "silent agreement" come to mean to them and how did they know when they had achieved it?
- How much did the group find themselves "rooting" for Kitty or exchangers as a move was being made? Why? How does empathy play a role in that?
- How sensitive did the group become to one another's energy? Did they notice that they could "sense" someone about to move before they did, that they felt their energy rise?

Appendix M

The Name Game

The players stand in a circle. It starts with a player, let's call her Karen, looking across the circle and making eye contact with someone else, Collin. At the same time, she says, "Collin?" Collin must respond by saying, "Yes." Essentially, Karen is asking Collin for permission to take his spot on the circle and Collin agrees to give it. Once she has permission, she begins walking toward Collin. Collin now must seek permission from someone else, so that he can vacate his existing space for the approaching Karen. He makes eye contact with Marge and says, "Marge?" Marge replies, "Yes," at which point Collin begins walking toward Marge. As Collin begins walking, the spot he occupied on the circle becomes vacant. When Karen reaches it, she rejoins the circle and waits for someone else to call her name. This process continues – Collin takes Marge's spot, and so on. The idea is for the group to maintain a smoothly flowing perpetual motion machine. Encourage them to walk slowly, thus not rushing the next person (pressuring them). It's about supporting your partner(s).

It is common to have difficulty in the early going as players get the hang of it. Here are issues that you will encounter: players forget to say "Yes." They walk toward someone before actually hearing their "Yes"; or begin walking without having established eye contact. One of the most common missteps is after having said "Yes," a player begins walking toward the player they just said "Yes" to, rather than finding a new person. That is, they attempt to switch with the person who called their name.

This exercise demonstrates to the players how we tend to work and respond as individuals, even in a group setting. We exhibit behaviors that benefit the individual. It also reveals players who feel a need to be "right." They are so eager to fulfill the instruction correctly, that they act alone rather than connecting to the others. This drive can make them blind to choices and behavior that the group requires. Fortunately, with gentle reminders from you, everyone is able to adjust and in a matter of minutes, the machine begins flowing smoothly as individual behaviors give way to behaviors that support the group.

After a few more minutes, the players are likely to have "solved" the challenge and may look somewhat bored. At this point, it's helpful to offer a character adjustment or "as if." You might tell them to continue the exercise as if they were all pirates or as if they have just won the lottery. The exercise becomes fun again as they all enjoy playing the adjustment. The language tends to change (from "Yes" to "Arrrr, aye aye, matey!" in a southern accent, and so on), as does the physicality. The structure of the perpetual motion machine continues to run smoothly for the most part.

When a glitch occurs, the players almost seamlessly support each other and make adjustments to keep the machine on track. After offering two or three "as ifs," pause the exercise. Ask for a volunteer who has a suggestion for a new "as if." Instead of having them announce their choice, let them begin the exercise with it. Instruct all the others to agree with the choice and all continue with the new "as if." In addition, tell them that the "as if" can change, in the moment, if someone feels the impulse to establish a new "as if." The only caveat is that each "as if" must be continued by a minimum of three players before it can change. In this way, no choice is abandoned too soon, and no one is made to feel that their choice went unsupported. If a player establishes a wholly original "as if" (that is, one unrecognizable to the others), sometimes another player will freeze, unsure of how to proceed. The answer is to simply copy (mirror) the choice as closely as possible. In this way, players realize that it isn't necessary to understand a choice in order to support it. Soon the players are connected, living moment to moment, actively playing a shared choice, and silently adjusting to impulses, initiations, changes, and glitches. The Name Game nurtures:

- Not thinking ahead, but listening to your partner and picking up their signals.
- Being present, in the moment.
- Agreement.
- Communicating ideas clearly.
- Being open and sensitive to the energy of the group.
- Working as an ensemble toward a group goal.

Discussion:

- Initially, were you able to wait for your partner's response of "Yes" before proceeding?
- Did you have difficulty communicating or understanding any of the "as ifs"?
- Were you able to see your work in terms of how it affected the group activity and other players?
- Did someone try a response other than "Yes"? What happened to the flow of the game? What happened to the focus?
- How did you feel when you thought you might not "get a space"?
- How did you feel when you observed others trying to make contact with someone, only to be "shaken off"?
- Did you "speed up"? If so, why? Did that put pressure on your partner to vacate the spot quickly? (Slowing down shows an awareness of your partner and the willingness to adjust as a means of support.)

Appendix N

Mindfulness Awareness Practice (as based on the teachings of Pema Chodron)

Start with the space. An acting room with a lot of clutter all around isn't supportive. Roger teaches meditation in a wide, open airy room. He's lucky. Try your best to get the room as uncluttered as possible. It doesn't have to be huge; a feeling of spaciousness can be achieved with a tidy area. Be sure not to have mirrors in front of the students, as the temptation for distraction will be great.

Encourage students to purchase a Zafu. A Zafu is a cushion that allows the students to sit more comfortably. A buckwheat Zafu offers more comfort, and one with a removable cotton cover can be washed. Zafus are also great to use in deepening a stretch across the chest and can be used in other voice and movement classes.

We all come with different aches and pains, so be sure to assess the physical abilities of each of your students. First, ask your students to sit cross-legged on the Zafu. That's ideal, but again, if somebody has physical limitations, then a chair is great. Meditation is not punishment. Once they are seated, have them reach back and pull the cheeks of their rear open on both sides so they're resting on their sitting bones with the rectum slightly open. The torso is upright, straight, and relaxed. Keep a watchful eye for students who are thrusting their spine forward. The shoulders are relaxed. The main thing here is that the chest is open. Forward. Available. The belly is released, no sucking in or holding of the abdominal muscles. The palms can be resting down on the knees, or palms up with the index fingers meeting the thumbs in what is called Guyan Mudra.

The eyes are open, so the student is fully in contact with reality, right now, as it is occurring. They are open, and their gaze is down toward the floor, about four to six feet in front of the student. The gaze toward the floor is part of the practice, and not to be confused with the habit of a downward gaze as a result of excessive smartphone use. The mouth is slightly open.

Encourage the student to do a check-in. Where are they right now? What are they bringing to the cushion this morning? And can they have a moment of unconditional kindness for themselves? Encourage the check-in along with an acknowledgment of where the day has brought them so far. This is what they have and they are bringing it to the cushion in that moment.

Bring their attention to the breath. Nobody has to take deep gulps or count to ten on each inhale and exhale. The breath will do its thing, and deepen over time. Focus particularly on the out breath. When they are exhaling, bring their awareness fully to that exhale.

The mind is going to move with an endless array of chatter, especially if this is a student's first time meditating. It's comical to hear a meditation teacher say, "Clear your mind." Instruct your students that each time they catch themselves moving away from the breath and their mind wanders, silently label it "thinking," bring the focus back to the breath. What's important here is that the label of "thinking" be gentle, non-judgmental. Kindness toward oneself is what we're encouraging. Thoughts are like clouds in the sky. Encourage the students to witness themselves thinking, nicely call it such, and then come back to the breath. The open, vast blue sky is what our mind is, and the clouds are all the thoughts coming and going. Some days it is clear as day up there, other days it's a Category 5 hurricane. Some days it's possible to notice the mind within seconds of floating off to some conversation or fight or work situation. Other days, the timer will go off and 15 minutes have flown by without one moment of being with the breath. Let your students know it's okay, and to be compassionate with themselves. These thoughts and emotions are going to arise; encourage the students to allow them to. And then, upon witnessing the mind's chatter, let them go as well. A student may say, "As soon as I label 'thinking' and let the thought go, the very next second a new thought pops up, or even worse, the same one!" Encourage them not to label their thoughts "good" or "bad," or "right" or "wrong." Simply reassure them it's all part of the process. When Roger first started out with this practice, he would joke that his mind was on one continual loop of, "Thinking, thinking, thinking, thinking!!"

Initially start with a small duration of time; we suggest three minutes. In Roger's Kundalini class he guides the students in a three-minute meditation for the first 3–4 weeks. He gradually adds to the time period, and by semester's end builds up to twenty to thirty minutes. We suggest assigning a daily meditation on your syllabus as part of the class assignments. A plain, old digital timer is best, as it takes the temptation away from checking their phone or tablet. Roger uses a meditation app on his iPhone (oh, the irony) that adds Tibetan Singing Bowls at the start and finish of the meditation. If a student chooses to use a meditation app when meditating at home, remind them to keep their device on airplane mode.

Experience has shown that students will want to fidget. A lot. Of course, if they are in pain, let them move. It's not meditation hostage time; however, fidgeting is often a distraction from being still with whatever is arising. In your discussion afterward, encourage them to stay still in their practice a few more seconds before moving. And if they have to move, move consciously, maintaining their focus on the breath. Mindfulness Awareness Practice nurtures:

- Being present in the moment.
- Self-awareness.
- Acknowledgment of one's surroundings.
- Stress and worry reduction.
- Concentration.

- Emotional well-being.
- Focus and attention.

Discussion:

- What came to the surface during your meditation? Any recurring thoughts?
- Was it challenging, both physically and mentally?
- Were you able to last the whole three minutes?
- Are you taking time to start each day with the practice?
- Are you noticing any changes in your day-to-day routine, focus, sleep, retention, and commitments from your daily practice?
- Keep a daily journal and share your experiences with meditation both on and off the cushion.

You'll hear some incredible feedback here, and most often the students will increase the time by a few minutes on their own.

Appendix O

Meisner's Repetition Exercise

Have the students close their eyes and listen to the sounds all around them: in the room, the hallway, outside. Have them mentally take note of all the sounds they hear. After a minute or so, ask them to share some of the sounds they heard. Then ask, "Were you *really* listening?" They'll most likely unanimously respond with "yes." Have them do another exercise: ask them to multiply two numbers in their heads without using paper and pen. For example, 684 × 348. Don't give them longer than one minute. In all likelihood, nobody will have the correct answer. Who cares? Whether they are right or wrong is irrelevant. What's important is the actual *doing*. Again, ask them, "Were you *really* multiplying? Were you *really* doing it?" Some may confess to have given up. Remind them it's always okay to fail, but never okay to stop trying.

Next, ask the students to repeat exactly what you say. For example, you may say, "I want a cup of coffee"; ask them to repeat that back, and do that a few times with different phrases.

Next, break them in to pairs, with each pair sitting in their individual chairs, facing one another. Have each set of pairs look at their partner, and make concrete observations about their partner. Nothing opinionated, stay to the facts. For example, "She is wearing a white scarf." Have them make a list in their minds of these concrete observations. Let them do that for about 30 seconds. Afterward, have them share some of their observations. Listen for phrases like, "She has beautiful eyes," or, "His beard needs to be trimmed." At this early stage, encourage them to stay with non-disputable facts versus opinions.

Call two students up to the playing area. Have them face one another about six feet apart, arms relaxed at the sides. No hands in pockets or arms crossed in front. Have student A make a concrete observation about student B, and student B repeat exactly what they heard student A say. Then student A repeats exactly what they heard student B say, and continue that way. For example, A might say, "You have on a green shirt." B replies, "You have on a green shirt." A replies back, "You have on a green shirt." Whatever one partner hears the other partner say, they repeat. There are no new pieces of concrete facts injected into the exercise at this stage. Students may feel the need to become louder or stress certain words to add variety. Discourage that behavior. Be sure they're allowing each other to finish what each person is saying before the next person speaks, otherwise how can they repeat if it hasn't been said yet? Notice if the students take long pauses, and instruct them to respond immediately. The brain has no place in this exercise. It's a ping-pong game. Let the exercise continue for a few minutes, and then begin again with student B initiating.

Anyone who has ever done Meisner training knows how thrilling this first day is. This beginning exercise immediately focuses and connects the partners to one another. It brings them actively listening in to the present moment. This exercise is conducted on the first day of a two-year training program at The Neighborhood Playhouse, where Sanford Meisner developed his technique. The technique goes into much more depth, but never without the tenets of this foundation. For more information on the full Meisner training, check out the work of Bill Esper, Larry Silverberg, and, of course, Sanford Meisner. Meisner's Repetition Exercise nurtures:

- Listening.
- Focus and awareness.
- Empathy.
- Vulnerability.
- Eye contact.
- Connection to one's partner.
- Impulses.
- Spontaneity.
- Being present in the moment.

Discussion:

- Was the direct gaze of another person uncomfortable?
- Did you find yourself fidgeting, crossing your arms in front of the chest, rocking back and forth, avoiding eye contact?

- Were you bored?
- Did you look for new things instead of simply repeating what your partner offered?

Appendix P

Kundalini yoga exercise set for balancing the head and the heart (as based on the teachings of Yogi Bhajan)

The head is where logic lives and the heart is where feelings live. When these two parts of the body begin to work in balance with one another, a greater sense of security, grounding, and presence is generated.

Before any Kundalini yoga set, it is important to warm the body up in order to engage in the rigorous physical demands of the work. There are many specific ways to do this in Kundalini yoga, and we encourage each teacher to discover those exercises they feel best bring the student to a place of readiness. Here is one example of a warm-up.

Students sit cross-legged, preferably on a cushion of some sort. A pillow or Zafu is best, as the elevation allows for a more comfortable seated posture. All the breathing in Kundalini yoga is done through the nose unless otherwise specified. Close the eyes, and focus them up, about half an inch above the center of the eyebrows right above the bridge of the nose. This upward gaze causes a pressure above that stimulates the pituitary gland, which is known as the "master gland" as it regulates many other glands in the body. Take a deep breath in through the nose, hold that breath for a moment, and then completely exhale all the breath out by pulling the navel in toward the spine for a thorough exhale. Then inhale completely again, exhale completely again. This is done a total of three times.

Bring the hands together in prayer pose, with the palms meeting and the thumbs pressed into the sternum at the heart center. Briskly rub them together in an up and down motion. The movement will generate a lot of heat. Do this for ten seconds. After ten seconds, stop the movement, inhale deeply, hold the breath for a few seconds, then exhale completely.

Keep the hands still in front of the heart center in prayer pose. All Kundalini yoga begins with chanting the mantra "Ong Namo Guru Dev Namo." Inhale through the nose, then chant "Ong Namo." The "a" is short and the "o" is long in "Namo." Be sure to vibrate "ng" in the back of the throat, as if holding onto the last sound of "sing" for approximately five seconds. Then inhale through the mouth, lips puckered, as if sucking the air through a straw. Fill the lungs up, then chant "Guru Dev Namo." The "r" in "Guru" is pronounced like a "d" with the tip of the tongue striking the alveolar ridge. Both of the "u" sounds in "Guru" are long. The mantra translates to, "I call upon the infinite creative teacher within me to move me from darkness to light." Repeat three times.

Lower the hands to rest on the knees with the palms facing up and the index fingers touching the thumbs in a hand position called Guyan Mudra. The spine is straight, not rigid, with a slight tuck to the chin. The eyes remain closed with an upward focus. This is called Easy Pose. Lower the chin to the chest. Begin rotating the head counter-clockwise in a circle. Inhale as the left ear moves toward the left shoulder, continue to inhale as head moves up toward the ceiling. When the nose faces the ceiling, begin to exhale, coming down on the right side. The right ear moves toward the right shoulder, and the chin moves toward the chest. Inhale up to the left, exhale down on the right. Do this for 30 seconds, and then change direction for another 30 seconds. This time inhale up to the right, exhale down the left. When done, inhale deeply, and return to Easy Pose.

Stomach Churn. In Easy Pose, hold on to the knees. Arch the back so the spine looks like the letter "C," with arms straight. Keep hold of the knees. Inhale, and as if making a circle with the waist, begin to move the torso counter-clockwise in a circular motion. The arms will bend with the circular motion. When the chest faces completely forward, exhale as the circle continues on the left side until at the initial letter "C" position. At which point, repeat the movement and breath. Think about the movement occurring underneath the ribcage, a grinding motion. Thirty seconds. Repeat on the other side, moving clockwise. Inhale coming up on the left, exhale coming down on the right. When done, inhale deeply, and return to Easy Pose.

Spinal Flex. In Easy Pose, move the hands to hold the shins. Left hand on left shin, right hand on right shin. Inhale while pulling on the shins to bring the lower spine forward, opening up across the chest. There will be a curve of the spine at the lower vertebrae. Exhale and return to the initial position. It is a rhythmic movement – inhale forward, exhale back. Be mindful not to move the head up and down. Keep the chin stationary in the slightly tucked position of Easy Pose throughout. Continue for one minute. After one minute, inhale deeply, hold the breath for three seconds, exhale, and return to Easy Pose.

Cat/Cow. Begin on all fours. Inhale while bringing the chin up toward the ceiling. At the same time, scoop the buttocks toward the ceiling and the belly button toward the floor. Roger gives his students the image, "It's as if a very large person is sitting on your lower spine, pushing your belly down and your rear up."

Exhale while simultaneously bringing the chin to the chest and scoop the buttocks toward the floor. For this part of the exercise, Roger gives his students the image, "You should look like a Halloween cat on a pumpkin!" The movement is rhythmic. Continue for one minute. After the minute is up, inhale up into cow and hold the breath and posture for three seconds. Exhale down into cat, hold the breath out for three seconds. Inhale and return to Easy Pose.

Spinal Twist. In Easy Pose, bring the hands up to the shoulders. Right hand to right shoulder, left hand to left shoulder. With palms down, bring the four fingers to the front of the shoulder, the thumbs to the back. The arms are parallel to the floor, bent at the elbows. Inhale and twist the torso left, so the left elbow is trying to "look" at the wall behind it. Exhale and twist the torso right, this time with the right elbow trying to "look" at the wall behind it. Let the weight of the arms swing across the front of the chest, and allow for a deeper twist from side to side. Roger makes the analogy of this posture to the twisting device in the center of a washing machine. Inhale left, exhale right. Continue for one minute. After the minute is up, stop moving, face center, keep the arms and hands where they are, take a deep inhale. Hold for three seconds. Exhale, bring the hands down, and return to Easy Pose.

With the warm-up complete, you are now ready to begin Kundalini Yoga exercise set for balancing the head and the heart.

The following set is from the manual *Transitions to a Heart-Centered World Through the Kundalini Yoga and Meditations of Yogi Bhajan* by Gururattan Kaur Khalsa, Ph.D. and Ann Marie Maxwell. The manual is rich with various sets and meditations to bring students to a vital, connected, and creative state of being.

This exercise incorporates movement that will be done on a count. Begin in Easy Pose, with arms outstretched to the sides (parallel to the ground), hands bent up at wrists at a 90° angle, fingers together, palms facing out (1). On (2), rotate hands so that the fingers point straight forward. On (3), return them to the original position. On (4), rotate the pointing fingers straight back, moving rhythmically, one cycle in four seconds, for six to seven minutes. Inhale in first and third positions, exhale in second and fourth.

As before, arms straight out to the sides (parallel) palms out (1). Inhale and raise arms in an arch, palms crossing each other slightly in front of the top of head, without touching each other (2). Return arms to outstretched position on exhale (3). Inhaling, arch arms overhead, palms up as before, but slightly behind top of the head (4). Continue the cycle for one to two minutes.

Continuing the arm movements of the previous exercise, now add Crow Squats. Stand up, feet a little wider than hip length apart, arms above the head. As you exhale and squat down, bring the arms out to the sides, parallel to the ground. Try not to bend forward at the waist on the way down. Keep the spine erect with the gaze forward, not looking down to the ground. Inhale and stand up, arms overhead. Continue for three to four minutes at about one per second.

The first exercise in this set becomes very challenging in a short time. The students will want to place their arms down and rest quite quickly. Encourage them to get curious about the discomfort and to stay with the exercise. In between each of the exercises, come to Easy Pose and rest for two minutes.

After the last exercise, rest in Easy Pose for one to two minutes before instructing the students to lie on their backs, hands by their side, palms facing up, for anywhere from 5 to 11 minutes. This is called Savasana, or Corpse Pose. When the time is up, hug the knees into the chest, and rock back and forth along the spine at least five times, from the soles of the feet to top of the base of the head. Rock back up to Easy Pose and meditate for at least three minutes. Mindfulness Awareness Practice may be used (see Appendix N), or another meditation from the Kundalini manual. When the whole session is finished, including warm-up, exercise, rest, and meditation, return to Easy Pose and chant "Sat Nam." Inhale through the nose, then chant a long "Sat" for about 10 seconds. The "a" sounds like the "u" in "but." On the same breath, chant a very short "Nam." Kundalini Yoga nurtures:

- The nervous system.
- Mental clarity and focus.
- The endocrine system.
- Physical vitality and energy.
- Brain chemistry.
- A deeper connection with the breath and consciousness.
- A relationship with discomfort.

Discussion:

- What were some of your thoughts during the exercises?
- Did you keep up with the entire set without taking a break?
- Did you find yourself becoming emotional? Were you able to allow the emotion to come up?
- How do you feel after the work versus before you started?
- What relationship might Kundalini have to your acting?

Appendix Q

Blindfold Series: The Cobra (Augusto Boal)

The group stands in a tight circle. Have them put on blindfolds, turn to their right, and place their hands on the shoulders and back of the neck of the person now directly in front of them. They explore the back of the head, the neck, and shoulders of the person they're touching. Encourage them to be specific in their tactile observations – don't stop the observation at a ponytail (as several people may be wearing ponytails).

Allow a minute or so for observation, then call for the group to break the circle and move out into the space "bumper car style" (arms folded across the chest, no hands or fingertips protruding straight out into the air where someone can get their eyes poked). After you see the group has shuffled their order, call a freeze, then ask them to *reform* the circle in its exact order without talking or using sound. When they find the person they had explored, they should place their hands on their shoulders to connect that part of the circle, as that person may still need to find *their* person, and so on. It continues until the circle has completely re-linked. Once the circle has reformed, call a hold, ask everyone to drop their hands, remove the blindfolds, and see if they have re-formed the circle.

Remind participants that when they encounter someone during the seeking phase, they can break the bumper car pose to carefully examine the partner's neck, back of head, and so on. If they know who their partner is, discourage them from examining another part of the body that would confirm identity ("I know Helen was next to me, and she was wearing that bracelet with the knot work; I'll just identify that!"). Instruct them to allow others to explore their head, shoulders, etc. (unless there is already a person attached to their shoulders) to support everyone in their search.

You'll also have several reformed "segments," with the person at the head of each segment still seeking *their* partner. Once someone has found their partner and placed hands on their shoulders and back of neck, be sure they don't drop their hands/arms. This will guide those who are still seeking to know that this link is complete (many hands will swiftly move over the shoulders and arms of a specific link, looking for its end to see if their person is there). You may also need to keep encouraging those at the head of a segment to keep moving to find their partner, but at such a pace that everyone behind them can keep up. The Cobra nurtures:

- Heightened awareness of the five senses (sight, sound, touch, taste, smell).
- Heightened awareness of a "sixth sense"; that is, energy fields of the unseen people.
- Heightened awareness of environment.
- Listening.
- Trust.
- Attention to detail; observation.
- Vulnerability.

Discussion:

- What details did you notice about your partner?
- What did you notice about your senses, particularly hearing and touch?
- How did you feel when you found your partner? Did you confront any doubts that you actually *had* found your partner? If so, why?
- What were some obstacles you faced in pursuit of your objective?
- What tactics did you use?
- How aware were you of time passing?
- How well did you trust your observations of your partner?

In discussion, note who is self-defeating ("I just knew I would be the last to find my partner" – they're playing their obstacle) and who identifies actions they took that helped them find their partner (playing their objective)."

You will rarely have a greater experience than the moment when the circle has reformed, and everyone removes their blindfolds. The joy and sense of accomplishment is a beautiful thing to witness. For young actors, it's a moment of discovering how much they're capable of with the support of the ensemble. For mature actors, they discover that despite years of practical application, the wonder and beauty of what's achievable with the collaboration of an ensemble is still what it's all about.

Hunter and Hunted

Two participants are blindfolded; one is given a rolled-up newspaper and becomes The Hunter, the other is The Hunted. All other participants go to the walls or edges of the room to become spotters. The objective of The Hunter is to tap The Hunted with the rolled-up newspaper before they escape. The Hunted's objective is to escape. If your room has an easily accessible door, The Hunted must make it to the door, open it, and begin their exit (obviously, they should stop before walking down the hallway!). If there are dangerous level shifts in the floors of your room, or too much junk for the number of spotters available to you, you can also clear enough space for an open section of wall at the end of the room, and The Hunted's goal is to touch that wall to be "home free."

Spotters should be given a specific signal (two taps on the shoulder) to identify themselves to The Hunter/Hunted; they must otherwise be silent. If spotters are guarding a sharp edge or a protruding architectural element, and The Hunter/Hunted is in danger of bumping into it, the spotter taps, then gently turns them away from the danger. Be sure to announce in advance that spotters can't have "a horse in this race," that is, if they're rooting for The Hunter, they shouldn't turn The Hunted directly toward them. They should turn them away from any danger as neutrally as possible.

At the beginning, spin and place The Hunter and The Hunted appropriately in the room, and ask spotters to make noise and move around. Though all specific danger spots should be covered, encourage spotters to exchange places while they're making noise as you spin and place The Hunter/Hunted; this way the participants don't mark their place in the room by recognizing someone's voice ("I hear Ramona, and I know she was standing about five feet from the door. . ."). Lastly, tell The Hunter that if they find the door first, they can't block it as a tactic. It's more challenging to explore other options. Hunter/Hunted nurtures:

- The power of simple objectives.
- Heightened awareness of the five senses.

- Awareness of "sixth sense" (the energy fields and presence of others). As Peter Falk said in *Wings of Desire,* "I can't see you, but I know you're there.").
- Listening (which of course is also sensory awareness).
- Trust.
- Commitment.
- Simple conflicts. The clarity and simplicity of the conflict allows participants to engage in ways that they might struggle with without blindfolds. The blindfolds "erase" the imaginary audience, and intensify focus on actions and needs.

Discussion:

- Did Hunter/Hunted identify their tactics? What influenced those choices?
- Did they default to playing the obstacle vs. the objective ("I don't want to get caught" vs. "I want to escape")?
- What did Hunter/Hunted notice about their sensory awareness? About their listening and extrasensory skills in particular? Did they feel at some point that they could "see" or sense their opponent (or spotters)?
- What did they notice about their senses after they took the blindfolds off? What observations do they have about their reliance on sight in relationship to their other senses?
- What effect did the blindfold have on their focus, and ability to be present?

This is also a great exercise to focus on the role of the spectator. Many people say that Hunter/Hunted ranks as some of the most compelling theatre they've seen. The spotters are completely invested in every movement, every choice that Hunter/Hunted are making. The tension is *excruciating* as Hunted nears the door, or as they near the Hunter. Rose has witnessed spotters nearly *swoon* from giddy tension as they observe Hunted crouch low to the floor, as Hunter sweeps the rolled newspaper six inches above their head, missing them entirely. Ask: "Why were you so completely engaged?" Answers will range from the clarity of the conflict, to the depth of commitment of the Hunter/Hunted, to the primal nature of the exercise and the instinctual responses it triggers. Every human understands "to get" and "to escape"; these conflicts are ancient and universal, and trigger something deep within. Hunters/Hunteds describe that they *feel* the energy of the spotters. Inevitably you ask, "How can we strive to create that relationship between the story we're telling, and the audience we're telling it to, always?"

Appendix R

Digital Disconnect

The following series of documents and guidelines can be used as handouts and guides for students and teachers embarking on semester-long Digital Disconnect projects and policies.

Part I: Handout for Digital Disconnects

This document may be used in whole or in part as you initiate your own Digital Disconnect policies in your classes and programs. Teachers may add to or subtract from the lists of guiding questions for students to consider as they explore this assignment. We encourage teachers to include themselves in the project, practice their own Digital Disconnect, and complete their own Technology Log, at least once early in the semester.

THE HANDOUT

We are all training to be storytellers of the human experience, so we must fully experience all aspects of human behaviors, consistently and richly in our daily lives. We must heighten our awareness, and observe and experience our behaviors and those of others. Acting insists that we be present, mindful, spontaneous, connected with our community, connected to nature, and fully connected to our *own* human nature.

In the past ten years, social and behavioral sciences have been extensively studying how we use technology, and in particular, how we use smartphones. Actors can no longer afford to be uninvolved or unaware of the research and the information being revealed. We are swiftly moving from somewhat humorous stories about Benedict Cumberbatch pleading with his audiences to stop filming his performance of *Hamlet,* to alarming stories about the effects of excessive use of technology and its negative impact on a person's ability to be present and collaborative.

The work, life, and profession of an actor is profoundly vulnerable to the negative side effects of excessive technology use. Someone who is training to create truthful human behavior must be acutely connected to the human experience. There is no other side to that coin. Actors are the social anthropologists of the arts. Painters study the human form so they can express it artistically; actors study human behavior so they can create truth in imaginative circumstances. If a painter never looked at their own body or that of another's, they wouldn't be able to draw the human form as it truly exists. They might be able to create an *idea* of what they believe it to be – but without direct, personal experience of it, their work can't be fully realized. Likewise, an actor who removes themselves from face-to-face interaction and direct communal experiences won't be able to truly know what a human being behaves like. Those whose primary exposure to human behavior is filtered through a screen might believe that they're accurately studying people, but they would be missing a key ingredient that an actor needs in order to create another human being: empathy. That ability to understand and feel another person's pain or joy is diminished when it's filtered several generations down from the original behavior via screens.

The following policy and guidelines are based on extensive research and findings, as well as on far reaching conversations we've had with acting students and teachers. We are instituting this policy to help you investigate and discover your own patterns of use, and to help you develop healthy behaviors that support you in your work and in your daily life. As we review and discuss your discoveries together, these steps and policies may be subject to change in the months to come.

CELL PHONES IN THE CLASSROOM

- All cell phones must be turned off completely prior to every class. They will be checked in the appropriate plastic bins. Cell phones will *not* be used during the class break. They will be returned after the class has finished. If a student has an ongoing family emergency, the student can ask their teacher for their phone at break time.

    o An emergency is defined as a health condition with a family member, or a safety emergency that affects family members.
    o Checking a work or rehearsal schedule is *not* an emergency. Plan accordingly.

- If a student fails to turn off their phone and it rings or makes noise during the class, the student will receive a warning. If it happens a second time, the student will be prohibited from bringing the phone to the following class, and must leave it at home. No exceptions.
- No electronic devices will be permitted to be used during classes, except for specific assignments (if you have a compelling reason to use a device, please see your instructor immediately). Purchase a notebook; time will be set aside in classes for you to write your notes in longhand in your notebooks.

DIGITAL DISCONNECT POLICY

- All BFA acting students are required to completely turn off their cell phones for one full working day per week. A working day is defined as from 9:00 am until 6:00 pm. No texting, no checking for messages, no Internet, no exceptions. Your disconnect day will be scheduled by your current acting instructor depending on which year of the program you're in; that is, sophomores will all be assigned the same disconnect day, juniors will all share the same disconnect day, and so on. This is so your ensemble can experience the DD together, and verbally share your experiences and challenges throughout the day.

- o If you have a family emergency, you can request permission from your teacher prior to the start of the DD to carry your phone with you.
- o If you find that you've forgotten to notify a scene partner about a time change, or forgot to check your evening rehearsal schedule, that does not qualify as an emergency: that qualifies as poor planning. Plan accordingly.
- o You will write a journal/paper to detail your experiences during this nine-hour period and hand it in to your acting instructor at your next class meeting. Your instructors will tell you which format they prefer (an informal journal or more formal process paper).

- All BFA acting students will be required to turn off their cell phones completely for one full 24-hour period one day each month. Students may choose which day they will do this assignment.

- o You will write a journal/paper to detail your experiences during this 24-hour period and hand it in to your acting instructor at your next class meeting. Your instructors will tell you which format they prefer (an informal journal or more formal process paper). For example, if you choose Thursday, 17 September as your 24-hour Digital Disconnect day, and your next acting class is on Monday morning, you would write a report detailing your experiences of 17 September, and hand it in to your instructor on Monday 21 September.

DEFINITION OF DIGITAL DISCONNECT

- Smartphone, iPad, laptop, tablets, computer, and so on, are all turned off and put away. We encourage you not to carry them on your person during the Digital Disconnect time; you won't be using them, and it will help you avoid temptation.
- You cannot use another person's device for digital or online activities (that is, don't look for loopholes in the assignment by turning off your device and using one that belongs to someone *not* on a Digital Disconnect). All activities related to the use of your electronic devices such as texting, Internet searches, Facebook, and so on, are prohibited.
- If you work evenings or late at night, or drive long distances, of course, use common sense and carry your smartphone with you for safety purposes, even on a Digital Disconnect Day.

WRITTEN ASSIGNMENTS

- Journal entries/papers describing your experiences during the Digital Disconnect should be a minimum of one and a half to two pages in length. Please use the following questions as guidelines to respond to, especially in the early weeks of the assignment:

  o What did you notice during the time you were disconnected?

    ■ About your own behavior?
    ■ About the behavior of those around you?
    ■ About your environment?
    ■ About your relationships?

  o Did you notice any changes in your ability to focus, concentrate, or listen?
  o Were you aware of any shifts in your ability to be present and in the moment?
  o Did you notice anything about the amount of time you spent engaging in face-to-face exchanges or social activities?
  o How would you rate your skills of memory and retention?
  o Did you notice any changes in your sleep patterns?
  o Did you miss your device?
  o Did you experience any physical symptoms? (phantom vibrations, neck pain, hand strain?)
  o Did you find yourself "unconsciously" reaching for your smartphone at any time?
  o Did you experience any emotional response to not having your device available to you? Describe that in detail.
  o If you were not successful in completing your Digital Disconnect time, what was the reason you activated or used your device? Are any of the following statements (from previous students) relevant to your choice?

    ■ I forgot that I was on my Digital Disconnect.
    ■ I was afraid I was missing out on something important.
    ■ I had neglected to look up important information that I needed that day for an assignment before I started my DD.
    ■ I didn't want my friends to think I was ignoring them.
    ■ I was bored.
    ■ I needed to check the time.
    ■ My family was worried about not being able to reach me.
    ■ I thought the assignment was unnecessary.
    ■ I wanted to see if anyone had responded to something I had posted earlier on one of my social media accounts.
    ■ I wanted to take a picture of something I was doing and share it with a friend.

    o   If you were not able to successfully complete your Digital Disconnect, in retrospect, what might you have done to ensure your success?

- I could have worn my watch.
- Done better advance planning to make sure I had what I needed for any assignments/responsibilities for the DD day.
- Shared my thoughts/feelings with ensemble members who were also on their DD to get support.
- I could have reflected on why I was worried about missing out on things in order to gain perspective.
- I could have been more patient.

- When you hand in your first DD paper/assignment, you will also submit a Technology Log from a "typical" day of your use. Try not to purposely choose a day that you might be camping or playing sports, something that would reduce the amount of time you would normally spend using a device. Chart/log the amount of time spent: writing and sending texts, doing online research, online entertainment, checking social media accounts (Facebook, Instagram, Snapchat, etc.), gaming, watching Netflix, and any other activity that necessitates the use of your devices. There are also apps that you can get for your smartphone that will help you chart the number of hours you spend using that specific device.

- After the first three to four weeks of Digital Disconnects, we will be asking you to additionally consider the following questions in your written reports:

    o   What are some of the activities you did during your DD times?

    o   Would you have consistently been doing these activities whether you were on a DD or not?

    o   Have you noticed anything as it relates to your senses (hearing, sight, taste, touch, smell)? Have you experienced anything differently? Less? More?

    o   What have you noticed regarding your communication skills with others (including friends, family, strangers)?

    o   Has anyone close to you shared their observations of differences they have noted in you while you're doing your DD? For example, has a parent noted anything about your use of time, your presence in the family, or anything regarding your social or collaborative skills?

    o   Have you noticed anything specific as it relates to listening, empathy, time management, observation, or productivity as you've continued your Digital Disconnects?

    o   Have you noticed anything about your immediate environment: that is, anything about your apartment or home, anything about familiar routes that you travel to work or to home?

- o After the past three to four weeks of doing Digital Disconnects, how would you now rate your skills of memory and retention? Do you notice anything about the relationship between hours spent on your device and the strength of those skills?
- o What are you noticing about smartphone use in others while on your DD?

- In the final two to three weeks of your semester-long Digital Disconnect, we will ask you to consider the following questions (in addition to any and all discoveries and observations you may want to share).

  - o Have you experienced any changes in your acting work? Specifically as it relates to the following skills:

    - Time management.
    - Taking responsibility for actions.
    - Listening.
    - Empathy.
    - Eye contact.
    - Being present and in the moment.
    - Memory and retention.
    - Spontaneity.

  - o Complete a new Technology Log for a typical day. Compare it with your first Technology Log. What differences, if any, do you note?
  - o What are your responses to considering the following topics as they relate (or not) to your personal use of technology?

    - Fear of missing out.
    - Avoiding (people, conversation, discomfort, work).
    - Fear of judgment or rejection (not wanting to be seen as weird or different).
    - Boredom.
    - Loneliness.

- If you could go back in time to the first day you tried this assignment, what advice would you give yourself that would be supportive throughout the semester?

Part II: Research handout for the classroom

This handout contains a summation of some of the most recent, and relevant, data regarding the extent to which smartphones are being used in today's population as well as data on the impact of excessive technology use on people and collaborative behaviors. For full descriptions of studies, please refer to Chapters 2, 3, and 4 where the referenced data is described in greater detail and is cited.

AVERAGE AMOUNT OF TIME SPENT USING SMARTPHONES

- Among Americans, 92 percent of individuals between the ages of 18 and 29 owned smartphones; in 2011, that figure was just 35 percent.
- The average reported technology use of undergraduate college students is ten hours daily for females (most popular activity being texting), and eight hours daily for males (most popular activity being gaming). That's roughly 75 percent to 80 percent of someone's waking hours.
- In the past ten years, there has been a 40 percent lessening of empathy among undergraduate college students aged 18 to 24.
- The iPhone was released in 2007.
- The current average age that a child receives their first smartphone is between the ages of ten and 12.
- The average daily use of smartphones for teenagers 13 to 18 is nine hours of entertainment media, while children aged 8 to 12 average six hours of use a day, not including time spent on homework.
- In 2016, only 41 percent of parents of underage children reported that they set limits on their children's activities on social media.

EFFECTS OF EXTENSIVE SMARTPHONE USE ON GRADES

- In a 2015 study at Kent State University of over 500 undergraduates, those who used their smartphones for an average of ten hours a day had GPAs of 2.84, while those who used their smartphones for an average of two hours daily had GPAs of 3.15.
- A study that asked thousands of teachers if digital technologies were having an impact on their students' writing responded as follows: 68 percent reported that digital tools make students more likely – as opposed to less likely or having no impact – to take shortcuts and not put effort into their writing, and 46 percent responded that these tools make students more likely to write too fast and too carelessly.

EFFECTS OF EXTENSIVE SMARTPHONE USE ON BEHAVIORS

- In a 2014 Pew Research Study of over 2000 smartphone owners, 77 percent reported that they used their phone to avoid being bored; 73 percent said that their phone made them feel "distracted"; 47 percent used their phone to avoid interacting with other people.
- A University of Virginia experiment found that 66 percent of men and 25 percent of women left alone in a room for 6 to 15 minutes would rather give themselves electric shocks than be left alone with their thoughts.
- In a study of over 500 college students, students who reported high smartphone use had low cardiorespiratory fitness, and overall had a more sedentary lifestyle, which would lead to them spending more time on their devices.

- Multi-tasking is a myth: the brain doesn't really do tasks simultaneously; in fact, we just switch tasks quickly. Each time we move from hearing music to writing a text or talking to someone, there is a stop/start process that goes on in the brain. That start/stop/start process rather than saving us time, costs time. It's less efficient, we make more mistakes, and over time it can be energy sapping.
- Even the presence of a smartphone (without using it) causes a drop in the focus and content of conversation. Conversation cultivates empathy, and the ability to read social signals in other people. The lack of willingness to have face-to-face conversations lessens someone's empathy, ability to listen, and ability to recognize social signals.
- The percentage of students who have experienced being cyber-bullied has doubled since 2007, from 18 percent to 36 percent.

EFFECTS OF SMARTPHONE DESIGN ON THE HUMAN BRAIN

- Smartphones are designed and programmed to make the user want to check in frequently. They capitalize on natural human brain chemistry and take advantage of it to alter behavior. The chemical dopamine, located in the brain's pleasure center, is released each time someone is rewarded with an action or activity on their device. Dopamine causes you to want, desire, seek out, and search, and increases your general level of arousal and your goal-directed behavior. Research shows that it is the opioid system that makes us feel pleasure.

EFFECTS OF SMARTPHONE HABITS ON SLEEP PATTERNS

- Seventy-eight percent of smartphone users reported keeping their phone or tablets next to their beds; additionally, those who kept them near and used them just before trying to fall asleep experienced disrupted sleep patterns. Smartphones and tablets emit "blue light" and tell the brain that it's morning. In effect, tricking the brain that it's time to wake up instead of time to go to sleep. Additionally, blue light suppresses the body's production of melatonin, a hormone that aids sleep and circadian rhythms.

Appendix S

Sample lesson plan of exercises to develop the specific skills of being present, vulnerable, and open

If your students are struggling to make eye contact, to listen to and be affected by their partner and their partner's choices:

- Murder Mystery (see Appendix A).
- Shepherd and Sheep (see Appendix B).

- Change Three Things (see Viola Spolin's *Improvisation*).
- Initiate, Copy, Heighten (see Appendix E).
- Syllables of Your Name with Gesture (see Appendix G).
- The Name Game (see Appendix M).
- Pass the Snap (see Appendix K).
- Mindfulness Awareness Practice (see Appendix N).
- Meisner's Repetition (see Appendix O).
- West Side Story (*Ensemble Theatre Making*, Appendix E, p. 196).
- What Are You Doing? (*Ensemble Theatre Making*, Appendix C, p. 193).
- It's Tuesday (see Appendix D).

Appendix T

Sample lesson plan of exercises to develop the specific skill of empathy

If your students are struggling with being aware of, and sensitive to, the feelings of others, if they are struggling to place themselves "in the shoes" of another person, and struggling to understand the emotions of another person; also may be challenged by time management, taking responsibility for their actions, and connecting the dots between actions they've taken and the consequences of those actions:

- Shepherd and Sheep (see Appendix B).
- Dinner Party (see Appendix C).
- Initiate, Copy, Heighten (see Appendix E).
- Why Were You Late? (see Appendix H).
- Meisner's Repetition (see Appendix O).
- What I Admire About You (*Ensemble Theatre Making*, Appendix V, p. 215).
- Blind Offers (*Impro* by Keith Johnstone, or *Ensemble Theatre Making*, Appendix A, p. 191).
- Family Portraits (*Ensemble Theatre Making*, Appendix J, p. 204).
- The Ad Campaign (via *Truth in Comedy*; also *Ensemble Theatre Making*, Appendix O, p. 208).

Appendix U

Sample lesson plan of exercises to develop the specific skills of awareness/physical awareness

Observation, physical expression, commitment, ownership, spatial awareness:

- Dinner Party (see Appendix C).
- Initiate, Copy, Heighten (see Appendix E).

- Syllables of Your Name with Gesture (see Appendix G).
- Walk and Rename Objects (see Appendix J).
- Pass the Snap (see Appendix K).
- Blindfold Series: Hunter/Hunted or The Cobra (see Appendix Q).
- Kitty Wants a Corner (see Appendix L).
- Family Portraits (*Ensemble Theatre Making*, Appendix J, p. 204).
- Come Join Me (*Ensemble Theatre Making*, Appendix B, p. 192).
- West Side Story (*Ensemble Theatre Making*, Appendix E, p. 196).

Appendix V

Sample lesson plan of exercises to develop the specific skills of risk taking, commitment

Listening to impulses, relinquishing desire to edit choices, taking responsibility for one's choices and one's partner:

- Kitty Wants a Corner (see Appendix L).
- Why Were You Late (see Appendix H).
- The Name Game (see Appendix M).
- Blindfold Series: Hunter/Hunted, The Cobra (see Appendix Q).
- Come Join Me (*Ensemble Theatre Making*, Appendix B, p. 192).
- Sound and Movement (*Ensemble Theatre Making*, Appendix D, p. 194).
- West Side Story (*Ensemble Theatre Making*, Appendix E, p. 196).
- Family Portraits (*Ensemble Theatre Making*, Appendix H, p. 202).
- The Hot Spot (via *Truth in Comedy*; also *Ensemble Theatre Making*, Appendix P, p. 209).

Appendix W

Sample lesson plan of exercises to develop the specific skills of memory and retention

Allowing one's self to truly experience and process the moment, allowing a person or event to leave a lasting impression:

- Dinner Party (see Appendix C).
- Going on a Picnic (see Appendix F).
- Syllables of Your Name with Gesture (see Appendix G).
- Multiple Pattern Juggling (see Appendix I).
- Initiate, Copy, Heighten (see Appendix E).
- One Word at a Time Storytelling (*Ensemble Theatre Making*, Appendix L, p. 206.)

Appendix X

Behaviors to look for in a possible technology addiction, along with resources to gain knowledge on the subject

It's best not to diagnose a student yourself. Stay attentive to their behavior, and what they're sharing in their journals/Digital Disconnects. If a student comes to you on their own or by invitation, simply listen, let them do most of the talking, and offer a supportive ear while they expand on their personal dilemmas. Allow them to find their own way with simple guidance through this tender subject. If you believe the student is in danger of harming themselves or others, then you have an obligation to reach out to the necessary help to ensure the safety of the student and those around them. What follows are suggestions for signs to look for, ways to initiate conversations, and guidance for both yourself and the student.

In his book *Cyber Junkie,* author and recovering video-game addict Kevin Roberts offers a comprehensive checklist of symptoms associated with technology addiction. He titles it "Warning Signs of Cyber Addiction," and says, "(I) developed this list from my professional experience and current addiction literature, as well as from conversations with colleagues all over the country" (65). He suggests reaching out for professional help when four or more of these behaviors become ongoing and continue for more than three months.

- Time warp – inability to determine time spent on cyber activities/ gaming.
- Lying about gaming/cyber activities.
- Changes or disruptions in sleep patterns.
- Craving games/cyber activities.
- Withdrawing from family and friends.
- Losing interest in other hobbies and recreational activities.
- Internet/gaming use for more than two hours a day, more than four days a week.
- Poor performance in school or at work.
- Physical ailments: backache, carpal tunnel syndrome, stiff neck, nerve pain, eye strain.
- Inability to see the negative consequences of cyber activity/gaming.
- Buying game items or skills with real money.
- Eating meals at the computer.
- Glorifying cyber activity/gaming.
- Emotional disturbance when electronic devices/games are taken away.
- Mood swings.
- Withdrawal symptoms after cyber activity/games: headache, malaise, light-headedness.

- Continued cyber activity/gaming despite serious adverse consequences.
- Persistent inability to cut down cyber activity/gaming.
- Ever increasing amounts of time spent engaging in cyber activity/ gaming.
- Obsessing about cyber activity/gaming even when not playing/online.

Many people experience any variety of the above, and exhibiting one or more symptoms does not qualify as a diagnosis. Eating at the computer may be to save time while the student writes a theatre-history paper due the following day. The symptoms listed need to be considered in context. The list serves as a topic of conversation for those students who you feel might be struggling with technology addiction, or who may confide in you in their journals, or face-to-face, sharing their struggles. It's a good place to begin a dialogue about the student's technology use. As we wrote earlier, encourage them to develop a daily log of when they are and are not online. Together, come up with alternatives to fill their time when they are technology-free. What does the student enjoy besides online activities? It may be hiking, volunteering, cooking/baking, or athletics/exercise. Establish weekly check-ins between yourself and the student to aid in their accountability, and reassure them there is no judgment on your end. Continue with the Digital Disconnect papers.

As we shared previously, www.addiction.com is a resource for all addictions. The website offers research on technology addiction, as well as a toll-free confidential hotline.

The following resources are taken directly from Kevin Roberts' book (169). These organizations will also be able to provide additional literature on the topic of technology addiction.

Illinois Institute for Addiction Recovery
5409 N. Knoxville Avenue
Peoria, Illinois 61614
Phone: 800-522-3784
Website: www.addictionrecov.org

Center for Internet Addiction
P.O. Box 72
Bradford, Pennsylvania 16701
Phone: 814-451-2405
Website: http://netaddiction.com

reSTART Internet Addiction Recovery Program
1001 290th Avenue SE
Fall City, Washington 98024-7403
Phone: 425-417-1715
Website: www.netaddictionrecovery.com

Bibliography

Bonczek, Rose B. and David Storck. *Ensemble Theatre Making: A Practical Guide.* Routledge, 2013. Print.

Halpern, Charna, Del Close, and Kim "Howard" Johnson. *Truth in Comedy.* Meriwether Pub., 1994. Print.

Khalsa, Gururattan Kaur and Ann Marie Maxwell. *Transitions to a Heart-Centered World through The Kundalini Yoga and Meditations of Yogi Bhajan.* Self-published, 1988. Print.

Roberts, Kevin. *Cyber Junkie: Escape the Gaming and Internet Trap.* Minnesota: Hazelden. 2010. Print.

Wings of Desire (German: Der himmel uber Berlin). Dir. Wim Wenders. Orion Classics, 1987. Film.

Index

acknowledgment: in acting process 16, 103, 153–5; of behavior 98; in collaborative behavior 16, 47, 84–5; recommendations to strengthen 84–5, 97–101

acting/actors 96; analytic skills 53–4, 75, 78, 85, 91, *see also* writing; authenticity 32, 64–6, 138; awareness 2–3, 16, 20, 28–9, 31, 66–7, 76–7, 81, 85–96, 99, 107, 109–111, *see also* awareness; being present/in the moment 5, 10, 12, 15–17, 20, 25–6, 29, 31–2, 34, 50, 71–3, 77, 84, 88, 91, 94–8, 105, 108–12, 118, 134, 140, 149, 152–7, 166, 169, 171, *see also* behavior; body 24, 54–6, 102, 116, 141, 144, 157, *see also* movement; commitment 21, 91, 104, 148–50, 163, 173; discomfort 22, 71, 111–12, 159–60, 169; language 22, 31, 44, 91, 108; performance/ production 111, 117–18, 121, 164; rejection 47, 68, 70, 76, 96, 99–101, 104–5, 150, 169; risk-taking 47, 77–8, 88, 104, 109, 138–9, 145, 150, 173; scene partners 16, 21, 30, 33–4, 48, 50, 55, 65, 75, 78–9, 92, 97–100, 105–9, 116–17, 141–5, 150–2, 155–6, 161–2; skills 5, 15–18, 20–3, 31, 48, 54, 67–8, 74–6, 79–81, 83, 86, 88, 91, 94–5, 98–9, 108–9, 113, 127, 135, *see also* collaboration; smartphone use by actors 2–3, 10, 24–5, 27, 29, 33, 35, 50–1, 54–5, 64–70, 75–6, 88–9, 97, 99, 102, 116–17, 153, 164, 167–71; smartphone use with scripts 34, 52,

see also smartphone; susceptibility to smartphone dependency in actors 65–6, 70, 75, 86; trust 13–14, 21, 72, 78, 85, 88, 99, 104, 118, 121, 138, 145–8, 150, 161, 163; *see also* education; boredom; collaboration; emotion; empathy; ensemble; eye contact; focus; listening; memory; movement; observation; rehearsal; senses; spontaneity; stamina; vulnerability

addiction 18, 103; cyber addiction 60, 103–4, 174–5; dependency symptoms 58–9, 87, 89–90, 94, 174–5; internet 59–60, 103–4; smartphone 51, 58–9, 76, 94

American Pediatrics 43–4

Ansell, Steve 4–5

apps 26, 41–2, 65, 74, 89, 95, 115, 133, 168

Association for Theatre in Higher Education (ATHE) 120

avoidance 31; of being present/in the moment 26, 89, 105, 138, 156; of boredom 71–2, 170; of consequences 32–3, 130; of discomfort/pain 22, 30–1, 99, 111–13; of people 1–2, 22, 67–8, 72–4, 105, 129, 169–70; of social interaction 65, 67, 72, 89, 129, 169; of work 74

awareness 2–3, 21, 90, 96, 134–5, 148, 164; of environment 21, 77, 90, 141, 147; of excessive smartphone use 41, 50, 67–8, 76–8, 85–6, 90, 98, 112–14, 117; impact of excessive smartphone use on 20–1, 36, 41, 46, 52, 86, 99–100; recommendations to strengthen 24, 84–91, 93–4, 97–8,